Praise for Nikki Vargas

"*Call You When I Land* is a beautiful memoir that not only takes you on a journey around the world through the vivid descriptions of the places she's been, but we see Nikki's transformation and how giving herself permission to live life for herself completely changes the trajectory of her life. It is inspiring for anyone who is questioning whether or not to stick with the status quo or take a leap of faith!"

—Jessica Nabongo, author of *The Catch Me If You Can: One Woman's Journey to Every Country in the World*

"Witty and incisive, Vargas captures the universal quest to learn who we are, what we want, and how much baggage we can afford to carry. *Call You When I Land* reads like an over-due catch up with your most audacious girlfriend."

—Alicia Menendez, MSNBC anchor and author of *The Likeability Trap: How to Break Free and Succeed as You Are*

"Like the planes she watches as a little girl, Vargas' story soars, a tender and thrilling voyage of self-discovery. Her far-flung adventures and moments of revelation will leave readers with full hearts (and possibly, packed suitcases)."

—Nicole C. Kear, author of *Now I See You: A Memoir*

"In this unflinchingly raw tale of self-discovery, infused with the lushest wanderlust-inducing descriptions, Vargas transparently takes you along on her vulnerable, messy, and courageous journey towards self-love, living your true calling, and the bravery it requires of you. Thank you for putting into words what fellow kindred spirits will instantly recognize—the healing, freeing, and transformative power of travel. This memoir is a true testament to showing up fully as yourself in this world."

—Lola Akinmade Åkerström, author of *In Every Mirror She's Black*

NIKKI VARGAS

A memoir

CALL YOU WHEN I LAND

HANOVER
SQUARE
PRESS

**HANOVER
SQUARE
PRESS™**

Recycling programs
for this product may
not exist in your area.

ISBN-13: 978-1-335-45509-3

Call You When I Land

Hanover Square Press
22 Adelaide St. West, 41st Floor
Toronto, Ontario M5H 4E3, Canada
HanoverSqPress.com
BookClubbish.com

Printed in U.S.A.

For all the twentysomething women out there
finding themselves, one of whom is my little sister.

Bebe, I promise you'll figure it all out one day
and have your own whirlwind story to look back on.

ALSO BY NIKKI VARGAS

Wanderess (coauthor)

CALL YOU WHEN I LAND

Contents

INTRODUCTION

My family has always been one for superstition.

We throw salt over our left shoulder. We "knock on wood" to stave off tragedy. We wear yellow underwear on December 31st to secure good luck in the coming year. We sit down before leaving the house on a trip, to ensure safe travels. And we always text each other before takeoff, with the simple promise of "I'll call you when I land." This phrase holds all the magic in the world to me, as though it casts a force field around the plane, guaranteeing it will blissfully sail through the clouds and reach its destination. It's a wish to hear my loved ones' voices again and a comfort that I'll feel connected to them even from 39,000 feet in the air.

In my twenties, when traveling became my way of running away from reality, this phrase took on another meaning entirely. It became a promise that one day, when I eventually figured everything out (whenever *that* would be), I'd call my loved ones and let them know that I had finally arrived. That I had not only returned to New York City, but that I'd landed on the woman I hoped to become, the career I strived to have, and the relationship that felt right.

This book is a journey over ten years in the making; an adventure marked by landings and takeoffs, epiphanies and revelations, beautiful countries and crowded hostels. My memoir details the many ways travel has shaped my life and morphed me into the woman I am today, and how the simple act of traveling has the power to completely transform us on an almost molecular level, bringing us to new places far from where we started.

I dedicate this book to the people still out there searching for themselves. But above all else, this book is for the people in my life: those met along the way, the broken hearts left in my wake, my family and friends who watched my evolution from afar, and everyone who waited for me to call them when I landed.

PROLOGUE

Iguazú National Park, Argentina

"I'm not in love!"

These words that erupt from my mouth seem to shake the misty jungle around me. A few startled capuchin monkeys leap from the branches. Colorful birds peer down curiously, likely wondering about the lone hiker yelling into the trees. I am standing in Iguazú National Park, a picturesque part of the world where Argentina meets Brazil. Here, at the border between two countries, a series of cascading waterfalls is considered the largest on earth and comprises one of the seven natural wonders of the world. Aside from the roar of falling water, it's quiet where I am. Or, at least it was, until my outburst moments ago.

In Argentina, a local legend describes an Indigenous woman named Naipí who was once engaged to a god besotted by her beauty. Despite the deity's power, Naipí fell in love with a simple mortal man named Tarobá. The two fled in a small wooden canoe only to have the god thwart their escape by furiously slashing the river in half, creating a series of dramatic cascades and condemning the lovers to an eternity of falling, which are the Iguazú waterfalls we see today.

I don't have a canoe, but I've run like hell from New York City at the prospect of facing my own upcoming wedding. Up until this point, my summer has been a blur of stressful dress fittings, menu tastings, and florist meetings. While all the other twenty-six-year-olds I know are concerning themselves with next weekend's bottomless brunch plans, I've been facing a slew of existential questions about motherhood, marriage, and what exactly I want in life. I try to picture myself living in the suburbs: a white picket fence and golden retriever, a silver minivan loaded with smelly soccer cleats from the three rowdy boys I'd be raising, a tired-looking husband who sits with his feet perched on our frosted glass coffee table as I float around the kitchen making dinner. While there's nothing inherently wrong with this vision of marriage and motherhood, it's admittedly tantamount to a 1950s sitcom, and starting to feel like my own personal horror movie playing on repeat the closer my wedding date looms.

"I don't want to do this. I don't want any of this."

I've gone through the motions of wedding planning on autopilot: nodding at the tailor's suggestions about how short to trim my veil, shrugging indifferently at the idea of having a DJ versus a live band. I've passively participated in every step leading up to my wedding day, trying to play the part of the happy bride while simultaneously burying my doubts. I helped choose the venue, an upstate New York lodge flanked by the Catskill Mountains. I picked the theme, a rustic fall fete that pays homage to all my favorite seasonal ingredients of the Hudson Valley. I even had my wedding menu tasting, devouring a butternut squash ravioli topped with crispy sage leaves and toasted walnuts.

My efforts to craft the perfect wedding are at odds with my desire to run away from saying "I do," making everything all the more confusing. In fact, the only detail I've actively fought for is opting for a wedding pie over a wedding cake. Having always celebrated my birthday with a slice of apple pie topped with a cinnamon crumble, I figure if I must get married, I might as well have my favorite dessert waiting for me. Throughout these past few months, I've kept thinking how it's not meant to be this way. In the myriad rom-coms and love stories I've grown up ingesting, brides had always seemed to operate on two speeds: wistfully romantic or an outright bonkers bridezilla. But never in all of these stories are the brides depicted as disinterested.

The only joy I've clung to these past few months is my budding passion for travel, an improbable love that has blossomed in the corner of my life like an irresistible affair. Between work calls at my entry-level office job, I printed out photos of far-flung countries to tape up in my cubicle. While my colleagues had framed pictures of smiling spouses and children, I surrounded my workspace with imagery of sunsets in Bali, beaches in the Caribbean, and the cerulean waters of Lake Como in Italy, places I hoped to one day see in person. I passed my lunch breaks trying to trace a clear path between my current career in advertising and that of becoming a writer, desperate to pull my love of travel from the shadowy corners of my life and thrust it into the sunlight. At night, I would spend hours writing for my no-name travel blog, *The Pin the Map Project*, indulging in my passion for travel writing like I was meeting a secret lover. Knowing that I may one day explore the world on the wings of my writing has been my only escape from wedding planning.

Of course, up until this point, it was a metaphorical escape.

I've been in Argentina for a week now, playing a game of cat and mouse between my heart and mind. With my wedding date on the horizon, my emotions have been fighting against my sense of duty. I feel the question like an ache in my chest—why am I currently alone in South America rather than back in New York with my fiancé? In turn, my brain responds by sprinting to the nearest glass of Malbec, determined to avoid the one thing I had yet to admit.

For days now, I've been defiantly sidestepping my reality back home. I've savored choripan sandwiches in San Telmo, wiping the sweet juices of the grilled chorizo from my lips while watching a handsome Spanish guitarist serenade the streets of Buenos Aires' oldest barrio. I took an impromptu day trip to Uruguay, catching the one-hour ferry to Colonia del Sacramento, where I aimlessly wandered the cobbled streets of the UNESCO World Heritage city for a day. I attended a local asado, devouring grilled steak slathered with chimichurri and clinking glasses with Argentine expats. I even made (and promptly ran away from) a tattoo appointment where a bored-looking teenager sat ready to ink my wrist with the words, *To travel is to live.*

Officially, I'm in Argentina on a freelance assignment to write about Palermo's blossoming café scene for *The Daily Meal*, a food-focused publication based in New York. Unofficially, I am a runaway bride. The title "runaway bride" rubs against my skin like an itchy sweater. The term has become a cliché that immediately conjures up romanticized images of Julia Roberts in a wedding dress, escaping by horseback with her frantic fiancé chasing her through the fields in a rented tuxedo. I can't help but wince at the thought.

To those around me, my love of travel is a silly dalliance, an unrealistic side fling that I'm meant to get out of my system before I don a veil, saunter down the aisle, and grow up. This changes when I announce my plans to travel to Argentina solo a mere two weeks before my wedding day. I am greeted with quizzical looks tinged with concern. My family thinks I'm suffering a mental breakdown. I assuaged their worries with reassurances that I'm simply chasing that next byline, flying to Buenos Aires in pursuit of a story—and hopefully the first step towards a career as a travel writer. In reality, I'm here because the very oxygen in New York City ran out for me.

Just two days ago, I was returning to my hostel after checking out a particularly charming bookstore-café hybrid tucked at the end of an alley in Palermo. I met an English-Italian traveler in the hostel common area, flipping through photos of waterfalls he had taken on a recent trip. Curious, I struck up a conversation with the wayfaring stranger and quickly learned the pictures were of Iguazú. Within an hour, I had booked a flight to the border.

Now, as I hike through Iguazú National Park alone, the weight of my backpack hangs loosely on my shoulders as my scuffed sneakers crunch along the jungle's dirt-packed trails. My dark brown hair is soaked, my navy blue T-shirt damp from the zodiac boat ride I just took to get closer to the crashing cascades. I walk through the jungle quietly now, without armor or distraction. Out here beneath the canopy of trees, I finally consider the question I've been avoiding all these months, the question I have exactly one week left to answer before I walk down that aisle.

"What is it you have to say?"

I ask the question aloud, the same way I would pose it to a fellow traveler I've been steamrolling this entire trip. The words barely escape my lips before a response roars out of me with such ferocity that I nearly stumble.

"I'm not in love!"

Every suppressed feeling I pushed aside these past few months feels like it's bursting from my chest, nearly shaking the trees around me. More than the words, what surprises me is their concreteness. There is no exasperation, no complaint, no doubt, no debate—there is simply a statement of fact. A truth that has coalesced beneath my skin despite my best efforts to ignore it.

"I don't want to get married!"

For months I had been fighting off these very words, even going so far as to board a plane to South America to outrun them. Yet they have followed me here. Trailing me all the way to the edges of Argentina and Brazil like a Pinkerton detective hot on a case. When I first speak them aloud, I stop walking, listening only to the soundtrack of the Iguazú jungle: the chitter of those birds, the "ooh-ahhs" of those little capuchin monkeys, the pulse of those majestic waterfalls reverberating through the trees. An undeniable gauntlet has just been thrown down. I know before I fully understand it that my life will forever be changed from this moment on.

PART ONE

Turbulence

Turbulence: An unsteady or irregular movement of air that, when flying, can cause erratic changes to an airplane's altitude or angle. This can result in passengers feeling bumps, choppiness, and other shifts in flight.

Chicago, Rouen, New York City, Cartagena

1

The Brick Ledge

Chicago, Illinois

I can trace everything back to that brick ledge by the garden.

On Kenneth Street, in a sleepy suburb of Chicago called Skokie, sits my childhood home. A low, two-story orange house that was inconsequential but for one unique detail: we had a small rose garden flanked by two short brick walls in the front yard. A thirty-second stroll from the driveway to the front door would take you through a tangle of roses and a low cacophony of sparrows, bumblebees, and flapping monarch butterflies. Looking back, I remember those plump, fuzzy bumblebees as though they were an emblem of my childhood. While they busily tended to their budding flowers, I'd run through the garden at top speed, squealing in delight as the bees chased me out onto the driveway and around my parents' Volvo like an old Italian nonna waving meddlesome kids off her lawn. Then, on lazy summer afternoons, I'd climb atop those low brick ledges and watch airplanes fly by.

My father, Axel Vargas, has always loved airplanes. I remember him being fascinated by their aerodynamics, obsessed with the idea of becoming a pilot, and how he'd romanticize the imagined thrill of landing a 747 jet. Growing up in Colombia, his first time flying was at the age of five on the now-defunct Super Constellation, a propeller-driven plane first introduced in 1949 and one of the first airliners to serve Latin America. As a kid, my dad would often fly with his two brothers and parents to the sun-kissed archipelago of San Andrés y Providencia off the coast of Nicaragua. Even at a young age, he was captivated by how a plane could transport him from one place to the next in just a matter of hours, allowing him to have a breakfast of scrambled huevos pericos in Bogotá and then sip coconut juice on an island later that afternoon. Flying always held a childlike wonder that never quite left my dad's side.

Throughout my childhood, my dad pushed his love of aviation to the corners of his life and medical career. Wearing his sky blue scrubs, he always had some indecipherable writing scribbled across the cotton fabric, a doctor's scrawl of notes he'd jotted down earlier that day. From his breast pocket would hang shiny Montblanc fountain pens, and on his waist was stationed a thick black beeper, its weight tugging at the thin material of his uniform.

In my dad's family, there are two things that have been seemingly passed down from generation to generation: the name Axel and a medical profession. It wasn't until I was born that both the chain of Axels and the chain of future Dr. Vargases was broken. My grandfather, Axel Senior, was a plastic surgeon in Colombia and, arguably, one of the best in the country. His father was a gynecologist, while his father's father was a neurosurgeon. By the time my dad, Axel Junior, arrived, it seemed only logical that he'd follow in the footsteps of his father, grandfather, and great-grandfather and become a doctor as well. And yet my dad still dreamed of flying planes, even going so far as to meet with a commercial airline pilot at a young age.

My dad arrived at this meeting hopeful, only for the pilot to completely dash his expectations.

"You must have the best job in the world!" I imagine my dad had gushed. "How often do you fly to Paris?" To which the pilot probably deadpanned, "I spent twenty years flying from Cleveland to Des Moines before I could finally work these international routes."

I can relate to this story. When I was young, after watching the film *Free Willy*, in which a captive orca whale is freed into the wild, I decided I must become a marine biologist. I imagined myself floating on dinghies off the coast of Norway, studying wild orca pods who would swim up alongside my boat for pets and kisses. I held on to this vision so hard that I eventually reached out to a bonafide marine biologist, asking for a phone call so I could learn more about his work.

"How often do you get to see the whales?" I asked excitedly. To which the marine biologist deadpanned, "I spend most of my time in a basement studying fish inside tanks." My childhood dream of working with whales ended right there, much as I imagine my dad's dream of flying ended after meeting that airline pilot. Instead, he chose a profession in anesthesiology and pain management, forever relegating his passion for flying to the evening hours spent playing *Flight Simulator* on his Windows 95 desktop computer.

My father would sit in his makeshift home office for hours—a cubicle separated from the TV room by a wall of towering plants—happily bent over a joystick, distracting himself from the never-ending patient charts he had to dictate as part of his job. At times, he'd call me over to his imaginary cockpit. Together we'd land Boeing jets, steadily approaching the virtual ground as the joystick vibrated in our hands with the imagined eddies of turbulent airflow.

On his birthdays when I was growing up, my dad wanted nothing more than to simply watch airplanes take off and land. My parents would pile my little sister, Natalie, and me into the family Volvo and drive the forty-five minutes to O'Hare International Airport to park by the landing strips. With a fleece blanket laid out beneath us, we would lie on the car's silver hood and watch in awe as the jets soared overhead, soon to land in countries as far-flung as Finland in mere hours.

"That's a 747 jumbo jet," he'd exclaim, the excitement palpable. "Do you know how something that weighs over two hundred tons can fly?" He'd show off his encyclopedic knowledge of aviation, explaining aerodynamics in layman's terms, eager to have us understand the power of what we were witnessing. While my dad found magic in aviation, captivated by how planes soar across the Atlantic Ocean, I found magic in the simple act of transporting yourself somewhere new. Even as a kid, it was never about flying for me—it was about travel.

Back in those pre-9/11 days, when a boarding pass wasn't required to get through security, my dad and I would grab lunch at the airport on special occasions and watch passengers rush by. I'd look around the terminal and think of that scene from Tim Burton's 1993 classic, *A Nightmare before Christmas*, where the king of "Halloween Town," Jack Skellington, finds himself standing amid a circle of trees, each boasting a delicately carved door in its trunk. One tree had a door depicting a heart—presumably concealing a world of red roses and plump cupids for Valentine's Day—while the others had a bunny for Easter, a four-leaf clover for St. Patty's Day, and, finally, a Christmas tree. Each door would lead Skellington to another realm entirely, one that promised to be a far cry from his own reality. What always struck me about this moment in the film was the thrill of crossing a barrier between a world you know and one you had yet to discover. In many ways, the airport reminds me of that fabled circle of trees, with each gate promising something different on the other side.

As we ate our sandwiches, my dad and I would sit side by side and listen to the final boarding calls for flights leaving for London, Miami, and Berlin.

"Which flight would you take?" my dad would ask me giddily, as though he considered just tossing his sandwich over his shoulder and casually strolling down any of the jet bridges, no boarding pass needed. If nothing else, Axel Vargas was—and remains—a dreamer.

★

Growing up, my dad and stepmom, Yana, saw the value in taking my younger sister and me traveling. Originally from Russia, Yana is a statuesque and undeniably beautiful woman with high cheekbones and black hair that she's always opted to keep cropped short and dyed an auburn hue. Her beauty was the sort to make people stop dead in their tracks, but she never seemed to care about her looks. For her, true beauty came in the form of intelligence, an attribute she was determined to instill in my siblings and me through long-winded books, classical music, highbrow films, and season tickets to the opera and ballet.

Yana first met my dad at age twenty-five at the now-shuttered Mt. Sinai Hospital in Cleveland, where she had just finished dental school and was beginning her residency. While riding the elevator one cool September day in the early '90s, she spotted my dad, recognizing the *Axel* printed on the laminated name tag that hung off his scrubs. She knew the name from a mutual friend who suggested the two might hit it off, and so introduced herself to the charming surgical resident and her would-be future husband. My dad offered to show Yana around Mt. Sinai, puffing out his chest proudly as he promised to take her to in-the-know coffee shops and to meet fellow residents.

Their first date was technically not a date at all, or at least Yana didn't think of it as such. My dad invited Yana to dinner at his apartment in Cleveland, where she expected to meet him and his family. Instead, she found a single father standing alongside a meal comprised of heated canned beans and boxed macaroni and cheese, and there, peering from behind a door with nervous interest, stood four-year-old me. His lack of cooking skills aside, Yana and my dad seemed to recognize their counterparts in the other: both were immigrants from other countries, both were in the medical field trying to make a name for themselves, and both were fiercely intelligent, revering one another's intellect.

Ever since Yana entered my life early on, I have always called her by her first name. I imagine, in large part, this was because my birth mom, Karen, was omnipresent, always making a point to stay close so she could be a part of her daughter's upbringing. My dad and mom met back in Bogotá, Colombia—he was in his twenties, and she was just shy of nineteen. The two eloped and got pregnant (much to the chagrin of their families), moving to the United States where their relationship, once born of passion, soon fizzled into a marriage marked by tension and resentment. I don't remember my parents getting divorced so much as I remember their decision to stay friends. While I grew up living with Yana and my dad, my twentysomething mom would do her best to be present, showing up for holidays and birthdays, movie dates, and back-to-school shopping. Eventually, she went on to meet her future husband, Chris, a kind albeit nerdy tech guy with a quick wit, an insatiable appetite for knowledge, and terrible dance moves.

While fragments of my early childhood days float through my memory like a collection of incomplete sentences, I remember travel as being the constant. Yana and my dad would painstakingly plan unique family trips that would take us to local Mayan communities in Mexico, the Russian countryside outside St. Petersburg, or hiking in Washington's Lime Kiln Point State Park, where we'd watch orcas swim by the shore. Old photos from these trips depict me as a preteen with dirt-scuffed sneakers, stained overalls, and an off-brand Tamagotchi permanently slung around my neck on a hot-pink lanyard, standing next to my younger sister who'd be wearing a too-big baseball cap and one-piece swimsuit. My sister, who is ten years younger than me, was Yana and my dad's first child together followed by my brother, Jan (pronounced like *yawn*), who was born ten years later.

On these family trips, Natalie and I would groan at the half-day hikes Yana would take us on; we'd snatch my dad's clunky camcorder to film ourselves; we'd play pranks on each other or occasionally join forces to play pranks on our grandma, Amparo, who'd sometimes join these family getaways. From my parents, I learned to love the magic of travel, understanding that it promised the kind of adventure I was unlikely to find on the streets of Skokie.

Perched atop that low brick wall in the garden, I would keep watching planes fly by. I imagined myself en route to places like Borneo or Sri Lanka, which I had only seen plastered across the dusty covers of the *National Geographic* issues my parents collected in the basement. I would look up at the sky from the sleepy streets of Skokie, dreaming I was onboard one of those silver jets.

A shimmering gold thread unspooled at my feet then. Born from my dad's love of planes—only to grow thicker with each family trip we took—this golden thread would delicately weave its way throughout my life, wrapping around every relationship, career, and life decision I'd come to make. Stretching through time, from that brick ledge and into my adult years, that shimmering thread would find me living out of suitcases and gallivanting around the globe in pursuit of that magical, yet-to-be-identified *something* that I now see was scattered all throughout my childhood like pieces to a puzzle. Each day I spent on that brick ledge, the bumblebees tending to their garden of roses nearby, I had been reaching for that glittering strand, arms outstretched towards the sky, grasping for something that would shape the woman I'd become.

I'm No Joan of Arc

Rouen, France

The Yvonne display case is a carnival for the eyes. Neon yellow lemon tarts are topped with a delicate swirl of snowy meringue. Rows of plump choux sit enticingly behind glass, their cream filling hugged lovingly by two golden round puff pastries on either side. But it's the rainbow of macarons I've come here for, a dizzying display of vivid purple, baby pink, and mint-green pastries that appear almost fake in their perfection.

"Je veux un macaron aux framboises s'il vous plaît?" I nervously ask the woman behind the counter, pointing at a raspberry macaron.

I hear myself stumble, the French syllables sticking to the roof of my mouth like an overchewed piece of gum. Since graduating college a few months ago, I've been living in Normandy, where the French language remains a tongue twister I often get frustrated with. Even the city I'm staying in, Rouen, remains a mysterious jumble of vowels I can't quite master. While I pronounce Rouen as "roo-ann," Alex—my born-and-raised French boyfriend of less than one year—pronounces it with one swift guttural sound of "wroan," which sounds like he's swallowing the word "womp."

"Roo-ann," I try to say.

"Wroan," he recites patiently.

The exchange reminds me of being a little girl and learning how to read with Yana. Together, we'd spend our afternoons bent over a notebook staring at the oh-so-advanced word "brown." Yana would encourage me to sound out the word slowly, emphasizing each consonant and vowel.

"Brah-OWWN-ah," I would say as I looked up at her, hopeful that I could just return to playing with my Barbies. I desperately wanted her to grab that yellow highlighter she had been using to check off my correct pronunciations.

"Try again," said Yana sternly, pulling out the dreaded pink highlighter for the words I had gotten wrong. The more pink-colored words I racked up, the more we'd have to go back and practice reading them.

"Brah-OWWN-AH! Brah-OWWN-AH! Brah-OWWN-AH!" I tried, getting desperate as I eyed the advancing pink highlighter approaching the page. My dad, ever the comedian, lurked in the background behind the family camcorder, laughing until he finally called out, "BROWN!" This moment in my family's history has become a favorite memory, one that I seem to be reverting back to now at the not-so-cute age of twenty-three.

"Roo-ann," I try again with Alex.

"Wroan."

"Woo-*arnnnnn*," I fire back.

"Wroan," Alex responds emphatically. We volley back and

forth with our varying pronunciations until I give up and refer to the city simply as "here."

"Here" happens to be a historic medieval town and port city on the Seine River, found in France's northern Normandy region. Rouen is an odd juxtaposition of modern and historical that is best reflected by the McDonald's sitting on the Rue du Gros Horloge. Masked to look like one of the many timber-framed houses that make up Rouen's Old City, this McDonald's, which the locals call "McDo," is right around the corner from Place du Vieux-Marche, where Joan of Arc was burned at the stake back in May 1431.

As a quick history refresher, Joan was a sixteen-year-old peasant girl living during the Hundred Years' War, fought between France and England between 1337 and 1453. When she was a teenager, Joan "heard voices" that instructed her to lead France to victory in battle, and so she defiantly stood up to authority and did just that. Convinced she was acting under the guidance of the divine, Joan led France to a shocking win at Orléans. To say Joan was brave is a serious understatement. Not only did this teenage girl from nowhere stroll up to the castle of Dauphin Charles (later known as Charles VII) and request an army, but then she went and dressed in men's clothing at a time when a woman caught having a mood swing would be dubbed "a witch."

When the English eventually captured Joan, she was imprisoned and burned at the stake at age nineteen in Rouen, unsurprisingly, as a witch. The fact that Le Big Mac is now neighbors with the landmark of France's favorite teenage martyr is just one of the many ways this city couples the past and present.

I arrived in Rouen back in early January and have since been living in a small apartment with Alex on the Rue Saint-Maur, about fifteen minutes walking from the tourist-filled

Old City. Overall, I like Rouen. The center of the Old City looks a bit like an ancient alpine village with its medieval half-timbered houses painted in faded hues of yellow, dusty orange, and rosy pink. The air is heavily scented with freshly made crepes and the unmistakable smell of calvados, that apple-infused brandy so unique to Normandy.

Unlike the Old City, I wouldn't call Rue Saint-Maur charming. Our street is a residential one where every cement building is a varying shade of depressing gray and muted egg-shell, resembling the business-formal sales rack at Ann Taylor Loft. The fact that it's winter makes Rue Saint-Maur even more drab. The door to our apartment opens to a small kitch-enette, which is barely big enough to fit the wooden two-person table and little sink we have. The kitchen leads to a larger area that doubles as our bedroom and living room, where the first thing to catch your eye is the bricked-up fireplace on the opposite wall with a large decorative mirror overhead. The entire space is awash in natural lighting that pours in from the floor-to-ceiling windows overlooking the street below. The daylight tosses a welcoming glow over the hardwood floors, our shared desk, and the black sofa bed that sits pushed in the corner next to a small side table. My favor-ite part of our apartment is actually not inside the apartment at all; instead, it's the front door to the building, painted a stunning bright blue that dramatically contrasts with the rest of the street.

*

I met Alex the previous summer in Manhattan while in-terning for the public relations team of the prominent fash-ion designer Donna Karan. At the time, I wasn't particularly interested in fashion or public relations, but had fallen in love with the idea of living in New York. On quiet mornings at Indiana University, I'd ride the campus bus and dream about the magic New York City promised—all of which seemed embodied by an anonymous fashion PR girl I followed on Twitter who shared snippets of her life via romantic tweets and filtered photos. Whether grabbing vanilla lattes in between celebrity fittings with Christina Ricci or Claire Danes, recounting dinners at chic restaurants like Nobu, or sharing moments from black-tie benefits and fashion shows, her life was an endless parade of glamour, a far cry from the cornfields of Bloomington where I was attending college.

One morning, she posted a job listing for an unpaid summer internship program with her public relations team. I jumped at the opportunity, even dressing up in my fanciest outfit and most stylish stilettos as though I'd be sitting across her desk on Fashion Avenue, despite this being a video interview. A week later, I snagged the position.

The anonymous PR girl turned out to be a fiery, no-bullshit redhead who was Senior Vice President of Global Communications at Donna Karan International. Donning towering designer heels and impeccable outfits (from Donna Karan, of course), she led a life that was every bit as fabulous as her anonymous online persona—the @dknyprgirl—promised. Meeting her was my first brush with a true New York powerhouse woman, the type to cut through the city with a glittering, unwavering confidence that commands a room. Unsurprisingly, my internship proved glamourous-adjacent. While @dknyprgirl ran off to magazine photo shoots—just as her Twitter had boasted—my days were spent sitting in a windowless back room, sandwiched at a desk with two other interns. For hours, I'd divvy my time between our small office, registering product returns, or organizing shoe-boxes in the fashion closet.

I quickly learned I didn't care for fashion and couldn't give two hoots whether the brand was featured in *Vogue*—a fact that didn't bode well for a future career in public relations. My fashion internship began to feel isolating. While the other interns would spend weekends perusing the designer racks at Century21 in the Financial District, spending every spare penny (of which there were few) on deeply discounted Chanel purses, I showed up at the office wearing repeat H&M outfits. While the PR girls ate their fancy arugula salads from the overpriced Guy & Gallard on the corner of 7th Avenue, I once showed up with a bagged McDonald's lunch, fending off looks of disgust from the models waiting to audition for the coming DKNY fashion shows. I had built New York up as this wondrous place, but the reality of living in Manhattan quickly eclipsed my imagination. I began to feel lonely, which was right about the time when Alex entered my life.

The first time I saw Alex, it was one of those humid New York nights when the stench of hot garbage lingers so thick you can practically taste it. I was due to meet my college friend John in SoHo, who was bringing his friend Marina, who, in turn, would be accompanied by her friend Alex, a fellow intern whom she had met while studying abroad in France. The four of us were new to New York and called upon any friend of a friend to meet for dinner in hopes of connecting with people in the city. The first thing I noticed about Alex was his French accent, which gave his English a cute sort of lilt. He had full lips and a kind smile that hovered between laugh-out-loud big and a mischievous smirk. I quickly learned that Alex was funny, if not a little awkward. He had a certain boyish innocence paired with an all-encompassing fascination with American culture. As he grew up in France, his romanticized view of the States had been shaped by watching reruns of American sitcoms, so his accented English was now peppered with the sort of ubiquitous one-liners pulled from shows like *How I Met Your Mother*. I was smitten.

It wasn't exactly love at first sight, so much as it was lust. I was attracted to Alex, that much was clear, and after that first dinner, I knew I wanted to see him again. I was hopeful we could enjoy a fling in the city before parting in the fall. That summer, we spent all our time together. Because we both had summer intern housing near Columbia, we'd sit on the university steps and eat frozen yogurts from Pinkberry as we listened with fascination to one another's upbringings. For me, Alex's childhood in France was something to be envied. My mind reeled at how he had grown up outside Paris, spending weekends in the shadow of the Eiffel Tower and taking road trips to quaint hamlets scattered throughout the Loire Valley. His upbringing seemed impossibly charming, riddled with crisp baguettes and stinky cheese, rolling lavender fields, and the sweeping Haussmann architecture of Paris. While I held on to my cliché of France, Alex held on to his cliché of the American dream. In a way, we each took for granted what the other desperately wanted. I was awestruck by his life in Europe—a far stretch from my formative years in the Midwest—while he lived vicariously through my classic American college experience replete with football tailgates, cheap Keystone Light beer, and frat parties.

The beginning of my and Alex's relationship played out like every romantic montage splashed across the silver screen. We had our first date at a hole-in-the-wall Cuban restaurant tucked away in the Upper West Side, where we indulged in ropa vieja—a succulent shredded beef dish served over rice—and watched the 2010 FIFA World Cup. We'd ride the N train to Coney Island on weekends, losing hours to the vintage roller coasters and arcade games before walking down the boardwalk for steamed pierogies in Brighton Beach. During the week, we sometimes played hooky from our internships to spend afternoons over bowls of spaghetti in Little Italy, washing it down with whatever house red wine was the cheapest.

Despite my hopes of having a simple summer fling, I was the first one to say, "I love you." The two of us were sitting at what had become our go-to Cuban spot on the Upper West Side, perched atop two barstools. The restaurant was lively that evening, swirling around us in a haze of sugary mojitos and Latin dancing. I remember an elderly man plopping down at the barstool next to me, instantly striking up a conversation, his eyes swimming with nostalgia. Although I can't remember his words, I remember the sentiment clearly: life is too short to wait. I was three or four mojitos in by that point, and this idea hit me like a shot of adrenaline.

Life is too short to wait, I repeated to myself.

I felt so alive at that moment, as though the very energy of New York was coursing through my veins. The man was right. Nothing in life is guaranteed, and our time on earth is too short not to say the things we want to say or do the things we hope to do. I put down my cocktail, turned to Alex, and blurted out the three words that had been building up inside me for weeks: "I love you." To which he replied back, "I love you too."

Alex and I hadn't planned on falling in love. Quite the opposite. Our summer fling had only deepened as the weeks wore on. Sitting on a city bus taking its route up Broadway to West 116th street for one last August evening, we ignored the realities of having short-term internships and temporary housing in a city we couldn't afford. We avoided the fact that I was due to return to college in September to complete my final semester while Alex would return to France to finish his last few months of business school. Wrapped in one another's arms, my legs folded atop the seat, we contemplated our future, finally facing the question of whether we'd be turning our summer fling into a serious thing. The odds were stacked against us.

"I love you and want to stay together," I said defiantly. "And if you want something different, tell me now before I waste another second."

"I love you too," said Alex, pulling me closer with a smile. "I want to try and make this work." By the time the uptown bus rolled to a slow stop outside the wrought-iron gates of Columbia University, we had our answer.

The plan was simple: I had exactly four months left in my senior year, and Alex had four months left in his New York internship. Through the fall and winter, we would cobble together a relationship consisting of video calls, text messages, emails, and strategically planned visits until I graduated that December. Alex would meet me for my graduation in Indiana and then spend the holidays with my family in Chicago before he flew back to France. I'd then meet him in Paris after the New Year and live with him in Rouen, while he finished his last semester of business school with plans to eventually work full-time for the company he had been interning for in New York. For as long as my tourist visa would allow, I'd stay in France, blogging and figuring out my own professional next steps, and then move to Manhattan, where I'd wait for Alex to join me so we could start our life together.

Everything about our grand plan felt wildly romantic. Granted, we had skimmed over a few obstacles, such as how we'd afford regular back-and-forth flights between New York and Indiana, or how I would convince my parents to let my new boyfriend spend the holidays with us. Nonetheless, I reveled in the spontaneity of my immediate future. While my classmates looked at entry-level jobs at insurance companies in Indianapolis and St. Louis, I planned ahead to weekends spent exploring Paris.

My family bristled at the idea of me going to France. They implored me to consider my future and think about getting a job. I would soon no longer be a college kid, they warned, but an adult saddled with student loans. Even worse, an aspiring *writer* saddled with student loans. Each parent chimed in with their own opinions.

"We did not invest in your education just for it to culminate in a joyride through France with a boyfriend," said Yana.

"Those student loan payments are going to start in six months. How do you plan to pay them without a job?" asked my stepdad, Chris.

"I want you to think long and hard about what you're doing," advised my mom.

By the time my college graduation rolled around, the family tension had reached an all-time fever pitch. I knew my parents felt betrayed, but the idea of me going to Europe had transcended a simple trip. Wherever my life would take me, I was convinced it had to start in France. While I had traveled abroad with my family in the past, this trip felt different; it would be me venturing out into the world alone. On a cold afternoon in early January, my dad—who had been largely quiet on my postgraduation plans—drove me to Chicago's O'Hare Airport, the site of so many hours we'd spent together, dreaming about travel. I felt nervous and excited as his car pulled up in front of the departures terminal.

"I'm proud of you," he said, smiling as I turned to hug him goodbye.

After the fights that broke out around my graduation, his words were like a warm salve over my heart. If nothing else, I knew my dad believed in me. It wasn't my France trip that made him proud (and it definitely wasn't the choice to follow a new boyfriend). Looking back, I'd like to think he was proud of my unwavering determination to forge my own path.

Perhaps he saw that same stubborn, unrelenting ambition that had carried him throughout his own life now reflected in me. Or maybe, he remembered those early days of my childhood when the two of us would sit at this very airport eating our sandwiches and listening to final boarding calls. Except this time, I would no longer be sitting at the gate dreaming of adventure; now, I'd be flying off into my future to have one.

★

My days in France are quiet. While Alex attends classes at the nearby Rouen Business School during the week, I have been mustering the courage to simply explore the neighborhood.

The thing is, I thought I'd be braver coming to France. In all the months I spent dreaming of and preparing for this trip, it had never occurred to me I'd be too much of a chickenshit to venture out on my own. It's as though the momentum of planning this adventure wore off when I disembarked at Charles de Gaulle Airport. Like my dad, I've always been a dreamer—losing myself to romantic notions of what life could be versus what it is. All those years spent dreaming about travel seem only to have eclipsed the complicated reality of navigating a foreign place like Rouen. Back at Indiana University, I had imagined walking along the Seine and conversing in French over warm croissants. While my friends attended career fairs, I listened to Édith Piaf and dropped any spare change I had into my piggy bank.

The piggy bank. I can still picture it now. It wasn't actually a pig at all, but a sky blue jar with an inspirational platitude about "all the places you'll see" painted across its front—with the unsaid implication of "if only you can afford it." I had taken a crap job working at one of those telephone banks where current students call and bother alums to donate to their alma mater. For months, I'd hold the phone receiver at arm's length as an enraged alumnus screamed about the idea of donating to a university for which they were still paying off student loans. I hated the job but kept working there anyway, hopeful I could squirrel away enough money to afford a ticket to France. At night, surrounded by pictures of Paris torn from travel magazines, I'd stare at the piggy bank that had become a shrine to traveling in my final months of senior year—another version of the brick wall I'd once perched on as a kid.

I imagined myself walking over to the Gare de Rouen station and taking the hour-and-a-half train ride to Paris's bustling Gare du Nord. I pictured afternoons in the Latin Quarter, roaming the dizzying bookshelves of Shakespeare and Company before heading to Café de Flore on Boulevard Saint-Germain, where I'd start conversations with other wayfaring strangers. I'd envisioned sipping a café au lait while discussing literary legends before bidding my new friends adieu and heading to the Louvre. I'd been so committed to this cliché vision that I had even insisted on buying a membership to the Louvre, convinced it would pay for itself with my regular museum visits. Having now stood up the *Mona Lisa* for weeks, that laminated card mocks me each time I open my wallet.

It's not to say I haven't been exploring Rouen. With Alex, we've explored on weekends, but when it comes to these lonely weekdays, my comfort zone seems to expand one block every couple of days. At this rate, I'll be confident walking around Rouen by age fifty. Despite him encouraging me to explore on my own or take the train into Paris, I can't explain why I feel the need to wait for Alex to explore France—as though I'm that little girl waiting for someone's permission to walk down the jet bridge. Maybe it's the language barrier. The fact that I can't pronounce Rouen correctly doesn't exactly bode well for my pronunciation of the rest of the French language. But I suspect it's something deeper than that. Maybe, even after all my preparation and planning, I'm feeling afraid of moving through the world solo more than I'd like to admit. Or perhaps I simply tend to let my imagination run wild, romanticizing expectations, only to find the reality more intimidating.

To pass the hours here, I've started a blog with the cringeworthy name *Le Post Grad*, where I document my time in France, sharing stories about my and Alex's weekends exploring the Normandy beaches or sampling cheese in Camembert. Today, my goal is to walk the five minutes over to Rue Jeanne d'Arc and simply order a macaron in French—alone. At least I'd made it as far as the bakery.

"Rien d'autre?" the woman behind the Yvonne display case asks me as the line of French locals steadily builds behind me, thinly veiling their impatience.

All morning as I practiced the art of ordering a single raspberry macaron, I hadn't prepared for a follow-up question. I want to slap my forehead and utter the only French phrase I seem to have mastered these days: *oh, merde…oh, shit.*

I smile awkwardly and switch gears to Frenglish.

"Um, je suis…sorry, what was that?"

I feel myself wanting to turn on my heel and run back to that blue door on Rue Saint-Maur, like a hermit crab retreating into its shell and scurrying down the beach. With flushed cheeks, I use a series of erratic hand gestures to point towards the display case and whatever macaron comes into focus. At this very moment, travel feels anything but magical.

Finally leaving the Yvonne pastry shop, I feel my cold sweat from this whole ordeal now drying in the cool morning air. As I shuffle down Rue Jeanne d'Arc, I decide to walk the four minutes over to the nearby Donjon de Rouen, a white brick building topped with what can only be described as the black cone of a witch's hat. In fact, the whole structure looked like someone from the heavens dropped a life-sized rook chess piece in the middle of town. This single castle tower stands almost comically on another drab residential street, separated by a wrought-iron gate. Windowless except for three ruler-sized slits, this thirteenth-century building can hardly be described as beautiful, but then again, why would it be? It was once a prison where Joan of Arc was held captive.

Since arriving in Rouen, I've been intrigued by the history of Joan of Arc, inspired by this headstrong teenager who seemed so sure of the world and her place in it. I once read a quote from her in which she said, "I do not fear the soldiers, for my road is made open to me." Like a centuries-long game of telephone, the original message had become a garble of what it once was, now the more popular quote, "I am not afraid; I was born to do this."

Thinking of Rouen's historical darling, I can't help but wish I felt braver. I had been so defiant when it came to dreaming of this trip. I stood up against my family, graduated college without a job, and flew across the world for a man I didn't know existed six months ago. Did I do all that just to now hide in my apartment?

I bet Joan wouldn't have panicked over ordering a macaron, I think to myself bitterly.

Turning away from the Donjon de Rouen, I make my way slowly back to Rue Saint-Maur, deciding I've had enough exploring for today. I turn onto my street and find the blue door of my building.

As I step inside, that warm sun-streaked kitchen welcomes me with its little table set against the white-painted walls. I pull out a plate and delicately place my hard-earned rose-pink macaron in its center. I glance at the clock: it's hardly lunchtime. I still have hours before Alex gets back from class. Another day in France stretches ahead of me. Another afternoon spent wrestling with myself: one side of me eager to walk the three blocks to the train station and go into Paris, the other side wanting only to stay within the warm confines of our cozy apartment.

I amble over to that small wooden desk positioned in front of the floor-to-ceiling windows and open my laptop. I have less than a month left in France before my tourist visa will expire and I'll have to board a one-way flight to New York. I can only hope I'll have more courage by the time I walk on that plane. I click open my *Le Post Grad* blog and open a new post, wondering if anyone is even reading these stories I keep sending into the virtual void. The apartment is silent save for the ticking clock—a constant reminder of how I'm wasting my time abroad. I type the first thing that comes to mind:

I'm no Joan of Arc.

3

I Wouldn't Wish This Hostel on My Worst Enemy

New York, New York

I hate Herald Square.

Standing on 34th Street in Midtown Manhattan, the rain only adds to the drama of us frantically hailing a cab with suitcases in hand. Anytime it starts to rain in the city, I could bank on stepping outside my apartment to see a horde of New Yorkers thrusting their Duane Reade umbrellas into the air as if taking a cue from a choreographer. The imposing black vinyl canopy will suddenly envelop the sidewalk, threatening to swallow up any pedestrian not quick enough to move out of the way.

I remember visiting New York with my dad while still in high school. The trip was meant to be a tour of East Coast Ivy League colleges we both knew I didn't have the grades for. On that first night, we rented a car at LaGuardia Airport and made our way into Manhattan, gliding over the East River towards the city lights that lay ahead. My dad opened the windows as we drove to let in the warm summer breeze; the air on the Queensboro Bridge smelled like a mix of exhaust fumes and salt emanating from the waters below. The river seemed to extend forever in both directions, crowned by the magnificent Williamsburg, Brooklyn, and Queensboro Bridges. My dad cranked up the volume of Frank Sinatra's "New York, New York," letting the vibrato of Ol' Blue Eyes serenade us on the drive. It didn't matter that we had just flown in from Chicago—another city with impressive skyscrapers. There was just something about New York that transcended the bricks and mortar it stood on.

The next day, while we were exploring Midtown, it began to pour. In an instant, I went from standing next to my dad to being pushed to the edge of the sidewalk by an endless stream of people. As I stood hovering between honking taxis and piles of rain-slicked trash bags, their smelly entrails spilling out onto the cement, I suddenly felt vulnerable. It wasn't the rain or even the crowds that intimidated me. It was the realization that, in a moment, this city could go from being the manifestation of your dreams to a cutthroat hell that would kick you to the sidelines if you didn't move quickly enough. I felt my dad's hand grab hold of my wrist and yank me through the crowd, pulling me back to the comfort of his side.

Standing here now, more than four years later, I'm just delirious enough to hope my dad will emerge from the rain-soaked New Yorkers and once again pull me to that same comfort. But no such luck.

Like I said, I hate Herald Square. It's a terrible place where tourists shove Saint Bernard–sized shopping bags past one another as they amble from Macy's to Sephora to Build-A-Bear. Sure, there are redeemable parts of Midtown, such as the stretch of karaoke joints and hot pot restaurants on Korea Way, but for the most part, this area is akin to an outdoor shopping center. Somewhere between the last Roy Rogers and Manhattan Mall, I have been living at a place called Herald Towers with my college friend Maryn. Or rather, I *was* living at a place called Herald Towers with my college friend Maryn, until about ten minutes ago when we were both unceremoniously given the boot.

Now here we are in the shadow of our building, fighting back tears. Pushing through that umbrella canopy, we try desperately to hail a cab to a last-minute hostel in the East Village. Maryn steps out into the street to wave down a taxi, while I'm frozen in place, unable to comprehend the shock of what's happening.

We have nowhere to live.

We have nowhere to live…in New York City.

I could blame my and Maryn's collective naivete, or the fact that we had only recently left the college bubble, but the truth is we just fucked up. Maryn had signed a six-month sublease for a one-bedroom apartment that she had been sharing with her roommate, Claire. When I landed in New York, I crashed at their place, grabbing one of four bunkbeds stacked side by side in the tiny room. We both assumed Claire would let us stay past Maryn's move-out date, allowing us extra time to figure out our next move. Instead, she kicked us out; in part due to rising tension, but mostly due to new roommates moving in, leaving Maryn and me without a place to live.

Already, I missed Herald Towers. Similar to my apartment in Rouen with the blue door I loved so much, the best part of Herald Towers was not inside the building. It was a fire escape facing the Empire State Building, which we could access from our floor at any time.

Most nights, Maryn and I would light up a joint and watch

the windows of the Empire State Building flick on as the sun set. To sit on the fire escape was to be so close to the Empire State Building that you had to crane your neck just to see the top of it. If you looked closely enough at night, you could see the camera flashes of tourists taking pictures from the eighty-sixth-floor observatory. There above the swirling crowds, Maryn and I would sit perched on that fire escape, looking up at the Empire State Building and out over the city. As our minds began to swim with the headiness of our shared sativa joint, we'd call out to the New York icon like an obnoxious neighbor.

"One day, I'll grab you by the fucking bricks!" we'd yell out, collapsing into a fit of marijuana-fueled laughter. "Just wait and see."

We'd point at the Empire State Building, pass the joint between us, and rattle off all the things we hoped to one day have: high-power editorial jobs, chic apartments overlooking Central Park, social calendars jam-packed with invitations to gallery openings in SoHo and dinner parties in the West Village. We'd toggle between reveling in our possible futures and reminiscing on our favorite college memories, a part of us still mourning the end of our time at Indiana University.

"Remember that night back at IU?" asked Maryn, her eyes glistening. "The night when we got drinks and talked about New York for all those hours?"

It had been a quiet Thursday in Bloomington, and Maryn—who had just turned twenty-one—went with me to grab a drink at one of the college bars overlooking Kirkwood Avenue, the town's main street. Maryn had plans to move to New York after graduation for an editorial internship, while I planned to move to Manhattan after France. Together, we sat at a high-top table facing the window, waxing poetic about the city we'd pinned all our dreams upon.

"I can't believe we're actually here," I'd say. We'd look out at New York for a few more moments before growing hungry and heading over to the twenty-four-hour Duane Reade across the street for a run of candy peach rings and dried mangoes.

★

Since arriving in New York, I have spent most of my time dreaming about my future with Alex. After three months of living together in Rouen, my tourist visa finally expired, and as planned, Alex had stayed in Normandy to finish his last semester of business school before he would join me in the States. In the meantime, I was supposed to go ahead and "set us up" in New York. A laughably monumental task we pretended was as simple as buying groceries. Those last few days in Rouen, we wallowed in the heartache of parting ways, promising we'd soon be reunited in our new life together. Now, blinded by that promise, I took on the responsibility of finding us an affordable apartment in New York while Alex focused on wrapping up university and sorting out his work visa.

From the moment I graduated college, it was made very clear that I was financially cut off from the family teat. There would be no safety net to pad my landing if I fell, and there would be no allowance to line my pockets if money was tight. I knew that as immigrants, my parents expected nothing less from me than the same resilience they had been forced to exhibit in their younger years. No one had stepped in to rescue either of them in their more challenging moments, and no one would swoop in to save me now.

Growing up, I remember my dad telling me about our immigration to the United States from Colombia. He recounted, in painstaking detail, how he had climbed the ladder from being a cashier at Burger King to becoming a doctor in Chicago. His evolution was always a fantastic one to recount, a story riddled with financial obstacles and racial discrimination, but one where he ultimately proved his naysayers wrong. His tale was outshone only by Yana, a Russian refugee who had spent a year self-schooling in Cuba before immigrating to the States to attend dental school.

Yana and my dad were the poster children for building something from nothing and weaving realities from ambitions. Throughout my childhood, my siblings and I had grown up with their anecdotes meant to either inspire us or underscore how flagrantly ungrateful we could be. The thing is, it was hard to imagine our parents as being anything other than, well, parents. It was as if both Yana and my dad had strolled out of the uterus with a 401(k), a mortgage, and the keys to a 1998 Volvo. They have always had the banality of adulthood figured out—filing taxes, picking health insurance plans, hiring the right landscaping service. It was impossible to picture them as wide-eyed twentysomething immigrants waking up with beer-fueled hangovers, partying with medical residents, and navigating new cities.

Their inbred certainty made adulthood feel all the more daunting to me. When I left for New York, I didn't have a job, a place to live, or more than $100 to my name—but I did have Maryn.

Maryn and I had met during my first year at Indiana University. She came from Alabama and had a Southern hospitality about her, but far from being disingenuous, her warmth arose from an earnest desire to please others. When I first met her, I admittedly bristled at Maryn's bubbly personality, which felt at odds with my own moody persona. She'd say all the right things, laugh at all the right times—but it wasn't until the two of us got closer that I saw (and loved) the cracks in her sunny facade. In Maryn, I saw that same tendency to protect my soft underbelly—she hid her vulnerability under a bed of extravagant kindness, and I masked mine with steely defiance.

The night I arrived at John F. Kennedy Airport, I was terrified. Without Alex by my side, I suddenly felt daunted by the task of trying to carve my way through New York. It wasn't until I was standing in JFK's baggage claim, collapsing into Maryn's hug under the weight of all the exhaustion, exhilaration, and fear that had been accumulating, that I began to truly understand aspects of my parents' stories. It was only then that I grasped what it probably felt like for them to arrive somewhere with nothing—no job, no money, and no place to call their own, just an unwavering ambition to start a life.

In those first few frightening days, Manhattan became riddled with emotional landmines. A subway pianist would begin playing the notes of Édith Piaf's "La Vie en Rose," and I'd feel the tears start to stream down my face as I looked on wistfully, missing Normandy—and Alex. The reality of living in Rouen had once again given way to the romance of it so that in hindsight, I missed everything about France—even the Yvonne pastry shop where I'd made an ass of myself ordering macarons. From the overpriced brasseries in Midtown to the cafés fueling the West Village, everywhere I looked, I spotted reminders of France and the man I had left across the Atlantic.

*

Maryn snaps me out of my catatonia, pulling me back to this sidewalk, this rain, and the fact that we have nowhere to live. While I have been standing in a daze, tasked with watching the suitcases, Maryn has been moving with the efficiency of a navy SEAL executing a rescue mission. I know the emotional gravitas of this day is bound to catch up with her, just as it's catching up with me, but right now, she is set on getting us out of the rain, into a cab, and over to the cheapest hostel we can find on short notice.

After what feels like hours of wandering through Herald Square, we are checking in at the street-level desk of some run-down hostel in the East Village. The building looks like a converted office space with an uncomfortable dampness in the air that sticks to your skin and makes everything—the bedsheets, your packed clothes, even the toilet paper—feel instantly sweaty. Our floor is made up of rows of makeshift rooms separated by thin partition walls not high enough to reach the ceiling. The air is musty like a high school boys' locker room, which comes as no surprise since the packed area seems to lack any ventilation. The entire hostel feels haphazardly thrown together, sidestepping all safety protocols as if designed on a lazy dare.

To call my and Maryn's room a "room" is a generous overstatement. A "cubicle" is more appropriate, just big enough to fit two sunken twin mattresses standing opposite each other on flimsy metal foundations. Between the beds, which touch the thin walls on three sides, there is a stretch of cement flooring just big enough for one person to stand, requiring constant maneuvering between us and the pile of suitcases we have stacked against the back. All around, I can hear the idle chatter of other guests, the bowel movements of people in the corner restrooms, and other assorted sounds through the flimsy walls that separate us. I wouldn't wish this hostel on my worst enemy.

I look over at Maryn and feel both of our resolves begin to crumble, but there is no time to process our situation. I have to go to work at my waitressing job.

Since arriving in New York, I have been serving cocktails at a glorified sports bar on West 26th Street, working with a motley crew of aspiring actresses, artists, and coke-snorting models in matching uniforms of off-brand Converse sneakers and tight black leggings. From the other girls, I quickly learned the value of flaunting beauty in exchange for decent tips. I invested in crimson lipstick and an overpriced push-up bra from Victoria's Secret that added at least two cup sizes to my bust. My earnings aren't much, but they're enough for me to begin putting away cash for my and Alex's future home.

The restaurant is expansive and mostly attracts young business crowds looking to blow off steam with half-priced margaritas. The front-of-house is reserved for regular diners, while the back-of-house is set up like a private VIP room for big spenders (read: big drinkers). When I first started working here, one of these big spenders made me cry. The kitchen was backed up, per usual, and the big spender in question was peeved that his steak was late and served at room temperature. In his frustration, he began to cut into me with the same ferocity he had been reserving for his well-done ribeye.

"How hard is it to do what you do?" His face was red from the happy hour Corona beers he'd been tossing back. "Goddamn waitress. You'll never be better than this."

As the man eviscerated me with words, I meekly promised to bring over the manager and offered to comp the cold beef, hoping this would assuage his grievances. My manager is a thirtysomething bald man whose face slightly resembles the British actor Damian Lewis. He is always dressed in a well-fitted suit and friendly with the waitresses, and is never one to turn down an end-of-shift drink (or "shift kick," as we call them). Flushed and trying to fight back tears, I recounted the customer's words to my manager. One look at me, and he let out a weary sigh that seemed to hold the weight of years of comforting New York novices fresh out of college.

You think this is bad? that sigh seemed to say. *Just you wait and see.*

"That guy is an asshole. Don't let it affect you," my manager said kindly. "You're really going to have to toughen up if you're going to live in this city."

As I mustered up a smile, I remembered how I used to spend ample time walking barefoot outdoors as a kid. I loved the feeling of the soft grass on my toes and the heat of the driveway pressed against my heels. The more time I spent running around our home barefoot, the more I began growing calluses on my feet. This fascinated me when I was younger, and I got it in my mind that by walking barefoot, I could magically turn my feet into something akin to shoes, so that if I ever stepped on so much as a pesky pebble, I wouldn't feel the pain. My toughened soles would act as a protective shell for my feet, allowing me to run carefree. Working at this restaurant has become like that driveway. Every shift, every shitty customer, every dropped tray, every lonely 2:00 a.m. walk after closing time seems to callus and toughen me up against New York.

Of course, even the most callused feet can still step on a nail, and today's sudden move-out has been one big fucking nail.

Arriving at the restaurant, I can still feel the dampness of the hostel clinging to my uniform, a visceral reminder that I have no place to live. We have a bed to sleep in tonight, but what about tomorrow? What about the night after? While I have managed to save most of my tips, I can hardly afford the deposit on a new apartment. These are the questions running through my mind when I bump into my manager. Every time I see this man, I seem to have tears in my eyes, and today is no exception. With the restaurant nearly empty and my shift just beginning, my manager knows full well these tears can't possibly be about another customer and their undercooked beef.

"Hold on...why are you crying?"

"I'm...I'm...HOMELESS!" I blurt out, mascara tears now streaming down my cheeks.

Immediately I am embarrassed. My situation is a far cry from the realities of being *actually* homeless, but all I can think of is that godforsaken hostel waiting for me. My words begin to spill out as I try to explain the morning of being kicked out of our apartment, hastily packing our bags, and checking into the East Village hellhole. My manager stares at me blankly.

"Maybe you should take the evening off and figure this out," he says with one of those world-weary sighs. Although I need the money, I accept his offer gratefully.

In the time it took me to go back uptown to the restaurant, break down in front of my boss, and head back downtown to the hostel, Maryn looks as though she hasn't moved a muscle. Upon second glance, the East Village hellhole is even worse than I remember—the lobby's linoleum flooring peels up at the corners, while a dust-covered staircase leads to that open space and its coffin-sized guest rooms. I find Maryn lying on the sunken mattress, just as shell-shocked as when we first arrived. The adrenaline of getting us here has worn off, and now there is only the daunting realization that we have nowhere to live.

"Oh, giiiiiiiirls?!"

I hear the flamboyant trill of one of the other hostel guests and open our flimsy door. Standing there is a tall and lanky stranger, not more than twenty-five years old, sporting a baby pink oxford shirt, a friendly smile, and a crop of curly dark hair.

"What brings you to New York City?" he asks in an Eastern European accent I can't quite place. I remember hearing his voice when we first arrived, flitting around from door to door, introducing himself to other guests. It occurs to me at this moment that while Maryn and I have been feeling like our world has collapsed, to everyone else in this hostel, we appear to be budget backpackers visiting New York for the first time.

The idea of telling this complete stranger the details of the day is simply too exhausting. Maryn and I swap a glance and silently decide it's just easier to play the part of travelers instead.

"We're visiting New York," I say flatly, too tired to come up with a more detailed backstory.

"Me too!" squeals the guy in that same excited trill. "Well, you'll have to come out with me and some of my new friends!"

I'm reminded, briefly, of the first time I met Alex—how the whole reason we had been brought together was through a string of acquaintances inviting whatever connection they had to dinner. Maybe Mr. Trill is just eager for a New York night with new friends, trying to assemble a group from the hostel to go out and enjoy the city.

I look back at Maryn, who is still sitting wide-eyed on the bed, and raise my eyebrows with a nonverbal *What do you think?* She responds with a defeated half shrug: *I don't care anymore.* We need to figure out our next steps and where we're going to live, but we are too emotionally frayed to come up with a game plan just yet. Sometimes, the only thing to do at times like these is to get rip-roaringly drunk.

A couple of hours later, Maryn and I are sitting at a table in French Roast a few blocks away from the hostel. The restaurant is a brasserie with locations scattered throughout Manhattan, serving up a menu of French classics like crispy duck confit and bottles of cheap Beaujolais. At our table sits an Australian backpacker from Perth who is in his twenties and has floppy brown hair and deep-set eyes. To his right, a young woman from England in a leather jacket. To her right is Mr. Trill. With a carafe of red wine on the table, Maryn and I listen as these backpackers swap travel stories while tearing into plates of garlicky escargot and dipping into our communal French onion soup with toasty baguettes. We have nothing in common but the city of New York, and there's a certain magic to being thrown together for the evening.

During the three months I spent in Normandy, I hadn't experienced such sudden camaraderie among strangers. At parties in Rouen, I was relegated to the role of Alex's American girlfriend, a novelty to his friends, left smiling and nodding on the fringes of French conversations I couldn't understand and didn't have the language skills to join. Because I had been in his country, surrounded by his language, living in his college town, and drinking among his friends, it had been too easy to stand behind Alex. I grew comfortable in his shadow, letting him take the lead rather than trying to navigate France myself. But now here I am, an ocean away from Alex's embrace and far from any sort of comfort zone. For the briefest moment, I am just one of these travelers, untethered in New York City, coasting by on a heady mix of adventure and anticipation for something new.

"Have you all been to the hostel rooftop yet?" says Mr. Trill, leaning conspiratorially over the empty glasses.

The rest of us exchange a look, our eyes twinkling with excitement, and soon enough we find ourselves back at the hostel and sneaking up the fire escape. When I climb up and set foot on the roof, it's immediately clear why one needs to sneak onto it. The silver-painted surface slopes downwards with only a small knee-high brick barrier separating us from the plunge to the sidewalk below. The five of us walk gingerly to a spot on the roof and huddle in a group with the brown-bagged beers we just purchased at a nearby bodega.

"How about a drinking game," suggests the Aussie. "Have you ever played G'Day Bruce?"

The rest of us stare back blankly as he begins to lay out the rules. Best I can tell, G'Day Bruce is a memory game in which each person goes around saying G'Day Bruce and then adds to it with a name. It's meant to challenge our wine- and beer-addled minds to recall everyone's addition, or risk chugging a Bud Light as punishment.

"I'll start," says the Aussie in his thick accent. "G'Day Bruce. Say G'Day to Angus."

"Angus!" laughs Mr. Trill. "What sort of name is that?"

"It's a popular name in Australia!" the Aussie fires back with a giddy smile.

Composing himself, Mr. Trill continues. "G'Day Bruce, G'Day Angus, Say G'Day to Galina."

"Galina?!" we echo in drunken laughter.

"That's a normal name where I come from!"

On and on we go, our group erupting into another giggly chorus of G'Day Bruces and yelling out to the city below. By the time it's my turn, the game has devolved into such a mix of foreign or nonsensical names that I end up being the one to chug my beer.

★

Tomorrow, the five of us will go our separate ways, these three travelers journeying on to whatever destination is up next on their great American trip. Meanwhile, Maryn and I will wake up with pounding headaches and stomach-curdling hangovers (never mix house wine, cheap beer, and French snails) and trek to a nearby Starbucks. We'll sit with our laptops opposite each other and scour Airbnb for any available and affordable apartments that we can book for upwards of two weeks, giving us time to figure out a longer-term living situation.

Eventually, we'll check out of our damp and crummy hostel and load our luggage into a taxi headed for a building in the East 30s along the river. We'll share a room within a two-bedroom apartment and soon become fast friends with the host, extending our Airbnb stay through the rest of the summer. Come fall, Maryn will move to Greenwich Village, finding a small but cute apartment off MacDougal Street that she'll share with a roommate, while I'll move into my and Alex's future home, a one-bedroom off 2nd Avenue and East 79th.

But for now, in this one sparkling moment, our realities are suspended in laughter, punctuated by G'Day Bruces filling the night sky. On that rooftop, in the company of travelers, I find myself smiling for the first time all day.

4

Just Say Yes

New York, New York

I can't hear the words coming out of Alex's mouth as he proposes. I see his lips moving, I can see the heartfelt warmth in his eyes, but try as I might, I simply cannot hear the words. His voice sounds muffled, like the warbled tones of an adult in a *Peanuts* cartoon. I could blame the wine or a heat flash from the sun bearing down on us, or maybe it's just the deafening pounding of my heart and the pumping of my blood that is drowning out his voice. Alex is kneeling in front of me on one knee, his dark jeans pressed into the soil of this vineyard out in Long Island's North Fork wine region.

The North Fork sits an hour-and-a-half drive from the streets of Manhattan. Flanked by the Long Island Sound to its north and the Peconic Bay to its south, the area is nicknamed Long Island's Bordeaux because of its incredible grape-growing climate. Back in the day, this part of Long Island was popular for its potato farms, but it has since given way to a slew of wineries that attract nature-starved New Yorkers from across the city. Today, Alex and I are two of them, courtesy of some cheap wine-tour tickets we found on Groupon. We've decided to take a break from emails and Excel spreadsheets to come drink wine instead.

We are alone amid an endless sea of leaves and vines of plump purple, red, and green grapes. Behind us sits the tasting room, from where we can hear the sounds of other mingling visitors drifting lazily on the breeze. After an afternoon of wine tastings, we decided to take a walk into the vineyard with two glasses and a bottle of semisweet rosé.

Now, Alex is looking up at me through squinted eyes blinded by the sun, delivering a speech I'm sure he has practiced many times, a speech that is falling on deaf ears.

*

Alex and I have been living together on Manhattan's Upper East Side for the past year. Our pre-war apartment is charming, albeit overpriced and unbearably small with "quirks" we chose to overlook upon renting, like a cracked mirror in the bathroom, the broken dial-up telephone circa 1955 mounted on the wall, and the kitchen that can only fit one person at a time. Looking for a place to live in New York was no easy feat—especially when searching with someone who was an ocean away.

Since our stint in that East Village hellhole hostel, I had been living with Maryn at that Airbnb in the East 30s. Between shifts at the restaurant, I'd hurry from one apartment viewing to another, only to leave each one increasingly horrified. From windowless subterranean basements to a building with a makeshift memorial comprised of flowers and teddy bears for a recently murdered tenant (you can't make this shit up), the task of finding Alex and myself a home had proved bleak. That is, until I came across the listing for a one-bedroom unicorn apartment that seemed to be somewhat affordable, well-located, and spacious enough by New York standards, which is to say, the bathtub wasn't in the same room as the bed and stove.

I moved in an entire month ahead of Alex, who remained in France tackling the logistics of securing his work visa. After paying my half of the security deposit and first month's rent, the remaining tips I had saved up from my shifts at the restaurant didn't leave much wiggle room for extravagances like, say, furniture. For those first few weeks, I lived in our apartment with a single mattress on the floor and a suitcase splayed out in the corner. On my nights off, I'd order Thai food from up the street and sit in that empty living room with my stir-fried noodles, drinking directly from a $10 bottle of pinot noir because we had yet to purchase any glasses. I'd lie atop my mattress and imagine how different our apartment would become once Alex moved in, how it would transform from bare walls and empty rooms and finally become a home.

As a waitress, my shifts seemed to be pulling in fewer and fewer tips as the weather warmed and New Yorkers opted to drink alfresco rather than in the dark recesses of an over-priced sports bar. These slow shifts found me staring at a sea of empty tables, scribbling down notes in my guest checkbook as I brainstormed ways to become a writer. I'd stand there for hours, my feet aching in those off-brand Converses, and jot down lists of publications I could pitch to, editorial internships I could apply for, jobs I could pursue, and stories I could write—any snatches of ideas that came to mind between bussing tables.

For as long as I can remember, I have wanted to be a writer. At age eight, I received my first journal, a blue Bugs

Bunny notebook from Six Flags Great America given to me by Yana. My early journals were filled with the sort of "cute" stories one would expect from a kid: suspicions that I'd been scammed into trading my brand new Barbie doll for my friend's worn stuffed dog (I had been) or the elbow bump from that boy in the library that I imagined had been an intentional love tap (it was not).

In junior high, my journal entries evolved into more existential questions, like when my boobs would come in so I could finally wear bras like all the other girls in school or whether I'd get my first period soon. As a teenager, my writing became a lighthouse in the storm of my angst, a way for me to navigate my mind and the unhinged emotions flying around inside it. It was in high school that the pages of my journals *actually* became scintillating. I wrote about losing my virginity to Ray, the high school "bad boy"—a blond-haired and blue-eyed fifteen-year-old who wore oversized puffy jackets and listened to Eminem on his Sony Walkman. I detailed how I'd occasionally smoke weed before classes with my friend Matt ("wake and bakes," as we'd call them). I'd divulge stories of sneaking out of our German shepherd's dog door and going to parties, and mortifying details of "shotgunning" my first Bud Light, shrinking in embarrassment as the beer splashed across my T-shirt and left a lake-sized wet stain in its wake. I wrote it all down—every kiss, every drink, every joint, every hookup—and would come home to find my little sister, Natalie, poring over the pages of my diary as though it were a gripping YA novel.

My journaling evolved again during college, when I declared myself a journalism major and began exploring writing as a career instead of just an outlet for my feelings. I started small by reporting stories for the *Indiana Daily Student*, covering town events ("Pets ALIVE celebrates annual Spay Day!")

and the occasional campus gossip ("Local student artist to appear on hot new MTV series *Truth Riders!*"). I soon fell in love with telling people's stories and the ability to transport a reader to another place—even if that place was just an animal shelter across campus. I spent four years pursuing a journalism degree and reporting for the student newspaper, only to graduate college at the same time that bloggers were going from basement dwellers to respected writers now quoted on CNN.

The blogs of the early '90s were mostly written off as "online diaries" and "weblogs." It wasn't until 2002 that blogging began reshaping the media landscape. It came in waves. First, mommy bloggers took off with their parenting advice that read like emails from a close friend. For new parents especially, those tips from reliable, rosy-cheeked Susan in North Dakota felt more human than a listicle from the parenting section of *USA Today*. Soon after, *Newsweek* predicted blogs would replace traditional media, and while they weren't exactly right, they weren't exactly wrong either.

Blogs began to saddle up right next to formal news sources, and soon the floodgates opened. Google debuted AdSense, effectively turning blogs into a business and bloggers into at-home professionals able to monetize their words. *The Guardian* became the first outlet to debut live blogging in 2003, and even the White House rolled out its official blog, sharing everything from foreign policy breakdowns to Christmas decorations. By the time the film *Julie & Julia* came out in late 2009 (for any film novices, Amy Adams stars as a food blogger trying to cook her way through Julia Child's recipes), blogging had officially pierced the pop culture fabric.

I remember sitting in my Media Ethics 101 class when I first heard of the eleven-year-old fashion blogger Tavi Gevinson and her website, *Style Rookie*, which had earned her front-row seats to New York Fashion Week alongside *Vogue*'s Anna

Wintour and the late André Leon Talley. For better or worse, Gevinson represented a crop of writers who could now gain access to the upper echelons of media by simply picking up a pen (or keyboard)—no degree needed. Blogging was meant to democratize publishing and allow the Davids of the world to stand up against the Goliath of media, but it had also blurred the lines of what defined professional writing and a hobby.

Surrounded by the cornfields of Indiana University in that media ethics class, paying $40,000 a year, my classmates and I witnessed the blogging revolution and collectively thought: *fuck.* Whether pulling from student loans or our parents' savings, we were paying out the wazoo for a journalism degree that now seemed obsolete. By the time I graduated college and flew to France, there were no writing jobs to be found, and so I started blogging in my spare time. As the old adage goes—"If you can't beat 'em, join 'em."

On those slow shifts at the restaurant in New York, I'd stare at my notes and try to trace a line between serving tables and becoming a bona fide writer. One afternoon, a twentysomething blonde girl and her friend strolled in for a late brunch. As I served them champagne flutes, I couldn't help but catch snippets of their conversation: they were celebrating the blonde's recent work promotion. It was another perfect summer day, which meant another quiet afternoon at the restaurant (and its lousy tips). Sunlight poured in from the big bay windows, illuminating my empty front-of-house section where only the two girls sat. As their brunch-fueled smiles grew wider, I looked at them and felt a tinge of envy. They were toasting to professional success, and here I was, manically drawing up notes to try and start my nonexistent career. When the time came to deliver their check, the blonde one slapped down a Chase credit card with a Chicago skyline printed across its front.

"Are you from Chicago?" I asked before I could help myself.

She looked up, really noticing me for the first time. "Yes, I am."

"Me too!" I squealed a little too loud. "I grew up just outside Chicago in the suburbs and moved to New York a few months ago."

Maybe it was the slow shift or the fact that I hadn't actually spoken to anyone but the busboy since arriving at 9:00 a.m., but I really let loose on this customer, rambling on about Chicago, my graduation from Indiana University, and how I had come to New York to look for a job but was having a tough time. By the time I stopped monologuing, I noticed the blonde girl looking up at me with a guarded curiosity. After a pause, she whipped out a white-and-red business card with the words Inventif Media printed across its front.

"We're looking for assistant media buyers and planners right now," she said casually. "Send me your résumé."

Before I could respond, the girl drowned the last dregs of champagne in her glass, bid me goodbye, and flounced out of the restaurant with her friend in tow.

As I stood there staring at the empty table and business card in my hand, all I could manage to think was: *What the hell is a media buyer?*

I didn't know anything about Inventif Media, but if it meant never having to serve another red-faced dude dribbling whiskey down his L.L. Bean vest, then I was sold.

A few weeks later, I quit my job at the restaurant and started working at a sleek office building in the Financial District. As it turns out, a media buyer is exactly as it sounds: a person who plans and buys media. At Inventif, I learned that those pesky internet pop-up ads *actually* have a purpose beyond being annoying scams. Thousands upon thousands of dollars are spent to have that 300 × 250 pixel ad pop up on your

screen at just the right moment, alongside just the right article, so you'll stop and think: *Yes, I should book a trip to Cancun.*
Chances are, most of those ads were strategically planned by
a group of twenty- and thirtysomething media buyers who
were probably aspiring writers too.

My days quickly became a blur of never-ending meetings to
discuss the best websites to buy ad space for clients like Evian
and Mexico Tourism. I soon learned things like the exorbitant cost of buying a home page ad on *The New York Times*
website or the wrath of a client like Volvo, whose beloved ad
would sometimes accidentally pop up on a porn site. I have
to convince myself daily that Inventif Media is but a brief detour on my path to becoming a writer.

I had left Rouen back in early spring, anticipating that Alex
would join me in New York a month or so later, but a bevy
of visa complications and paperwork kept us apart until late
August. By the time his plane touched down at JFK, an entire summer had slipped past. Yet somehow, I had managed
to do exactly what I set out to do when boarding that one-
way flight from Paris to New York. Despite the many challenges, I found an apartment, found a steady job (although in
an entirely different industry), and secured a paycheck (steady,
however measly) that barely covers my half of the rent. It's
been a year since Alex moved in with me, and in that time,
we've settled into a comfy routine, one in which it feels like
we've been married for decades rather than dating for fewer
than twenty-four months.

*

As I look down at Alex on his knee now, my body feels
slightly wobbly. There are many reasons why I want to marry
Alex. I love his laugh and the joy he brings to any given room,
from the happy hours at the Stumble Inn on 2nd Avenue to
standing in line at UPS. I love our life and the little nicknames

we have for each other, like how he calls me "cub," inspired by a small brown teddy bear we won off an arcade game in Coney Island during our first summer together. I love his family and how they've become an extension of my own. I especially love his mom, the quintessential French woman, exuding a flow of warmth and kindness wrapped in unattainable Parisian class. I love having someone to split the rent with because, without Alex, I'm fairly certain I'd be living with fourteen roommates on the fringes of Brooklyn, or worse, staying at that East Village hostel.

The reasons why I want to marry him are clear and quantifiable. But the reasons why I might not want to marry Alex? Those are harder to make sense of; they sit in my mind like a mess of wires I keep procrastinating untangling. It's impossible to say what exactly I'm feeling about this proposal, other than an incongruous feeling that something is out of place.

My mouth feels impossibly dry as the sun beats down on us in the vineyard. Alex is still kneeling in the dirt before me, delivering his speech, as I wonder exactly how much time has passed since we left the tasting room.

"Will you marry me?" asks Alex, pulling out a small ring box.

A kaleidoscope of images flashes across my mind. I see the pair of us as interns, locking eyes for the first time at that SoHo restaurant. I watch our love blossom over ropa vieja at that Cuban spot on the Upper West Side. I see the evenings of sharing frozen yogurt on the steps of Columbia University and the lazy mornings spent tangled up in sheets at his intern apartment on Amsterdam Avenue. The emails and love letters that spanned the distance between New York and Indiana as I wrapped up my last semester of college. The months spent living in Normandy in that tiny studio with the bright blue door on Rue Saint-Maur, and how Alex had been my comfort zone in a foreign place.

I remember the joy of having Alex finally arrive at JFK after so much time apart, walking through the terminal with his suitcases in tow. I see our entire story then—the good, the bad, the beautiful, and the ugly—and I know I have my answer. I love this man. To say no to marrying Alex would be to end our story, which I'm not ready to do. I push aside my wobbly doubts, reasoning they'll work themselves out along the way. I look down at Alex and just say yes.

He Was Never Really There

New York, New York

I know what I'm doing is wrong, and yet here I am, zipping up a too-tight black pleather dress and slathering on crimson lipstick. There are many reasons why I shouldn't like Jasper; the top one being that I'm engaged to his coworker. And yet something about this man has crept into my mind like poison ivy, its gnarled vines wrapping around my every thought. I tell myself it's a harmless crush, but deep down, I know it's more. Now here I am on the subway, avoiding my reflection in the window as I take the 6 train down to Solas Bar in the East Village. I'd texted Jasper a choice: meet me by 9:00 p.m. if you feel the way I do and I'll call off my engagement, or don't show up and I'll be history.

★

My Jasper story began a few months after Alex proposed. Hurricane Sandy had swept through New York City with such destructive force that it left $70 billion in damages and over two hundred people dead in its wake. In Manhattan, the hurricane played out in the most Shakespearean of ways, with everything below 14th Street plunged into watery darkness and everything uptown seemingly unaffected.

Because Hurricane Sandy had made landfall in New Jersey's Atlantic City, it ferociously swept north towards lower Manhattan. To be south of Union Square was to find yourself without running water or electricity. Subway stations swelled with water that submerged the platforms and tracks. The FDR highway that snakes along Manhattan's east side was flooded with roaring currents of the East River. Neighbors huddled around battery-powered charging stations, running extension cords across water-slicked brownstone stoops. Late-night hosts like Jon Stewart painted downtown dwellers as Herculean survivors hunting rats for dinner and uptowners as pompous asses complaining about canceled Broadway shows and sprinkle shortages at Serendipity. In most comedies, there is a grain of truth, and here, the jokes were not far off.

Up on 79th Street, Alex and I hadn't seen so much as a light flicker. With our bathtub full of "just in case" water jugs and our kitchen bursting with nonperishable food supplies, we were more than happy to take in our downtown friends who came seeking refuge from the storm—one of whom was Jasper.

Given the flooded subways, stalled city buses, and out-of-commission taxis, our trio of guests had to walk the thirty or so blocks from their East Village apartments, carrying bags of clothes and toiletries with them. For days, they had gone without plumbing or electricity until they arrived at our front door. As I greeted them, all three faces lit up at the sight of our working lamps and television, as they dropped their bags and practically sprinted to our shower.

I can't say I felt anything when I first truly got a look at Jasper. Like Alex, he was a French expat in New York on a work visa. Jasper was handsome in a sort of unconventional way; he had a similar build to Alex but tousled light brown hair and deep-set arctic-blue eyes that were at once brooding and playful. I don't know what Jasper—or Alex, for that matter—did at their company, only that it required they both wear stuffy suits and stare for hours, with glazed eyes, at endless spreadsheets. Because I had only known Jasper in one capacity, he existed in my mind with surface-level labels: French, expat, coworker. That all changed the moment I heard Jasper speak about travel.

As Hurricane Sandy raged outside our dusty windows, we turned my and Alex's one-bedroom home into a mini staycation pad. We didn't have much space, but we did have beer, cheap snacks, and bad television. With nothing to do, we'd move from lounging and day drinking to drinking games, which always escalated into the sort of heart-to-heart conversations typical of a conditionally boozy day. This was when Jasper would begin to light up as he recalled vacationing in places like Mexico or Thailand, where he'd visited to indulge in his passion for photography. His favorite destination was Playa del Carmen, which he found to be both affordable and easily accessible from New York. There, on sandy beaches filled with nighttime bonfires and oceanfront margaritas, Jasper would spend every spare penny and vacation day.

He spoke of palm-tree-shaded beach haunts in Central America, their thatched roofs and sand-strewn floors mere feet from the ocean, and recalled energetic hostels in Southeast Asia, drinking cold Singhas alongside other backpackers.

To hear him was to listen to a travel-filled saga that took us far from the realities of our hurricane-imposed quarantine. When his words failed him, Jasper could always be counted on for his photography and videos. He would excitedly toggle between shots of Bangkok's busy streets and GoPro surfing clips (these he especially could not get enough of). I remember being struck by Jasper's passion for life, a feeling so electric it could power up lower Manhattan. Sandy (and I) didn't stand a chance.

The more I listened to Jasper gush, the more I felt a thrill creep in. Was it jealousy I was feeling? Attraction? Admiration? It might have been all three mixed together like a cocktail I'd enjoy now but regret later. What I can say with certainty is that this was the moment I realized one undeniable truth: I wasn't happy. Listening to Jasper wax poetic about travel had held up a mirror to my own life, showing me a reflection I didn't recognize. I couldn't pinpoint exactly what was making me feel unhappy, just that I'd become acutely aware of how alive Jasper seemed in comparison to me.

I was bored with my career. What the hell had happened to my dreams of writing? And I had doubts about my engagement that I couldn't quite articulate. Compared to Jasper's stories, my life felt colorless and passionless. I couldn't blame Alex, my employer, or anyone else, because I had chosen this. Day after day, I woke up and made the forty-five-minute commute to the Financial District, where I'd spend eight hours talking about internet ads. I then returned to this same apartment that we could barely afford and washed those same dirty dishes left in the sink and put away that same pile of clothes Alex had left crumpled on the floor by his side of the bed.

Surely, I told myself, all relationships eventually become monotonous, filled with rising arguments and dwindling sex lives, right? And becoming a writer wouldn't pay the bills, so it made sense to stick to the media buyer role I detested. I turned away from my dreams of traveling and writing, blaming the measly paychecks and limited vacation time that came with my entry-level job. Now here was Jasper, challenging my excuses; he was my age and equally stuck in an entry-level position, without a trust fund to fall back on, chasing adventure around the globe while fueling his passion for photography. I wanted *exactly* what Jasper had. I, too, wanted to have experiences that kept listeners rapt with attention. I, too, wanted to chase my creative passions to the corners of the globe. I, too, wanted to travel.

In hindsight, this was the moment I should have taken my life back. I'd like to tell you that I slammed my Bud Light on our chipped Ikea coffee table, brushed the tortilla chips off my sweatpants, hugged Jasper, and said, "Thank you." I'd like to tell you that I then turned to Alex and said, "I'm sorry, but this isn't working." I'd love to tell you I then waltzed out the front door—hurricane be damned—and began living my best life right then and there, but I didn't do any of that. Instead, I turned towards Jasper and decided that the only way I could take back *my* life was by being with *him*.

★

During Jasper's stay at our apartment, I picked up on the most subtle of flirtatious signals, typically limited to the twilight hours when another day of drinking had rendered everyone too tipsy to notice. One evening, when everyone had fallen asleep, the two of us went out into the stairwell to keep talking. It was then I noticed his lingering looks sweeping across my body, and the light touches that seemed to last a second too long. When it came time to say good-night, he leaned in for a hug, pinning me against the gray cement wall of the stairwell. His arms pulled me in tight and his breath brushed the crook of my neck, leaving no doubt in my mind that an attraction had sparked between us.

The first time Jasper and I kissed came one night after the hurricane ended, after he'd returned to his East Village apartment. Alex had opted to stay home while my friends and I went dancing in a restaurant-turned-bar in Midtown East. Inside the bar, blue lights rippled across the venue, giving the disconcerting impression of drowning in an ocean. As the music swelled and the cerulean light danced across the walls, I spotted Jasper. He was next to me within a moment, extending his hand out in a "come dance with me" gesture.

Moments later, I was in his arms, our bodies pressed against each other, moving in tandem. With no space between us, I could feel his breath on my neck, his body heat sending electric waves across my body as the music pulsed. Every fiber of my body stood on end as those blue eyes locked onto mine, and his grip tightened around my waist. Our faces hovering centimeters from each other, we both seemed to pause before diving into a kiss that filled my chest with butterflies, lasting only a few seconds before he pulled himself away. A line had been crossed.

We both felt the guilt from the moment our lips parted. Jasper seemed horrified at having kissed his coworker's fiancée. I imagine, for him, what had transpired was a minute indiscretion he'd quickly forget, chalking it up to a night of heavy drinking in a dark club. For me, I felt my heart rip in half—one side paralyzed by a debilitating guilt and the other side ignited with passion. I began to obsess over our kiss, replaying it on a loop throughout the monotonous parade of my days, jonesing for another hit. I can't say I'm proud of how I behaved—"desperate" is the word that comes to mind—but for the next month, that kiss blossomed into a one-sided emotional affair that consumed my mind. I looked for any excuse to spend time with Jasper, hoping his thirst for life would somehow translate into my own.

I pretended to have a sudden interest in photography, flirtatiously asking if he'd teach me the basics of using a DSLR camera. I'd ask to come over and flip through his vacation photos. I'd study his Facebook albums and come up with reasons to text him, staring helplessly at my phone when days would go by without a response. As my attention turned towards Jasper, I felt certain that Alex remained none the wiser. The fact that Alex trusted me intrinsically only amplified my guilt tenfold. But I couldn't stop. I was drawn to Jasper and everything that a relationship with him seemed to promise: travel, adventure, and passion.

For the most part, Jasper remained aloof, only reaching out when a night of drinking had knocked over his wall of common sense. I'd thrill at the ping of Jasper's text messages on those nights. When we'd meet up, Jasper never spoke about what was unfolding between us, only pulling me in for a dance or kiss one moment and pushing me away the next. I both desired and resented Jasper, furious that he had been the one to spark this, only to withhold his affection now that I was hooked. I began to feel like Jasper's yo-yo, always unraveling at his feet before he quickly wrapped me up and tossed me away. Did he have feelings for me? I needed to know, and so I presented him with my ultimatum.

*

Riding on the subway en route to Solas Bar, I feel flushed and sweaty. My pleather dress is unforgiving, probably squeezing the common sense out of me as I steady myself with the cool metal pole. I can't say whether I truly intend to leave Alex for another man—but at this moment, my life feels uniquely thrilling, which is something I haven't felt in a while.

If I press Pause on this ridiculous drama I've orchestrated, I know Alex doesn't deserve this. Beneath the river of problems that has been plaguing our relationship, I know I'm taking for granted that steady and reliable love that's waiting for me at home. Whatever is making me unhappy is not entirely his fault, but rather than speak up, I've turned towards another. Jasper arrived at what felt like a burning building, throwing open a window and letting in the fresh air. And now he had become my singular obsession, my dreams incarnate, an un-suspecting man on whom I'd projected every desperate need for a new beginning.

With just a handful of stops standing between me and Solas Bar, I suddenly feel my phone vibrate. I know before I check the message that it's from Jasper.

I'm not coming. Sorry.

In an instant, my vision tunnels. The air in the subway car evaporates. *He said no.*

I want to scream and rip off my dress in one swoop, but I stay glued to my seat. It feels impossible that the other pas-sengers around me can't sense the pain that has just erupted in my chest like a grenade throwing out shrapnel.

The subway pulls into the 14th Street station. I will myself to place one foot in front of the other and cross the platform to catch the uptown train back to 77th. As I barrel through the underbelly of New York, I reread his message.

I'm not coming. Sorry.

Beyond the words, it's their indifference that cuts deep. I had imagined myself sipping margaritas alongside Jasper on the beaches of Playa del Carmen, flipping through his photos while he read through my writing. I day dreamed of the life we could have together, an exciting relationship marked by travel and creativity, a dream now shattered with a four-word text message. I realize in one crystalized moment how idiotic I had been to pin all my hopes on Jasper. Suddenly, every text, clandestine meeting, kiss, and sideways glance seems different, like a bar flipping on the lights at last call. What was once dimly lit and romantic now feels tacky and overexposed. I had been playing with myself this entire time—he was never really there.

I wearily climb the stairs of the 77th Street station and step out into the brisk night air. My dress sticks to the cold sweat dripping down my body as I walk the three or four blocks to my and Alex's apartment. For as wonderful a man as Alex can be, I can't help but feel as though I'm marching back to a cage of my own making—a relationship skyrocketing towards a marriage I'm not sure I want.

Thankfully, Alex isn't home when I arrive, likely tied up at a sports bar with friends. I walk to our bedroom, unzip the sausage casing of a dress, and collapse to the floor in tears as my thoughts berate me.

What were you thinking?

How could you be so fucking stupid?

How could you be so goddamn desperate?

How could you do this to Alex?

How could you do this to yourself?

What makes Jasper so special, anyway?

I linger on that last question. It occurs to me now that everything that had attracted me to Jasper—from his travels to his creativity—had nothing to do with his personality. In fact, if you asked me to describe Jasper as a person, I'm not sure I'd have anything to say beyond the man likes GoPro videos, Mexican beaches, and cameras. Why had I convinced myself that I needed him—or anyone else, for that matter—to book a flight or to be more adventurous? Why had I decided that the only way to reclaim my life from one man was by handing it over to another? I am beyond frustrated with myself.

At the same time, a series of images flashes across my mind: me as a kid sitting with my dad in the airport, watching passengers run for their final boarding calls. Me in France, alone in that apartment, afraid to explore without Alex holding my hand. Me in New York, saying yes to all the wrong things, desperately pining for Jasper so I could have permission to pursue my own passions.

Suddenly, I am gripped by a red-hot defiance. Right now, I have something to prove to that harshest of all critics: myself. I stride over to my laptop and flip open the screen, my hands shaking with adrenaline.

I look up a flight for next month and am relieved to see that ticket prices are not nearly as expensive as I had imagined (apparently, you *can* travel on an entry-level salary). I reach for my wallet and grab my debit card, punching in the number before I can reason against it. I take a deep breath and click "Book." The confirmation for a round-trip flight to Cartagena appears on the screen.

It will be my first time returning to Colombia since I was a little girl, and my first time taking a trip without family or a boyfriend in tow. I slam the laptop shut and sit for a moment, feeling every thought of Jasper and the last month fall away from my skin. Soon enough, I'll be traveling, and I didn't need a man to do it with me.

6

El Pájaro Libre (The Free Bird)

Cartagena, Colombia

Growing up, I wished I looked and sounded more Colombian. It felt almost unfair that I should hail from such a beautiful and mysterious country only to come out looking like the Coppertone baby. My skin is white (like yogurt, as my very Colombian-looking dad likes to tease), and my hair oscillates between rolling waves, a frizzy nest, and hanging limp. I'm disappointed to say I don't have a hint of an accent unless I'm ordering something like a burrito, in which case I'll roll those *R*s as though my life depends on it.

To see celebrity women like Sofía Vergara and Shakira would only make me feel less Colombian. I don't pronounce "Jesus" like "cheeses" as Vergara does in her punchline jokes on *Modern Family*. I don't spell my "haha haha" as "jaja jaja," the way my Colombian relatives do in their emails, and I sure as hell don't move my hips the way Shakira can in her music videos. When people hear I am Colombian and was born in Bogotá, they tend to raise their eyebrows and say something along the lines of, "I would *never* have guessed that." The truth is, I don't know what it means to be Colombian, only that I desperately want to *feel* Colombian.

Coming up in a predominantly white neighborhood, I shamelessly flaunted my Colombian heritage in hopes of separating myself from the rest of the kids in my school. Let it be a testament to the bubble that is Chicago's North Shore suburbs that even a hardly-Colombian can be "exotic." But looking back, there was nothing really exotic about me. I was a white-passing Latina who was about as Colombian as an Olive Garden might be considered authentic Italian. In high school, my Colombian background may have failed to shine through my Limited Too bell-bottoms and Abercrombie & Fitch polo shirts, but it sparkled around my home. Throughout my childhood, my heritage existed like ají picante slathered on an otherwise bland meal—adding spice to every family gathering, dinner, and conversation. I didn't need to look far to find Colombia, as it seemed the entire country had been distilled into my grandma, Amparo Abad.

In Spanish, you add the diminutive suffix "ito" or "ita" to indicate affection and love, so we lovingly called my grandma Amparito. In my early childhood, Amparito lived with my family, even sharing a bunkbed with me. Eventually, she sought out her own apartment, a one-bedroom in Skokie about fifteen minutes driving from our house. It seems to me that Amparito had always been a grandmother. For as long as I can remember, she wore her gray-white hair in that classic grandma bob and preferred generously sized T-shirts in the warmer months and large fleece sweaters in the winter. I remember hugging her and being nuzzled against her fleece-clad breasts like I was hugging a giant teddy bear. Yes, she was cozy, but always managed to add a pop of old-school glamour to her outfits, with a delicate pinned brooch or a gold necklace placed just so. Born and raised in Colombia, she had been instilled with a classic sophistication and impeccable manners—the kind only taught in the bygone days of etiquette schools—and would guffaw at how I'd shovel cereal into my mouth or wipe my hands on my ripped jeans in lieu of a napkin. To Amparito, a lack of social grace was a cardinal sin; she never forgot a birthday, never ate with her elbows on the table, and always thanked her hosts for a good meal.

Amparito and my dad shared a lot of common traits: both could light up a room with their laughter and roll with the punches better than most. Together, they had a sort of comedy shtick going, where my dad would lovingly tease my grandma, and in turn, she'd playfully slap his arm and say, "No me molestes" (Don't bother me). Mostly, I loved hearing their rapid-fire Spanish bouncing off the kitchen walls as Amparito warmed up mini chocolate eclairs she'd bought on sale from Sam's Club earlier that week.

Because her English was limited, being with Amparito often meant being thrown into an impromptu tandem language exchange. For nearly all the questions she'd ask me, my lazy teenage response was invariably, "yo no sé" (I don't know). I was indifferent to learning Spanish and shrugged at her gentle corrections, choosing instead to watch Carson Daly introduce the day's top music videos on TRL. When you're sitting in your childhood kitchen, watching your grandma dance to cumbia, making a "ssst st st ssst" sound as she shakes her hips, it feels like that moment will last forever. And so, you reason, there's plenty of time to learn Spanish phrases beyond "yo no sé." Of course, life moves quick, the present becomes past, and people become memories; suddenly, you kick yourself for all the times you should have flicked off MTV, given your grandma your undivided attention, and asked her to teach you more.

Through Amparito and my dad, I could taste, hear, and feel what it means to be Colombian. I'd taste it in the banana leaf–wrapped bocadillos my dad and I would eat standing side by side in the kitchen, always pairing the sticky sugar-covered guava treat with queso blanco. I'd hear it in the telenovelas my grandma would watch on hot summer afternoons, the swell of music overlaying a passionate argument between an often voluptuous woman and her dark-eyed suitor. I'd feel it in the energetic conversations over wine-fueled family dinners, my dad's eyes twinkling as he translated a dirty joke from Spanish to English. Colombia may have been over 2,700 miles away from Chicago, but in that house, I managed to feel connected to a place I had yet to fully understand.

Of course, there was a darker side to Colombia too, one I'd only heard about between the pan-fried arepas and Carlos Vives songs. Through hushed voices, I'd catch snippets of conversations about relatives who had been forced to flee the country due to volatile politics, civil unrest, and an acronym I would only later come to understand: FARC.

FARC, or the Revolutionary Armed Forces of Colombia, was a narco-terrorist organization formed in 1964. As an adult, I learned that the FARC was a political movement founded on Marxist ideologies and that, at its peak, had controlled over 40 percent of Colombia. The FARC financed its military operations and civil war using narco-trafficking, kidnapping, and taxing of the local people, bringing in an estimated $600 million annually. In its heyday, FARC was one of the richest terrorist organizations in the world and would recruit from small Indigenous communities scattered across rural Colombia. More than 11,000 FARC fighters joined the guerrilla movement as minors, lured with the promise of food, shelter, and education—many of whom would go on to commit unspeakable acts.

Throughout my life, I thought of the FARC as the metaphorical big, bad wolf behind every misfortune my family had. As a kid, whenever a relative showed up at our Chicago doorstep, it seemed to be because the FARC had driven them out of Colombia. It appeared the FARC was to blame for my uncle's kidnapping when he left his work one day at the embassy in Bogotá, only to be taken to a field, stripped of his belongings, and held at gunpoint. He left the country shortly after due to trauma and concerns for his safety. The FARC also appeared to be why my grandfather fled Colombia after receiving threats from the guerrillas. But of all the family miseries that could be credited to the FARC, the story of my great aunt, Adita, haunted me the most.

I don't remember Adita. Because I met her before age six, details of her escape me—as do most of my memories from Bogotá—but what I do recall is the summer of 2004. That year, my dad and Yana had suffered just enough of my teenage antics and decided to send me to Colombia for a few weeks to stay with Adita. While the trip was meant to be a cultural experience that would connect me to my Colombian heritage, to my teen self, it was a punishment meant to cruelly cut me off from my high school friends. My dad spent weeks planning the trip, only to receive an odd email from Adita days before my departure flight that read: No envíes a Nicole aquí.

Don't send Nicole here.

A few days later, Adita was dead. Hundreds of questions surrounded the strange circumstances of her death. I'd listen as family speculated at the sordid details, always guessing that the FARC had somehow been involved. The questions swirling around Adita's death would haunt me for years to come, until one day, as an adult, I'd return to Bogotá to revisit them.

These stories created a duality of what Colombia meant to me growing up: on the one hand, the country seemed a lively place that existed in the music and cooking of my jubilant relatives, and on the other, a dangerous war zone one needed to escape.

★

Of the many photos I have of my early years in Colombia, one in particular has always stood out to me. It is slightly yellowed and bent around the edges, depicting my smiling, twentysomething dad while he's holding a baby wrapped in a white cotton onesie. Behind him, mountains rise in the background, a city sprawled out beneath the balcony with weathered Spanish signs barely visible from the streets below. On the back of the photo, seven words are written in a child's handwriting: *Daddy and me in Colombia or Miami*. Today, looking at the mountainous backdrop, it's obvious this photo was not taken in Miami, yet the words are a testament to how little I know about my early childhood, unable to place where I was and when I was in Colombia.

As they say, happiness comes from knowing who you are and what you want—two questions I have been grappling with since the Jasper ultimatum. I try to tackle question number one first, throwing myself into planning my Cartagena trip, using it as a way to distract myself from the emotional roller coaster I had ridden since Hurricane Sandy and to finally jump-start my writing career. Because I hadn't written for my blog since returning from Rouen, letting *Le Post Grad* fall into obscurity, I sought to cultivate the passions I had left gathering dust. If there was any silver lining to my job in media buying, it was the connections I had to sales teams at publications I admired, like *Travel + Leisure* and *Food &*

Wine magazine. With an email, I gained an introduction to the *Food & Wine* editorial team, who generously threw me a freelance assignment. My article would be a brief slideshow of ten dishes to try in Cartagena, inspired by my upcoming trip. Just like that, I had my first bona fide byline.

★

In Cartagena's Old City, narrow cobblestone streets are flanked by colonial homes painted in vibrant hues of yellow, orange, green, and blue. Wooden balconies hover overhead, intertwined with hot-pink bougainvillea flowers dripping from the banisters like a diamond necklace hanging off a wealthy woman's neck. Street vendors stand on the corner selling sizzling arepas, made fresh on the spot.

I watch as a plump woman with a friendly smile slaps dough between her hands before dropping it into a vat of oil. She instinctively knows when the dough is ready to be plucked from the vat, opened up into a pocket for the egg, and then dropped in the glistening oil once again. The arepa comes out a startling yellow, like the color of Velveeta cheese, and the texture is impossibly crispy. The egg center is perfectly gooey, and the trio of salsas sitting on the cart give it the "oomph" needed to elevate the entire meal. As far as I'm concerned, this $2 arepa—which is now the crown jewel of my *Food & Wine* article—is on par with any overpriced dinner back in New York City.

Sitting on the northern coast of Colombia, Cartagena is a historic port city that differs significantly from its inland neighbors like Bogotá and Medellín. As I scour Cartagena for dishes to feature in my article, I learn how varied Colombian cuisine can be. In Bogotá—where the climate is cooler, and the city sits tucked between mountains—the food is more hearty (think beef, vegetables, and stews). Cartagena's cuisine, on the other hand, is brighter and louder, with Caribbean-inspired dishes using ingredients like sweet plantains, tropical red snapper, and crisp coconut shavings.

Wiping the arepa crumbs from my lips, I'm walking around the Old City when I spot a trio of Palenqueras wearing ruffled dresses in the red, blue, and yellow of the Colombian flag. Large plastic bowls of tropical fruit sit balanced atop each of their heads as they smile and wave their floor-length skirts. The Palenqueras are more than beautiful; they are emblematic of Cartagena and its history. Hailing from nearby San Basilio de Palenque—the first town made up of freed Black slaves in Latin America—they are direct descendants of slaves brought to Cartagena during the Spanish colonial era who managed to run away to the nearby mountains. Formally known as Cartagena de Indias, the seaside city was a Spanish colony up until its independence on November 11 (which also happens to be my birthday) in 1811.

You wouldn't know it looking at the city now, but Cartagena's tumultuous history is one marked by wars, revolutions, pirate attacks, witch hunts, and slavery. One million slaves were traded and sold in Plaza de los Coches, which today is a main square that—somewhat eerily, I might add—covers its painful past with rows and rows of stalls selling sugary sweets and homemade confections, like guava cocadas. Those who escaped slavery built the village of San Basilio de Palenque, a place where former slaves could protect their customs, culture, cuisine, and freedom from the Spanish settlers.

The Palenquera women stand proudly throughout the Plaza de los Coches, selling fresh fruit and posing for photos, reclaiming a space that once sought to trade and sell their ancestors like cattle. It's a beautiful symbol of strength and resilience, not to mention an opportunity to have a seriously refreshing treat.

"¿Puedo tener un tazón de fruta por favor?" I ask one of

the Palenqueras, pointing at the bowl atop her head, eager to try the fresh fruit.

"Claro, mami!" says the woman with a warm smile, her bright red lipstick contrasting with her sun-kissed skin. "A la orden."

This last phrase is often used in Colombia—heard in every exchange, whether you're asking for la cuenta from the server at the end of a meal or direcciones from a stranger on the street. Colombians are famously accommodating, and "a la orden" is a phrase that exemplifies that trait. Once a military term that translated to "at your command," used to show respect to senior officers, the words have evolved to now mean "at your service."

In one swift movement, the woman pulls the bowl off her head and plops down on a bright blue plastic stool that materializes from nowhere. Like a surgeon wielding a scalpel, the Palenquera expertly cuts and slices through papaya, pineapple, kiwi, guava, mangoes, banana, and passion fruit in rapid succession, arranging the fruit in a bouquet inside a white Styrofoam bowl for me. One bite and I'm already having a spiritual crisis. Notes of sweet and tart mingle into a syrupy juice oozing from each slice of fruit. I want to weep for all the times I have stood under the fluorescent lights of a Manhattan office and eaten flavorless melon and cantaloupe for lunch. Fruit simply doesn't taste like this back in New York.

As I move through Cartagena's Old City, I follow my senses in a frenzied sort of way, running from taste to sight to smell, touching and eating everything as though trying to inhale the very essence of Colombia. If every city had one word with which to describe it, Cartagena's word must be "alive." Everything here is teeming with life—from the tantalizing food to the electrifying music. New York is worlds away now. Alex, Jasper, the apartment I can barely afford, the engagement I'm not sure of, the career I stumbled into, the dreams I failed to pursue—all of it is minimized by distance and pushed aside by travel.

Colors and buildings blur as I walk down narrow streets and charming alleys in search of my next great bite. I start to imagine how I would spend a year in Colombia and whether I could convince Alex to come with me. Would he love it here as much as I do? Would he be as moved by the music, the culture, the food, the people? Would he be willing to ditch New York and travel for a while?

Probably not, I think to myself, remembering our last silly fight from a few weeks ago.

It had been a weekend afternoon, and Alex and I were headed to our local Key Food supermarket. I hated grocery shopping with Alex as it always ended in an argument, with one of us (usually me) stomping away in frustration down the produce aisle. Every time, Alex would shop according to the weekly coupon catalog, letting only the deals dictate exactly what we'd buy. If sliced bologna was $3 off, we were getting it, regardless if we actually wanted (or needed) to buy the lunch meat. I didn't care for the coupons one way or another, filling our cart with a box of granola bars or a package of frozen gnocchi, only for it to be vetoed by Alex because "it's not on sale this week." I'd roll my eyes, annoyed at his militaristic approach to grocery shopping, wishing we could just buy the fucking gnocchi.

Between the two of us, Alex is the more financially responsible one. While he handles our mutual bills, pulling from a joint checking account we both funnel the lion's share of our paychecks into, somewhere along the line, he has also become controlling of my personal spending. Or maybe, I've relinquished control to him—it's hard to say. When I want to buy something for myself—a $25 Laura Mercier lipstick from Sephora or a $38 black cable-knit sweater from Zara—I feel the need to ask permission, creating a constantly buzzing stream of resentment. And when I actually *do* buy something for myself—like, say, a last-minute flight to Cartagena—it comes with the added price of guilt and arguing.

We were on our way to pick up groceries that afternoon when a question popped into my mind. I asked, "If you could have any superpower, what would it be?"

"Instant teleportation," he said immediately.

"Imagine all the things we could do if we could snap our fingers and transport ourselves anywhere!" I mused. "Paris for lunch? Dinner in Chiang Mai? A drink in Barcelona?"

"I was thinking more along the lines of instant commutes," said Alex. "Like if we could get a big house upstate and just snap our fingers and be in the city, how awesome would that be?"

Clearly, what Alex wanted and what I wanted were at odds: his dream of practical financial stability and a lovely home crashed against my dreams of backpacking in South America and becoming a travel writer. My passion for travel had become a hot-button issue between us in recent months. No matter the flight deals or travel hacks I shared, he seemed less than interested in prioritizing travel beyond holiday visits to family.

I was desperate to show him our life together didn't need to follow a society-approved road map or be relegated to Westchester just yet. I'd been following bloggers who detailed full-time traveling as a couple, and all their stories boiled down to one takeaway: if you're willing to let go of your comfort zone, you can travel the world. While I hadn't worked out the logistics, I imagined we could live in cheap Airbnbs and hotels, turning away from our soul-sucking nine-to-fives to work odd jobs in Bangkok instead, earning just enough to keep traveling. I pictured us mingling with expats, living abroad in communities of creative transplants.

"When are you going to get this out of your system?!" Alex asked me one night, exasperated.

Deep down, I knew it wasn't a matter of convincing Alex on logistics, because he didn't want that life—any of it. And there seemed to lie our problem: we were building a future together while ignoring the fact that we longed to walk entirely different paths.

★

Feeling wildly optimistic and even slightly manic, I find myself sitting in an unassuming square in Getsemani called Plaza de la Trinidad. The plaza is a short ten-minute walk from the Old City that takes you through Centenario Park, where lazy sloths and curious monkeys move slowly through the trees. Compared to the Old City, Getsemani feels like an artist's haunt. It's less polished than its touristic counterpart but just as beautiful, with art-splashed walls and balconies adorned with pink-and-orange flowers. During the day, Plaza de la Trinidad is a quiet square surrounded by no-frills cafés, but come nightfall —like most of Cartagena—it becomes a gathering spot for locals and travelers alike. Colombian music floats on the evening breeze from one of the nearby bars, reminding me of Amparito dancing in the kitchen of my childhood. Couples go from nuzzling on cement benches nearby to pressing their bodies together in rhythmic cumbia. Outdoor tables trickle out from the restaurants onto the cobbled streets surrounding the plaza, and the air is infused with the smell of stewed potatoes, yucca, plantains, and shredded chicken from the bowls of brothy sancocho they're serving. Nearby, I see some teenagers playing an impromptu match of fútbol, stealing sips of cheap Aguila beers in between kicks.

I love this. I *really* love this. I love who I am out here. I love how I *feel* out here. I have a flashback to those stormy hurricane nights listening to Jasper talking about his trips. I get it. If *this* is what traveling means, then I want to chase this feeling around the world.

The following day—my last one in Cartagena—I am sitting on a beach in Bocagrande (which translates to "big mouth" in Spanish). Compared to the Old City, Bocagrande is all modern, lined with sleek hotels, shining glass condominiums, and upscale Japanese and Colombian restaurants. Although this part of town is largely residential, it offers one key thing the rest of Cartagena does not: a beach. Visiting Cartagena, I had expected the sort of beaches ubiquitous in the Caribbean— white sugary sand, swaying palm trees, turquoise water, and cocktails served out of coconuts—but you won't find that here. Instead, the sliver of beach by the Old City is marked by rocks, while Playa Bocagrande is lined by skyscrapers and shrouded in hawkers selling everything from knock-off Ray-Bans to foot massages.

Because I've booked a cheap apartment in Bocagrande, I wake up each morning and walk the two or three blocks to the Olimpica grocery store, where I pair a few freshly made pan de bono (a sweet pastry-like bread made from cassava starch, cheese, and eggs) with granadilla (passion fruit's sweeter cousin). With my loot in hand, I walk the half block over to Playa Bocagrande, where I sit down on the sand and watch the waves crashing against the shore. As I break the paper-like skin of the orange granadilla, its sweet pulp and seeds spilling out onto my hands, I pull out my journal and jot down any impressions or thoughts I want to remember. This morning routine has become a sort of meditation, a way for me to build a bridge between the country I'm in and the emotions I'm holding. On this particular morning, the cloudy sky reflects the melancholy I feel about flying back to New York tomorrow. I don't want to leave. I feel as though I've merely scratched the surface of Colombia.

I push my bare toes deep into the sand and begin to write in my journal. I am trying to draw up a game plan for how I can return and stay in Colombia—with or without Alex. I jot down year-long volunteer opportunities, publications I can pitch to for future travel assignments, and even a check-list of things needed to claim my dual citizenship at the Colombian embassy back in New York. If I must board a plane tomorrow, I am determined to have some sort of action plan that promises to bring me back to this country. I'm so distracted by my writing that I barely notice the fifteen-year-old girl standing over me, peering at my journal curiously. I look up and squint, her silhouette framed by the sun peeking out from between the clouds.

"¡Hola! ¿Qué estás haciendo?" she asks in a friendly tone.

Thanks to Amparito and all the times she corrected my broken Spanish, I have a baseline understanding of the language, and even a rather extensive vocabulary to pull from. I'm not exactly confident in my Spanish, but unlike my ill attempts at speaking French, I'm eager for the opportunity to try my hand at conversation and connect to my heritage.

"Solo estoy escribiendo en mi diario," I explain to the girl, pointing at my journal and pen to show her what I'm doing.

"¿De donde eres?" she asks me curiously, clearly picking up on my American accent and wondering from where I've come.

The way the girl playfully plops down on the sand is immediately endearing. It's clear she is teetering on the edge between a child and a full-fledged teen. She is wearing a one-piece bathing suit, her dark wet hair messy from the seawater and sticking out every which way. When I say I'm from New York, her eyes widen as though I've just told her I'm visiting from Mars. Her Spanish quickens as she excitedly begins referencing every song, television show, and movie she's seen or heard that has ever mentioned or pictured New York. I can't keep up with her Spanish now—only catching snippets here and there—but on some unspoken level, I know exactly what she is saying. Her excitement emanates from her body language. I find it funny that my home is a place she dreams of going to while her home is a place I'm trying to stay in. I gather from our conversation that she's from nearby Barranquilla, a city farther up the coast. She talks about her school life there and points to a family lying under umbrellas nearby, peering over occasionally to see who their daughter is speaking to.

"Mi familia," she says proudly. "¿Dónde está su familia?"

I look at her face, now illuminated by the sun, and explain I am here without family. For the second time, her eyes widen. She considers me for a moment before nodding decidedly.

"Eres un pájaro libre," she says, as though she's finally figured out this stranger on the beach.

You are a free bird.

Beholden to a job I hate and committed to an engagement I nearly blew apart for a crush, I have felt anything but free these past few months. I find myself reveling in this girl's four words, seeing myself through her eyes: a traveler sitting on the black-gray sand alone, hailing from a city often synonymous with wayward dreamers.

You are a free bird.

I relish the words, trying my best to remember them and internalize them. Not because I feel I am a free bird but because, at this moment, I know I can become one.

7

Tattered Bracelets

New York, New York

"Are you not happy with the dress?"

From down on the floor where she's been hemming my gown, the tailor looks up at me, concerned. A tape measure hangs from her neck like a yellow bow tie while a pin—held precariously between her front teeth—reminds me of the long, thin cigarettes I'd see women smoking in Le Marais back in Paris.

"What?! No! The dress is stunning!"

My words come out too eager, a clear overcompensation. The tailor looks at me dubiously before turning her attention back to the hem with a shrug. I am standing on a pedestal surrounded by four full-length mirrors, each offering a different perspective of the $6,000 wedding dress draped across my body. The gown is strapless with a sweetheart neckline and a silhouette that is a cross between an A-line and a trumpet. A delicate lace applique rests atop the buttery ivory fabric with light-catching sequins dusted across the surface like powder. The entire ensemble is classic, romantic, and gorgeous, but the reflection staring back at me is anything but.

Under this fluorescent lighting, my skin's pallor is a sickly green, outmatched only by my facial expression oscillating from a steely scowl to pure panic. I am the opposite of what a bride should look like. My glow is less angelic and feels more like that of a radioactive comic book monster, glowing green. On my wrist are several woven bracelets, adding a pop of faded rainbow colors standing out against the ivory of the gown.

I study my reflection and lock eyes with my mom sitting behind me, nestled in a plush chair and observing the fitting like a royal surveying a ballroom.

I can tell from her expression that she's frustrated; all her efforts have not yielded a happy-looking bride. She's pulled out all the stops: a three-tier red velvet cake wrapped in a dazzling white cream cheese frosting. A reception with homemade decor and Etsy-found elements inspired by the wedding's upstate-New-York-meets-travel theme. Even a vintage-looking globe, which she thought would be the perfect way for guests to scribble their good wishes and give a nod to my newfound love of travel. She's paid homage to the fall season, finding a wooden stand for cider donuts, small apple pies (my favorite), locally made honey (in tiny jars with personalized labels that read "Meant to Bee"), and a signature "Apple-y Ever After" cocktail. No detail has been spared, which makes my lack of enthusiasm that much worse.

Everything is seemingly beautiful in my mom's world. She has always exuded love through two things: attention to detail and good food. Gift bags are never just filled but lovingly stuffed with an array of color-coordinated tissue fluffed to perfection. For every occasion, she sends a carefully chosen card with a handwritten note. For every meal, there's a curated menu designed with the guests in mind—lobster tails with individual ramekins of heated butter or a homemade trifle overflowing with fresh berries and whipped cream. She is more thoughtful than most, always surprising people with gifts they didn't know they needed: a backpack complete with a checkered blanket and plastic wineglasses so that I can have picnics in Central Park, or a ceramic bowl for storing garlic at the ideal temperature to make sure I have fresh cloves for cooking. For my mom, planning this wedding is like stepping into the Olympic arena, an opportunity to put all of her talents to the test. It's an occasion to dazzle, entertain, and show everyone we know a good time. She is *so* ready for this, but I am not.

Having had me in her late teens, my mom is younger than most other moms I know and is often mistaken for being my older sister. We share the same hair texture, though hers is dyed jet black and cut in a short bob. We share the same eyebrow arches and almond-shaped eyes, but where her eyes are a dark brown, mine are hazel like my dad's. Looks aside, my mom and I are a lot alike. We both can be too generous, often overextending ourselves and overpromising favors. We tend to pick up the check more than we should, and offer more than we can deliver. Despite our innate desire to please, she and I are part of a motley crew of fiery Latinas that can be traced across three generations to my maternal grandma, Clarita, a firecracker of a woman. Because we are both Scorpios—Latina Scorpios, which should really be its own brand of crazy—we operate on our own volatile yet sensitive emotional wavelengths. We read the feelings of others the way seismographs can pick up on earthquake vibrations from miles away. Because of this, I know before I look that she is trying to "figure out" what's unfolding inside my head.

She's undoubtedly wondering why I don't look happy and whether it's about the dress or something more serious. Through my guilt, I can practically see her thoughts unspooling around her black patent leather Gucci loafers, and I know what's on her mind: that I'm a child playing dress-up rather than a woman on the cusp of becoming a wife. And then I see her eyes settle on my wrist.

"You'll have to cut those bracelets off."

Defensively, I wrap my hand around my wrist and cover the woven bands.

"Forget it. I'm *not* going to do that."

My voice is edgier than intended. I know how I sound—hell, I know how I *look*—but I can't quite articulate any of the feelings parkouring off my rib cage. Didn't I choose this gown? Didn't I send out those save-the-dates? Didn't I say yes to Alex kneeling in that vineyard? I took part in every step leading up to this moment: this gown. This reflection. This fitting. This wedding. Everything feels off—everything, that is, except these tattered bracelets.

I look down at the strands woven into different patterns and tenderly finger their frayed strings, now hanging like the branches of a weeping willow. Some of them have long ago lost their color, stripped down to gray-brown strands, while the newer bracelets retain their vibrancy, held together by sparkling little plastic beads. Each of these bracelets represents a place, moment, and time in which I felt happy these past few months, a feeling that has been in short supply lately.

This sky blue one—my first bracelet—was purchased under an archway in Cartagena's Old City. It caught my eye while I was out exploring, making my way towards the Plaza de Los Coches for fruity cocadas. As I walked under the faded canary yellow wall surrounding La Ciudad Vieja, I spotted an artisan selling an array of hand-painted figurines and bracelets he was weaving on the spot. I chose a simple blue one whose color matched the sky and sea surrounding Cartagena. As I was buying the bracelet, I suddenly imagined myself in that monochrome office in downtown Manhattan, eating a lackluster kale salad alone in my cubicle. Everything in New York felt lonely and colorless, and I would inevitably have to return to that reality. I wanted a reminder wrapped around my wrist that could transport me to *this* moment when everything felt alive.

I'd like to think my mom would understand. She is, after all, the one who bought me that map last Christmas. It was a framed world map from *National Geographic* with a carefully chosen quote she'd had inscribed across the bottom: "To travel is to live." It's a fragment from the larger Hans Christian Andersen quote that reads:

> To move, to breathe, to fly, to float,
> To gain all while you give,
> To roam the roads of lands remote,
> To travel is to live.

With the map came a little Ziploc baggie of small multi-colored pins meant to mark all the places I'd been, would go, or hoped to one day see. I hung it and eagerly placed pins in countries where I had traveled so far. Canada with my family to stay in an Airbnb on San Juan Island, where we'd watch whales swim by the coast. Mexico on Yana's babymoon, when she was nearly eight months pregnant with my brother and my little sister got such a bad sunburn, her face swelled up to look like the Kool-Aid Man. France with Alex, where we lived in

that medieval town in Normandy. And finally, Colombia—
the first place I'd visited as an adult on my own dime.

"Looks nice," Alex had said, absent-mindedly eyeing the
map as I hung it above our black Ikea couch. But all I could
see was how devoid of pins the map was.

It seemed to me I had about five minutes left to see the
world before Alex and I exchanged our vows, and I wasn't
about to waste a second of it, so I started a new travel blog
with a mission to fill the map on my wall with pins. The blog
was named, aptly, *The Pin the Map Project*. I fawned over its
home page in the twilight hours while Alex slept. I tinkered
with its design between conference calls at the office. I fun-
neled what little extra cash I had into spoiling that blog with
upgrades and custom artwork, a watercolor logo of a paper
airplane flying around a pile of suitcases. When I wasn't actively working on my travel blog, I was constantly thinking
about ways to enhance it, grow its following, and fill it with
stories. *The Pin the Map Project* became my virtual playground,
one in which I felt closer to the person I wanted to become
but had somehow lost sight of.

In the year or so since I first received the map, I'd used
a mix of social media following and connecting with other
bloggers to grow *The Pin the Map Project*'s readership. Soon
enough, I amassed enough of an audience to be introduced
to the concept of a press trip. A press trip is when journalists, bloggers, and other content creators (read: influencers)
are invited to a destination at the behest of a tourism board,
hotel brand, or PR firm representing travel clients. It's a tit-
for-tat arrangement for writers to spotlight a destination or
hotel in exchange for comped flights, meals, and accommo-
dations. As far as journalism standards go, the ethics behind a
press trip are up for debate. Some publications refuse to work
with writers whose stories are inspired by a press trip, arguing

that their work is biased if their travel expenses are paid for. On the other side of the argument is the fact that travel writers are grossly underpaid. Press trips not only provide writers with fresh content, but they allow them the opportunity to travel without maxing out a credit card. For me, discovering press trips meant I could venture to destinations I'd otherwise never afford and gain fresh content for my budding travel blog while doing it.

And so, I swung from press trip to press trip like a monkey from tree to tree, collecting bracelets along the way and actively avoiding my wedding planning. With each trip I had taken, I collected a woven bracelet that could transport me back to a time and place in which I'd been filled with joy. To cut them off—and for this wedding, no less—felt like sacrilege. Traveling had become my personal brand of religion, a port in the storm from which I could escape the mounting questions around this wedding and the questions—from myself and others—about why I didn't look happy.

I wish I could say I recognized these emotions as being something more than just pre-wedding jitters. I wish I'd had the wisdom to realize that travel had become an act of running away, and the bracelets a symbol of a crutch in an unhappy situation. Instead, I've continued avoiding my swirling hurricane of doubts, because the thing is, I *do* love Alex. Despite all evidence to the contrary—Jasper, my wedding hesitations, my impulse to keep flying away—I love my fiancé. He is my best friend and by far the only person I'd want to spend a cozy Friday night with. Sure, our love has morphed from the sizzling "can't get out of bed" passion it once was to something more comparable to, say, the comfort of a baby blanket, but it is still love—a love I'm not sure I'm ready to lose.

Standing in my wedding dress atop this pedestal, I know that losing Alex is as terrifying as spending my life with him.

Everything about this feels confusing, and so I've kept turning to travel, which has created a duplicity in my life. Arriving in a new country has felt like one big, desperate gulp of fresh air, pressing Pause on my reality back home. Navigating foreign cities has introduced me to another, more independent version of myself. Out *there*, I romp about the globe with wild abandon—feeling lighter, sexier, and more spontaneous—temporarily free from the title of fiancée and my career in advertising. Crossing time zones has been like stepping into Instagram's Valencia filter, and through the lens of travel, my life looks brighter and warmer. Whenever I travel, I've relished living in that suspended animation where wedding planning and engagements simply don't exist only to come back *here* and feel the chains of reality as soon as my plane's wheels touch the tarmac. Yanked from Technicolor Oz back to colorless Kansas, I don't know what to say or think.

★

"Okay, the hem is done. Let's try on the veil."

In one swift motion, the tailor stands up and smooths her smart black trousers. She reaches for the veil hanging on the wall behind her, and delicately places it atop my head, its airy netting falling lightly over my shoulders. The veil has a demure blusher, an extra piece of sheer fabric meant to cover my face until it's revealed to my groom. The tradition of veils can be traced back to Rome when brides would wear them to hide from evil spirits as they walked down the aisle. It was meant to be a shield from any nefarious entities that might thwart the bride's impending happiness, which was to be ultimately found in her husband's arms. Over time, veils became symbolic of purity and chastity. Today, it seems their sole purpose is for women to hide their perfectly made-up faces behind them until they reach the altar.

"Now, doesn't that look nice?" says the tailor, fastening the veil to my head and stepping back to admire the look.

The tailor and my mom nod in satisfied agreement. Yes, the veil *does* look nice. Like the gown, it's delicate with a dusting of sequins that catch the light with every little movement. But for something meant to protect a bride's happiness, it seems to do just the opposite for me, as though someone has thrown a pile of tulle and lace over my strained face, so no one has to acknowledge what's underneath.

"It looks great," I say flatly. I reach for my wrist and begin rubbing those tattered bracelets, hoping to transport myself anywhere in the world but here.

PART TWO

Changing Pitch

Pitch: A pitch is the nodding motion of an airplane's nose and tail. Controlled by pilots, the pitch can move the plane upwards or downwards, ultimately changing the direction of flight.

Bocas del Toro, Buenos Aires, Iguazú, Borneo, Paris, Hanoi, Bali, Bogotá

PRIORYTET
PRIORITAIRE

8

Three Sheets to the Wind

Bocas del Toro, Panama

Everything feels chaotic right now—sandy, sweaty, and messy. If I wasn't standing in Panama, this might bother me, but travel has a funny way of reframing things to feel more beautiful than they are. Out here, throwing back whiskey-ginger cocktails beneath a Panamanian moon at a bar named Iguana, my skin still warm to the touch from the midday sun, I am free from all of the emotional baggage I've left behind in New York, every bag brimming with poor choices, all the unsaid words to Alex and my family, and the relentless nerves about the direction my life is going.

Running from mounting pressures has become my modus operandi, and throwing myself into new, far-flung destinations has become my coping mechanism, so here I am. Anxiety has been following me everywhere these days, popping up in the unlikeliest of places: an abandoned ghost town in California, on a speedboat in Miami, in a bridal salon in New York. I'm not surprised it has followed me here to Panama, trailing me to this expat haunt on Isla Colón in Bocas del Toro.

Iguana is like Bocas del Toro's answer to a New York dive bar, a no-frills, no-fuss joint where dressing up might be tantamount to wearing a tuxedo at a Taco Bell. The entire venue is made of wood, with a sagging ceiling crafted from strips of beige canvas. Standing inside the bar, I get the sense I'm on a moored ship, one of those old-timey ones Captain Cook might have sailed around the Caribbean once upon a time. Twinkling blue fairy lights wrap around every weathered banister and column, but it's the outside deck that is the most memorable (and liable). There, smack-dab in the middle of the dance floor, is a carved-out "pool" that drops into the ocean below. The whole set-up looks like a suburban dad's home improvement project gone awry. It's a strategically placed water trap waiting to swallow up unsuspecting backpackers.

"Nikki! Where the hell is Melanie?" asks my friend Alyssa, suddenly at my side. "I don't see her!"

"Have you checked the ocean?" I ask dumbly, pointing at the water trap. I'm fixated on that pool, which looks more like an ominous black hole as the night darkens. I'm about three sheets to the wind, on my third (fourth?) drink, and trying to avoid the sharp pangs of anxiety hitting my stomach as they so often do these days.

"I checked the bathroom and the pool," replies Alyssa, getting frantic. "She's not here! We need to find her!"

I scan Iguana and spot our friends, who have fanned out across the bar. I see one friend dancing precariously close to the pool's edge, gyrating her hips to the Latin pop music blaring over the speakers. I spot another tossing back a vodka shot before swiping through photos taken earlier that day, probably the ones of our group grinning wide while cartwheeling down the sugary beach. Everyone is distracted by whatever cocktail, pop song, or conversation has monopolized their attention. Sure enough, Melanie is gone.

Shit, I think, trying to gather my already scattered thoughts. *We've lost Melanie.*

★

I've come to Central America with a group of girlfriends whom I met throughout my two-and-a-half years of working at Inventif Media. We're an obnoxious gaggle of twenty-something, PowerPoint-hating, whiskey-loving, fast-talking Manhattan women on a mission to enjoy this island before we return to our own chaotic one. We are staying in a city called Bocas del Toro Town (nicknamed Bocas Town), part of a larger archipelago and province named Bocas del Toro off Panama's Caribbean coast. Bocas Town is precisely what I had expected when we planned this trip: it's laid-back in a no-shoes, no-shirt kind of way and just rustic enough to be endearing without being uncomfortable. Unlike other beach towns overrun by all-inclusive resorts and travelers wearing pastel-colored shirts from Tommy Bahama, this island feels different. To stay in Bocas Town is to be inducted into a community of backpackers, surfers, and American expats selling half-price yoga sessions on the beach.

It's said that back in the day, sailors once relied on the seclusion of these islands to serve as a pit stop to repair their ships. It's this very promise of seclusion that has brought our group here. Bocas Town is the perfect jumping-off point for exploring the archipelago and its uninhabited islands and pristine beaches. Since arriving a few days ago, we have let Bocas del Toro reveal itself in all its wondrous beauty. We traveled by boat to the mainland to visit a locally run cocoa farm, where we hiked through the verdant jungle in pursuit

of football-sized red cocoa pods, from which the most delicious chocolate is derived. We've ridden our bicycles around
Isla Colón, discovering tucked-away bluffs and quiet beachside shacks serving crisp fried red snapper and coconut rice.
We pass our days lazily, exploring the island and moving at a
relaxed pace juxtaposed with our wild evenings spent dancing at overwater bars.

I love it here in Bocas del Toro, even with my tailing anxiety. It's not just the island's natural beauty or the beaches and
bike rides; it's the overall vibe of the place. "The vibes, man,
the vibes," as the expats would say, are so calm here compared to what I left simmering back in New York. It has been
a month or two since that uncomfortable wedding dress fitting with my mom, and things have only become more stressful with the arrival of spring. As my mom likes to remind
me constantly these days, we are now narrowing in on my
and Alex's September wedding date, with only a handful of
months left to hammer out the final details.

Every day I'm bombarded with more wedding to-dos: con-
firm the menu with the caterer, get a final guest count, block
off hotel rooms for out-of-town visitors, schedule a wedding
hair and makeup trial, decide on wedding favors. I have begun
to feel like a lobster in a pot of boiling water, the rising tem-
peratures draining the very life out of me. Meanwhile, the
tension between Alex and me has reached an all-time high,
our apartment becoming a boxing ring where we throw our
words like punches. Everyone is frustrated with me these days.
Hell, even I'm frustrated with myself. I'm not only an unhappy bride but an avoidant one, turning to travel with each
chance I get, always running away, and never explaining why.

Panama is like a breath of fresh air. No one here gives
a damn about my career, the direction my life is (or isn't)
going, or any of my wedding plans. As a traveler in Bocas

Town, nothing matters beyond the good surfing conditions and whether you want that cocktail shaken or stirred. Each morning, I've woken up to birds singing as Melanie strums her ukulele from a hammock strung across our shared wooden balcony. As the rest of our group ambles out of bed, I listen to Melanie lazily plucking the chords of "I'm Yours" by Jason Mraz as I watch hummingbirds flit from flower to flower in the nearby trees.

As much as I love my work friends, the truth is that none of them quite understand what I'm going through. None, that is, except maybe Melanie. Like me, Melanie is in a serious relationship with a perfectly lovely man whom she has seemingly been dating for an eternity. While not yet engaged, their future promises perfect children wearing perfect Janie and Jack pastel onesies playing in their perfect color-coordinated playroom in their perfect Westchester home. When Melanie and I grew closer, I realized that while her partner's eyes were trained on their glimmering horizon, her eyes were beginning to look over her shoulder towards something else. It was a something else I recognized, an unknown but overpowering force that kept pulling me from the paved path ahead and out to the craggy wilderness surrounding me.

Together, Melanie and I have bonded over words we cannot find and feelings we cannot escape, instead running with our single friends, staying out late and throwing back Fireball shots until our teeth are slick with the sticky cinnamon liquor. Unable to articulate just what we're feeling, we instead step between two opposing sides of ourselves: the girls smiling placidly on their partners' arms and the women trying to break free in all the wrong ways. Despite being surrounded by friends here in Panama, some of whom I've even asked to be my bridesmaids, I feel utterly alone. I am on an island of my own making. I desperately wish I could make sense of myself to somebody—be it my mom, my fiancé, or friends—but all I can do is fidget uncomfortably in this growing unrest.

It's just the wedding planning, suggests my mom.

It's pre-wedding jitters, assumes Alex.

Everyone feels this way right before marriage, guess my friends.

Their reassurances all point to one truth: whatever is "going on with me" is transient, something that will work itself out before I reach the altar, so long as I'm patient. And so, I've concocted a solution made up of three parts travel, one part whiskey, and ten parts avoidance meant to silence my doubts and bury my discontent until the moment they magically dissipate.

I remember being a kid and visiting Cabos San Lucas with my family one summer, when we took a day trip to the very tip of Mexico's Baja California Peninsula to a rock formation known as El Arco. To reach this unique arch, you need to take a boat to a secluded spit of sand called Lover's Beach, sandwiched between two jagged rock towers. While visiting Lover's Beach, I got caught in a riptide. I had been standing in shin-deep water, looking at the large checkerboard-like waves crisscrossing around my legs. Unbeknownst to me at the time, these "cross sea" waves occur when two swells converge, forming a pattern that is widely considered one of the most dangerous sights a swimmer can see.

It happened quickly: a current knocked me over, and within a moment, I was pulled about a foot out, still within reach of the sand but precariously close to the open sea. Despite the shallow water level, the current felt like an invisible hand pushing my face under the waves. From beneath the surface, I could look up and see the sunlight sparkling above, but try as I might, I couldn't break through the water and reach the air. It took four grown men, including my dad, to rush out into the ocean and physically lift my body up, my swimsuit hanging off awkwardly. As a kid, all I could feel was mortification, but looking back, I now realize how dangerously close I had come to being claimed by the Pacific.

In some ways, everything now feels like that riptide holding my head beneath the waves. Except no one is rushing into the surf to rescue me, and for reasons I can't quite work out, I'm not saving myself. Instead, I stay beneath the surface, looking desperately at the sunlight dancing above the water, willing myself to stand up and breathe, only to push myself further beneath the waves. To make matters more complicated, there is Augustino.

★

Two days ago, my friends and I spent the afternoon at the famed Starfish Beach, where a constellation of chunky orange starfish sit scattered beneath the water. As I waded through the ocean, scanning the seafloor, I walked right into a stranger, who was likewise distracted by the slow-moving marine invertebrates. One look and I knew the man was a fellow traveler. He looked ridiculous at first glance, strolling through knee-high water wearing a full snorkel mask, the breathing tube held in his mouth, while carefully balancing an expensive-looking camera wrapped in a waterproof bag. After bumping into me, he pushed his goggles up, revealing small red imprints on his forehead and light brown hair that stuck out like the ruffled feathers of a cockatoo.

"Ah, lo siento!" he said apologetically. "I am…eh…how do you say…seeing los starfish?"

That accent. Those eyes. That smile. I knew I liked him immediately.

"¡No hay problema!" I exclaimed, hoping to impress him with my subpar Spanish. "¿De donde eres?"

"¡Tu hablas español!" he said, relieved to not have to stumble through English. "Soy de Buenos Aires y estoy aquí con dos amigos de Argentina."

Although he spoke too fast for me to fully comprehend him, I soon learned that Augustino hailed from Buenos Aires and was traveling through Central America with two close friends who had also come from Argentina. Augustino and I had an easygoing chemistry that soon found us sitting on the seafloor, waves lapping over our knees, as we indulged in the two questions that matter most to travelers: where you've been and where you're going. Those two starting points open up a world of conversation that can lead to stories of train rides spanning the distance from Rome to Venice, memories of getting lost in Tokyo, and unfulfilled romances that thrived among the rice paddies of Indonesia. As my friends looked on curiously from their towels on the beach, Augustino and I exchanged numbers in hopes of meeting up again during our trip.

That evening, my friends and I arrived at a popular oceanfront bar whose dance floor not only sits perched above the ocean but whose balcony is fixed with a wobbly trampoline from which you can leap directly into the water. And there in the dancing crowds, I saw Augustino. Without his snorkel mask, I finally got a good look at him. He was classically handsome with short, light brown hair, sun-kissed skin, and deep brown eyes. His full lips stretched out into a goofy smile that made him (and those good looks) endearing and instantly approachable. And then, of course, there was that accent with its cute lilt of Spanish. I quickly swooned at the way Augustino would pepper his sentences with Argentine slang like "dale" (a common word for "okay") before modestly apologizing for his "not-so-good English." Augustino was flirtatious in a cautionary sort of way, one that seemed to ask, *Is this alright with you?*—and it was alright because, with him, I felt a delicious jolt of passion that had eluded me since, well, Jasper.

Augustino and I spent the night dancing together, swallowed up by a crowd of fellow travelers, their bodies swaying to the pulsating Latin music. Before we knew it, it was just the two of us standing on a nearby beach. We had wandered off the dance floor for water and fresh air and then for something else entirely: a quiet stretch of sand where we could be alone. As we walked down the moonlit sand, he stopped to face me. Gently tucking a stray hair behind my ear, he smiled softly and leaned in close, letting his other hand wrap around the small of my back, pulling me towards his body.

"I can kiss you now, dale?" he asked in a near whisper, his voice hopeful as his gaze drifted down to my lips.

I couldn't help but smile, and for just a moment, I hovered there on the edge, debating whether I wanted to get back on this carousel of passion, guilt, chaos, and emotion that I had barely survived with Jasper. I let the tension fill the space between our bodies, letting myself feel far removed from everything now: New York, Alex, my upcoming wedding. That's the thing about travel. Once you step on that jet bridge, the ropes that tether you seemingly slip off, leaving you feeling like an entirely different person. One look at the moon, the stars, those eyes, and I gave in to another illicit kiss.

"My hostel está cerca," he said, peeling his lips off mine. "¿Quieres venir?" he asked, pointing towards a row of beachfront cabins I hadn't noticed earlier. Nothing was lost in translation as Augustino gestured hopefully to his nearby hostel, eager for me to come over for the night.

"I'm sorry," I said, knowing full well what would happen if I followed him to his room. "Necesito buscar mis amigas."

If Augustino was disappointed, he hid it well. Instead, he hugged me close, kissed me goodbye, promised to keep in

NIKKI VARGAS · 118

touch via WhatsApp, and walked me back to the bar so I could find my friends. The truth is, I wanted to sleep with Augustino—badly. But that was a line I wasn't sure I was ready to cross. Granted, kissing him had already crossed a line, as had kissing Jasper.

★

"Can I have another whiskey and ginger ale, please?" I ask, waving down the Iguana bartender. I can feel my anxiety deepening as more questions arise.

If everything I have been feeling is, in fact, pre-wedding jitters, could I live with the guilt of kissing Jasper and Augustino before walking down the aisle? Perhaps I could write them both off as temporary lapses in judgment, hallmarks of a time in my twenties in which I'd felt lost and confused. Some part of me clearly hopes that I will pull it together for the big day and become the bride everyone wants me to be and the wife Alex needs me to become. I desperately want to believe what my friends and family have been saying all along; that this confusion will magically resolve itself by my wedding day.

Augustino returned to Argentina yesterday, and—true to form—I have begun to obsess over him in a way that feels uncomfortably similar to how I once obsessed over Jasper. I'm replaying the few moments we shared: sitting in the warm waters watching starfish pass by, dancing at the overwater bar, kissing on that beach. If insanity is defined as the act of repeating the same thing over and over again, expecting different results, then I would've had the word rubber-stamped on my forehead. I can already feel myself thinking of ways to get to Buenos Aires and see Augustino one more time. I'm desperate for another hit of that passion I'd felt on the beach. I'm a spinning top veering towards the edge of the table, but just like that riptide in Cabo San Lucas, I still don't know how to save myself.

Shit. I was so distracted by my torrid thoughts that I completely forgot the situation unfolding. *I'm a terrible friend.* After searching the bar for Melanie, Alyssa materializes next to me once again, her voice urgent. "C'mon! Let's grab the bikes and look for her."

I down my drink and nod at Alyssa, following her lead as she shepherds our drunken group towards the bar's exit like a flock of wayward sheep.

Typically, we'd send Melanie a flurry of text messages, but she had her iPhone stolen the other night when she wandered off with a backpacker for a midnight swim, leaving her belongings vulnerable at the end of a wooden pier. Even without a way to call her, we have a few things working in our favor. For starters, it's a weeknight in Bocas Town, meaning fewer crowds and emptier bars. Also, our homestay is about a five-minute bike ride from Iguana, making it very likely that Melanie pulled an Irish exit and snuck off to bed early from the bar. Then there's the main street, which extends just a few blocks before dissolving into unlit dirt roads, giving us a manageable search radius with a handful of places she could have wandered off to. Imagining Melanie's disappearance is anything more nefarious is to go to a dark place we cannot fathom, and so, we start searching.

Our group sets off on our bikes, pedaling slowly down sandy roads, stopping every so often to run into a bar and scan the crowd for our friend. After fifteen or so minutes, Alyssa calls out to us.

"Wait! Hold up!" She abruptly stops pedaling, waving the rest of us over to what looks like a private villa.

Why would Melanie be here? I think to myself. Then I hear it: Melanie's unmistakable laugh, a joy-filled chuckle emanating from the back of the house. A wave of relief washes over our group as we ditch our bikes and follow our friend's voice over to a wobbly white fence enclosing the villa's backyard. One knock on the flimsy wood, and we're greeted by a guy I immediately recognize as one of the "dude backpackers" (I never did catch his name) we'd been drinking with at Iguana Bar forty-five minutes earlier.

"Jesus Christ, Melanie, what the fuck were you thinking?" implores Alyssa angrily, pushing past the dude backpacker into the yard. "You can't just walk off like that!"

"I'm fine!" says Melanie lightly. Her eyebrow cocks daringly. "Want to go skinny-dipping?"

I can't help but laugh. Melanie's cool as a cucumber, sitting on a white lawn chair with her tanned legs draped over one side and a near-empty Corona bottle dangling from her right hand. It's only then I register that all of them—Melanie and the guys—are sopping wet. She casually nods in the direction of an elevated three-story wooden structure several feet away, standing on the edge of the ocean. If my time in Bocas Town has taught me anything, it's that every night of drinking seems to involve a rickety platform, trampoline, or dock from which to perilously jump into the water. This wooden structure is no exception: a series of three platforms overlooking the ocean, each connected by a set of stairs, with the highest one standing maybe ten feet above the surface.

A few minutes later, I am standing alongside Melanie atop that three-story structure—at the highest level and still a little drunk, mind you. To their credit, the dude backpackers have graciously opted to stay in their patio chairs, giving us some semblance of privacy as we prepare to ditch our clothes and soar through the air. The night is balmy and cloudless, with a dusting of stars. On the count of three, we fling ourselves off the dock, the air enveloping our bare bodies for a few seconds before we crash into the warm waters of the ocean below.

I am invigorated by the jump and electrified by the moment, swimming in wild abandon, feeling entirely weight-less as though every stress and doubt has slipped off me in the waves. I feel sexy and curvy, a wild woman in the throes of nature. *This* is a freedom I've only found hints of at the bottom of a glass or the end of a jet bridge. *This* is a freedom I want to spend my life chasing. As chaotic as my life feels right now, I know that one day, I'll have to confront everything I'm running from. I'll put down the whiskey, drop the suitcases, wipe away the smeared lipstick, and stop thinking of other men—or maybe I won't. Maybe all of my confusion will just float away right here on this night breeze, becoming a memory of a blurry albeit beautiful time in my life. All I know for sure is that right now, nuzzled in the warm embrace of Bocas del Toro, I can hide just a bit longer.

9

Roots & Wings

Iguazú National Park, Argentina

It's hard waiting for the words to flow. For too long, they've been clogged up inside me, a blocked artery cutting off oxygen to my brain. Out here, away from everything, I can finally say what I need to say. I'm truly alone for the first time in what feels like an eternity, stripped of my defenses and hidden from distractions. There is no tulle and lace to hide the ugly truth or glittery sequins to cover my fake smiles.

As I walk, I feel myself searching for an epiphany I can leave this country and continent with, something to carry across the 4,753 miles back to New York. My wedding is now less than one week away. I'm officially out of time. I had waited for what I assumed were pre-wedding jitters to slough off my skin, revealing a sparkling bride beneath. Instead, I've only twisted further into myself, trying to make sense of why I've been running since the day in the vineyard when I said yes to marrying Alex.

Looking back, my decision to travel solo didn't feel real until I sat on that American Airlines flight to Buenos Aires. Sitting in the darkness amid all the vacant plane seats, it felt like no one could see me, as though I had hurried out the back door of my life beneath the cloak of nighttime. But, of course, everyone in my life—my family, my friends, my bridesmaids, my future in-laws, my fiancé—are staring with bated breath, wondering whether I'll make it down the aisle in a few days. I shrink beneath their inquiring gazes, their eyes lined with panic and concern, wondering—always wondering—just what is going on with me.

What the hell am I doing?!

Until boarding the plane, I had moved solely on adrenaline, letting it propel me through airport security, check-in, and finally onto the jet bridge. Unable to explain what I was doing or why I was doing it, I knew only that I needed to run away this one last time. For months, I had chased some unknown truth across countries, all the while looking for something I couldn't name yet. Some sort of revelation that would clear the thick fog that had settled over my mind.

I now walk quietly beneath a canopy of trees, their leaves rustling in the breeze against the thunderous sound of the waterfalls roaring ahead. What I'm doing is admittedly cliché: a woman lost in the jungle of her mind on the wild borders of Argentina, Brazil, and Paraguay. I'm hiking along the trails of Iguazú National Park, where the god known as M'Boi is purported to have slashed the earth in a jealous rage after falling in love with an Indigenous woman named Naipí. It's said that Naipí's beauty was so arresting that it could halt the flowing waters of the Iguaçu River. Although she was to marry the deity, she tried to escape her fate by running away with a mortal man she loved named Tarobá. As the story goes, the god punished the lover's attempts to flee by violently slashing the river and creating the waterfalls we know today.

The main draw for Iguazú National Park is what is known as Devil's Throat, where the Iguaçu River looks as if it has been gouged with an ice cream scooper, revealing a half crescent of cascading falls draped by delicate wisps of misty rainbows. Local legend says that a certain rock jutting out of the falls and a particular tree hovering at the water's edge are the transmuted forms of Naipí and Tarobá, connected now by mere myth and rainbows, forever held in Iguazú's watery embrace.

Arriving at the park, I find myself instantly and deeply moved by Iguazú. I don't even mind the gang of sneaky striped-tail coati that rob me blind of my potato chips. I had pulled out a bag for a quick snack before hiking, only to find myself swarmed by coati, their elegant long snouts gently sniffing the air for treats. As I reached for my camera to snap a photo, one of the bandits snatched the bag and ran off, letting chips fly in its wake like confetti.

As I move through the jungle now, the overwhelming sound of crashing water grows louder. The trees part to reveal an astonishing scene: as the cascades of water crumble into another river below, the surface reflects the morning sunlight, generously tossing out rainbows over the water. The grin of Devil's Throat with those white gushing waterfalls looks more like an angel's smile. As if that isn't enough to make a traveler swoon, turquoise-colored swallows (known as swallow tanagers) swoop between the falls like shimmering orbs of neon blue.

I am devastated by Iguazú's beauty, frustrated even. It feels silly to stand here taking selfies—my arm outstretched at an odd angle and messy hair held back by a thrifted DKNY scarf—as though I should be paying homage to this view through sonnets and interpretive dance instead. A nearby family takes note of my struggle to snap a photo of myself and kindly offers to take my picture, capturing what would unknowingly become a defining moment in my travel journey. I drop my backpack to the ground and stand off to the side, not wanting to obstruct the waterfalls, smiling widely for the camera with a look that says, *I can't believe I did it. I can't believe I actually boarded the plane and came here alone.*

★

I have come to South America on assignment for a publication called *The Daily Meal*, a website covering culinary trends and food-related stories that run the gamut from the best slow-cooker recipes to how to make a buffalo chicken dip. Beneath the avalanche of chaos that has tumbled over my life—from a job I hate to a wedding I keep avoiding—the seeds of my travel blog have continued to blossom against all odds.

Through *The Pin the Map Project*, I snagged a few paid writing opportunities, including a regular gig as a contributing travel writer for *The Daily Meal*. So far, my articles haven't really been about travel, instead sharing New York–based experiences like a "buggy eats" event at the Explorer's Club on East 70th, where I cringed at the fried tarantulas and crispy cockroaches people ate in between sips of vodka martinis. This latest story is my first travel article for the publication, focusing on the best cafés to visit in the über-trendy Palermo neighborhood in Buenos Aires. While the pay isn't enough to pop champagne and quit my advertising job just yet, it does feel like the first bona fide step towards a career I have been doggedly pursuing for most of my twenties.

There's a quote from one of Emily Dickinson's poems that reads, "If your nerve deny you, go above your nerve." I came across the quote while reading Cheryl Strayed's *Wild*, a memoir I've clung to on this trip like the hand of a dear friend. I've internalized these words, transforming them into a personal mantra of sorts. For a week now, I've done my best to "go above my nerve"—the very nerve that held me back in Rouen—by letting Argentina introduce itself to me in kaleidoscopic waves of delicious meals, kind strangers, and the sort of travel stories that make for excellent dinner fodder.

One day, I ventured across Buenos Aires to the colorful La Boca neighborhood, where homes made of corrugated metal and scraps are decorated with leftover paint from the nearby ship docks. Another day, I roamed the open-air markets of San Telmo, the city's oldest barrio, where I met a dentist-turned-chef who now runs a choripan joint. I watched as the man grilled the savory sausages and sandwiched them between two halves of a crispy baguette slathered with homemade chimichurri. Choripan (a combo of the words "chori" for chorizo and "pan" for bread) is as common in the city as a traditional barbecue asado.

On one of my favorite nights, I crashed an asado. I'd been invited by one of the travelers in my hostel who knew a friend of a friend of a friend who was holding one. We arrived at a local's apartment, which recalled one of those cramped one-bedrooms back in Manhattan, except this one had access to a roof where slabs of marbled beef sat cooking upon a smoky grill. In many ways, the asado reminded me of a typical night with my friends back in New York: people gathered in a tight living room, with music blasting from a portable Bluetooth speaker, all of us talking excitedly between bites. But instead of eating $1 slices from the pizza joint on the edge of Tompkins Square Park and drinking the crappy wine from the East Village liquor store on 1st Avenue, the food and drinks of an Argentine asado are incomparable. Flimsy paper plates were piled high with juicy flank steak accompanied by skewered grilled veggies like sweet bell peppers and red onions, washed down with free-flowing Malbec boasting notes of black cherry and pomegranate.

At the asado, I found myself remembering Rouen and how I'd sit on the edges of French conversations at parties thrown by Alex's friends. I've come a long way from the girl who was trying to work up the courage to explore a new city solo, the girl who had heart palpitations over ordering a raspberry macaron in Normandy. Sure, having a basic grasp of Spanish does help, but sitting at that asado, amid a sea of expats, locals, and travelers, I felt more comfortable than I'd been feeling back home.

With each day, I settled into being solo, growing more confident and falling deeper in love with travel. So in love, that I booked a tattoo appointment in Palermo, where a bored-looking teenager stood ready to ink my skin with the words, *To travel is to live.* I had booked the appointment on a whim, eager to commemorate my solo trip with the same words printed on the pinned map my mom had given me for Christmas. I arrived at the tattoo parlor in Palermo Hollywood—a small space with black-painted walls decorated with crinkled Argentine rock band posters.

"I'd like to tattoo 'To travel is to live' on my inner left wrist," I explained in Spanglish.

"Dale, how about this?" The artist picked up a blue ball-point pen and sketched the words on my skin, letting the oversized font take up my whole forearm.

"Um… I think that's a little too big. Can we go smaller?" Clearly annoyed, the tattoo artist grabbed rubbing alcohol, wiped away the pen marks, and reapplied the sketch. This time the font stretched from my wrist halfway to my elbow.

"I think it's still too big," I winced, apologetically. "Can we go even smaller?"

"Any smaller and it won't be worth getting the tattoo," said the artist, rolling his eyes as he ran a hand through his bleach-blond hair.

"Sorry," I said, sheepishly, making a move towards the exit. "I've changed my mind."

As I walked back to my hostel in Palermo Soho, I looked down at that would-be tattoo whose blue pen marks still inked my left arm. Maybe I'd one day brush past my fear of needles and get a tattoo in Bangkok or at a tucked-away parlor in Amsterdam. Who knows? The point is that wherever and whenever it eventually happened, the tattoo's ink wasn't what mattered so much as the words. "To travel is to live" had already sunken deep below the surface of my skin, as had its meaning. Whatever happened next, I promised myself I'd keep right on traveling.

★

As I lost myself to Buenos Aires, falling more in love with the city and culture, I tried to push away the mounting pressures back home, their tendrils reaching across continents. For my family and friends, my writing assignment offered an "official" (albeit unsatisfactory) explanation for my pre-wedding disappearing act.

"The wedding is in two weeks. You have to go *now*?" Alex asked, reaching his limit. "Are you *sure* this is a good idea?"

"Yes," I told him. "I need to do this."

But the truth is, I didn't need to do it. I didn't need to fly to Argentina for my story. With no impending deadline or demanding editor, I could have just as quickly cobbled together a "10 Best Cafés in Palermo" article from the comfort of my Ikea couch back in Manhattan, pulling from a quick internet search and social media posts. It would have been cheaper too, since I'd opted to travel to Argentina on my own dime. No, I wanted to come here. I had pitched the story with the intention of having an excuse to travel. Whether I can admit it or not, I know this assignment is simply a front meant to give me one more chance to find myself before I say, "I do."

And then, just to thicken the plot, there is, of course, Augustino.

Since my trip to Panama a few months ago, our moment on that moon-soaked beach had only grown more romantic and extraordinary with time. Despite the many miles between us, he still existed within the pings of WhatsApp messages, his flirtatious banter distilled down to words on a screen. My Buenos Aires trip offered a collision of wants: a chance for me to run away from the wedding (albeit temporarily), a step closer to becoming a travel writer (hopefully), and an insatiable desire to see Augustino one more time.

I feel goose bumps running down my arms now as I think back to a few nights ago in Buenos Aires, when I saw Augustino for the first time since Panama. My hostel, Eco Pampa, is a bit of an eyesore on Avenida Guatemala. It is painted a startling lime green with matching wrought-iron fences and gates encasing its windows and doors. The color is a nod to its eco-conscious mission. I learned upon my arrival that Eco Pampa markets itself as the city's first green hostel (both literally and figuratively), where furniture is constructed from recycled materials, and light fixtures rely exclusively on low-energy bulbs. I had booked a single room with its own bathroom, affording myself a sliver of privacy in an otherwise crowded hostel touting ten-person dorm rooms and bunk beds.

From the moment I planned this trip, I must have known I would sleep with Augustino. When I agreed to meet him for a drink at an alfresco bar around the corner from my hostel, I surely sensed that the evening would end with him in my bed. I don't know if I stopped to question my actions or to contemplate what it meant to cross this moral line. No, I had been acting solely on impulse—just as I'd been doing these past few months. Whatever had held my desires at bay back in Panama had long since evaporated. I can feel a rush of adrenaline as I picture us tangled in my bedsheets, his fingers threading through my hair and gently tilting my head up towards his. I can still feel his arm snaking around my waist, pulling me closer to his bare chest while simultaneously pushing himself deeper inside me. I can still hear his breathless Spanish whispering in my ear.

Augustino didn't stick around after we finished having sex. Instead, he left me sitting on the edge of my bed, wrapped in nothing but one of those paper-thin white towels supplied by the hostel. He'd gotten what he wanted, and I had let him. I was a conquest he had been waiting to enjoy since Bocas del Toro, a box he could now check off his list. Our momentary passion was followed by an awkward and perfunctory good-bye. I knew I wouldn't see him again. And once more, I was alone, left with the fallout of my impulsive decisions.

In the time we'd spent chatting via WhatsApp, I made Augustino out to be so much more than he was—just as I had done with Jasper. I tried to justify my desire to see him as something that was simply "meant to be." I needed Augustino to be more than a kiss on a beach because it would rationalize my infatuation with him. It would make running away from my wedding better if I were running into the arms of "the one."

After he left, I listened to the sounds of Palermo spinning around me: the chatter from the hostel common area, the music from the wine bar next door, the honking of Fiats rumbling down the Avenida. Pulling the towel tighter around my naked body, I held my breath, waiting for my levees to break and release a flood of regret. I had slept with someone else. I had betrayed my fiancé. I had made a decision that I could not file away. I waited and waited, but only one emotion stepped forward: relief.

★

As an aspiring travel writer, I'm ashamed to admit that I didn't know about Iguazú National Park before arriving in Argentina. In fact, I hadn't even planned to visit the waterfalls until about two days ago, when a chance encounter inspired me to book a flight to the border. I was returning to my hostel from another afternoon spent perusing the cafés of Palermo, this time one found inside a quiet bookstore called Libros de Pasaje. From the street, Libros de Pasaje looks like a regular bookshop, but go inside and you'll discover a small dining area with a handful of tables sandwiched between copies of Jack Kerouac's *Lonesome Traveler* and Spanish translations of *The Great Gatsby*.

Libros de Pasaje quickly became my favorite haunt—a place where I could spend hours tucked away, sipping coffee and pretending I was just another Porteño. In Buenos Aires, Porteño is a nickname for city residents, a term that literally translates to "port city person." Oh, how I wish I could disappear into the crowd of these Porteños. Two days ago, after indulging in a few too many cappuccinos and Tortas Antonia—a homemade dessert concocted with nuts, red fruits, and chocolate—I returned to my hostel to find a man sitting in the common area, poring over photos of waterfalls. I guessed he was somewhere in his mid to late thirties from the light gray peppering his dark hair.

"It's Iguazú," he smiled, catching my not-so-subtle gaze. His accent was a unique blend of Italian and UK English, so I guessed he was a fellow traveler, perhaps with a Western European upbringing.

I quickly learned that Michaele (pronounced "Mick-ele-y") had just returned from Iguazú National Park that very morning as part of a larger South American adventure. In the past few weeks, he had ventured from Machu Picchu in Peru to the reflective salt flats of Bolivia and onward to the iconic Ipanema Beach of Brazil, but of all the wonders he had seen (of which there were many), it was the Iguazú waterfalls that had left a lasting impression on him.

"Wow. Those photos are absolutely amazing," I said, leaning in to get a better look. "How far are the waterfalls from Buenos Aires?"

"Not far at all!" exclaimed Michaele, excited to share details of his visit. "It's about an hour flight, and the domestic airport—Jorge Newbery Airport—is only twenty minutes away. You really should see the waterfalls for yourself."

After chatting for fifteen minutes, I walked away from Michaele armed with a recommended itinerary, a suggested hostel, and tips for navigating Iguazú National Park. An hour later, I booked my flight to the border.

Around me, families and couples are beginning to trickle down the elevated wooden walkways, picking up pace as the trees reveal Devil's Throat in all its glory. As tempting as it is to stay here by the falls, letting the swelling crowds and roaring water drown out my thoughts, I know I need to be alone. I've come to Iguazú National Park to finally stop avoiding myself.

I turn away from the waterfalls and hike down one of the circular trails winding through the jungle. The farther I walk, the more I am enveloped by wilderness, the roar of the cascades and the crowds of spectators slowly falling away, and suddenly, I am alone. Truly alone. So alone that if I stop moving, the unnerving silence is punctuated only by my breathing and the occasional call of the capuchin monkeys above me. I feel a surge of anxiety as I ask myself aloud:

"What is it you have to say?"

Admittedly, I've felt my inner voice tugging at my sleeve for months, trying to grab my attention and get me to stand still long enough to hear it. I am now far enough from other people that I feel comfortable talking to myself. I let the question linger for a second before an exasperated response roars out of me.

"I DON'T WANT TO GET MARRIED!"

I practically scream the words with such force that I spot a few plush-crested jays with their tuxedo-like markings flutter to the sky.

"I DON'T WANT TO GET MARRIED!"

I feel as though I've just kicked myself to the ocean's surface, inhaling for the first time, letting my body fill with oxygen as my mind starts to steady. I think back to Augustino, and how sleeping with him had been my point of no return. When I let him wrap his body around mine, on some level, I knew that everything—my engagement, this wedding, the pressure, the planning—was finally over. I had crossed a line I could not uncross and would not ignore, and I felt relieved for it. Now here was the final frontier, the words that have been floating in cloudy fragments these past few months, finally coalescing.

I don't want to get married because I'm not ready.

I don't want to get married because I'm not in love.

I don't want to get married because I'm not happy.

I don't *want* to get married.

For the first time, I truly understand why Alex and I cannot move forward. For too long, we've ignored that he's grown roots and I've grown wings, that our futures had long ago diverged. I love Alex the way one might love a childhood friend. It's this love that has kept me in place, afraid of the chasm that will be left in his absence, and it's this very fear that has pushed me into the arms of Jasper and Augustino, desperate for someone to catch me when I inevitably fall. But the painful truth is I'm no longer in love with Alex and, if he were to confront himself, I know he'd realize he is no longer in love with me. We are both clinging to a version of the other that no longer exists: the doe-eyed college kids on the steps of Columbia University, trying to prolong a summer romance that has long since run its course.

Despite it all, I knew Alex would stand there on our wedding day and say "I do" for all the times we had truly meant it when we said we wanted forever. He'd look past these tumultuous months and promise himself to a woman who had been running since the day he proposed. He would do what was expected of him—and us—pushing aside all doubts and flagrant warning signs. He would file away the fights, the growing lack of intimacy, and hope I'd somehow grow into the woman he wanted, rather than marry me for the woman I'd become. We both deserve to be with people who know—beyond a shadow of a doubt—that this is the relationship they want. Only now, in the Iguazú jungle, do I feel certain that the kindest thing I can do is give us back our futures, freeing up space in our lives for a love we both have yet to find.

I feel everything now: relieved, terrified, sad, exhilarated, inspired, defiant. But above all, I feel strong—a power that seems to infuse every part of my body. I had become complacent and avoidant. I had stayed in a career I hated and went through the motions of planning a wedding I didn't want. I drowned my doubts in alcohol and distraction, letting go of the steering wheel of my life long ago. Now I had only myself to blame for the direction my world had drifted, and no one—not Augustino, Jasper, Alex, my family, or my friends—could and would save me from the mess I had created.

My stomach is now twisting in knots. Going back to New York is going to be a shit show. I'll have to fly home and call off my engagement, break a wonderful man's heart, and cancel a wedding that is now days away. I can no longer avoid the turbulent river in front of me or keep looking for ways to get around it. Instead, I'll walk right in and face the current, pulling from a well of strength that has now been dug. I'll face it all—the vitriol and the disappointment, the confusion and the pain, the sadness and the loss—because I finally know that my life is worth fighting for, and that the woman I can become is waiting for me if only I'm strong enough to change course and reach for her.

And finally, after months of avoiding the arms of my fiancé by stumbling into the embrace of others. After months of hiding behind lace veils and sprinting down jet bridges. I know I am strong enough to just say no to getting married and walk away.

10

Earn This

New York, New York

My and Alex's apartment looks barren. Almost the way it did when I first moved in that summer after living in Rouen. It all feels a lifetime away now; saving tips from my serving job at the restaurant, counting the days until Alex joined me in New York. Looking at the empty living room, I stare at the red marbled bench that covers the radiator. I always loved to perch on that bench, reading my books in a sliver of sunlight that would push its way through our dusty windows every afternoon. Any trace of our life together has now disappeared, leaving only bare white walls and scattered black cable wires.

I'm suddenly unnerved by how quickly one can dismantle a life. If I close my eyes, I can see our apartment as it was a few weeks ago, when it still resembled a home. I can imagine every framed photo and piece of furniture in the exact place it once stood: the push-pin map hanging above the worn Ikea couch, the clothesline of photos over our shared bedroom desk with pictures of us and family smiling, the wine bar still holding that dusty bottle of uncorked champagne given to us as an engagement gift.

Canceling a wedding is like dropping a rock in a lake and being forced to watch the ripples fan out from the point of impact. The first ripple, of course, is the financial losses suffered by the bride's and groom's families. The canceled venue, the overpriced florists, the fall-themed decor, the upstate Hudson Valley–inspired menu, and the slew of other prepaid vendors with nonrefundable deposits. Then there are the financial losses endured by the nearly 120 guests who reserved hotels, rental cars, and flights for a wedding no longer taking place. More than canceled trips, there is the inconvenience of having asked over a hundred people to rearrange their schedules and take time off work for your special day for which outfits were purchased, plans were made, and—in the case of two family members—cosmetic surgery had been done.

After the financial fallout comes the next ripple: everything left behind. The nonrefundable and nonreturnable wedding gown altered to fit only my body. The myriad of registry gifts that require awkward mea culpa notes in place of thank-you cards: *I'm sorry about the inconvenience this has caused you and your family. Thank you for the Cuisinart toaster.* Then there are the other, more personal items like the Christian Louboutin stilettos my mom painstakingly bedazzled for months, sitting hunched at her kitchen table using tweezers to glue on the micro gems, all so she could surprise me with a one-of-a-kind pair of wedding shoes. There's the hand-painted red-and-yellow ceramic clock from Italy's Abruzzo region, gifted by my dad and Yana so that it would hang in our future home, and the family heirlooms, such as my great-grandmother's ring—a dazzling ruby set in a yellow gold band—so I'd have "something old" to wear when I said my vows.

After that comes another ripple: the gossip and speculation. A circle of hell in which everyone in my life wonders what happened and is curious as to why I didn't make it down the aisle. In the immediate aftermath of my announcement, I'd become persona non grata, a label that saw family and friends distancing themselves from me in droves. Family members stopped speaking to me, unable to look me in the eye. Friends dropped me, disappointed I hadn't confided in them sooner, unable to grasp I had only just admitted the truth to myself. But even that's not the worst of it. The last and most painful ripple is a large, far-reaching ring that encircles the rest. As the villain in the situation, I don't feel comfortable openly mourning the loss of a relationship I chose to plunge a stake through. It doesn't matter that I've lost my home, best friend, and fiancé in one fell swoop or that I've been pushed away by family and friends—the one who chose to walk away does not get to grieve.

I deserve this, I think to myself. *This is the price you pay.*

With guilt comes nostalgia. As it crumbles around me, I can't help but remember how our home once bore witness to laughter, frivolity, and play. These white walls watched us wear our Superman and Wonder Woman outfits on Halloween and saw me host my first-ever Thanksgiving in our too-small kitchen, roasting pre-cut turkey slices in a toaster oven. This apartment had played host to a revolving door of friends who'd drink and talk for hours in our living room. Apartment 2H beheld the evolution of two kids becoming adults, finding their footing in a city known for spitting people out. For all the fights that had unfolded and tears that'd been shed, there had also been levity here once. It didn't matter that my and Alex's story had been but one chapter; our relationship played out in this space like an entire lifetime.

"I guess that's all of it," says Alex, gesturing around the empty apartment.

He is getting ready to leave the city in search of a fresh start in Chicago. He has no interest in moving through a place whose every street now feels haunted by our story. There is no animosity between us now, just a weariness that befalls any couple in the process of disentangling their lives.

When I had first called off our wedding, there had been a week or so in which we'd stayed in limbo. While I had managed to say I didn't want to get married, I couldn't bring myself to utter the more painful truth I'd discovered back in Iguazú: I wasn't in love with Alex anymore. During that limbo week, I came home to find Alex waiting for me in a suit and tie, standing in front of a smorgasbord of my favorite foods. He had gone to Agata & Valentina—a pricey gourmet grocery store we only shopped at on special occasions—and bought every single item I loved: the fresh-squeezed juice made from Valencia oranges, the fancy chocolates hailing from Italy and Sweden, the stinky and expensive cheeses only purchased for holidays and birthdays. He had bought it all along with red roses, hopeful that this would somehow fix the unfixable.

Once, during a Monday night football game, I remember Alex explained a Hail Mary pass to me as the last-ditch effort to save the game. I recognized this gesture as his own Hail Mary pass; we had lost the wedding, but against all odds, Alex hoped this smorgasbord could save us. When I didn't throw my arms around him, covering him in kisses and tearful proclamations of love, he knew our relationship was over. His eyes were heavy with an aching sadness that would haunt me for years. As we stood there silently picking at our feast, I thought about how I had never wanted to hurt Alex. I had only wished to find a side exit and slip out of our lives unnoticed, as though sneaking out of a party. But of course, that wasn't possible, and now nothing, not even Agata & Valentina, could intervene.

I cross the room and hug Alex now, choking back tears as I officially cut the final rope tying us to this life we once shared. In all those months I'd spent running away, jumping at travel any chance I got, I had never thought of what it'd feel like to say goodbye—only what it would be like to be gone. I can almost see the delicate thread that had connected us, now falling to our feet. What unspooled one balmy night at a restaurant in SoHo, now severed in this empty one-bedroom apartment on East 79th Street, four years later.

"I hope you earn this," says Alex with a sad smile. "After all of this, I hope you go out there and do what it is you want to do and become who it is you want to be."

I nod, letting the words sink in. Since returning from Argentina, I had left nothing but heartbreak and disappointment in my wake. I had sacrificed everything—my family's approval, my friendships, our home, and Alex's heart—on the altar of something I had discovered while solo traveling: the desire for a new kind of future I was now determined to reach.

Giving Alex back the engagement ring was the first step on a journey that would see me tearing down and rebuilding my world so that it better resembled me. For too long, I had said "yes" when I meant "no" and had been looking off to the side when I should have been looking forward. I now needed to chase my dreams of travel writing, pushing it into the forefront of my career. I needed to venture far in continual pursuit of something that wasn't just an escape from my reality. I understood what Alex was saying; I needed to earn this pain—my own and others'—and make sure that *all of this* hadn't been for nothing. I needed to earn this moment—and keep earning it—showing everyone that the lost money, untouched gown, tossed-out flowers, and sea of tears surrounding me were not in vain.

"I better not find you married in a year," laughs Alex wryly. "Or see on Facebook that you're living in Connecticut with a baby next summer."

"Imagine," I say, smiling. The mere idea is ludicrous.

With one last look at our apartment, we close the door, exit our pre-war building, and walk outside. It's early evening now, the setting sun casting a glow over 2nd Avenue that bounces off the glass and steel of the surrounding buildings, an urban beauty. I take it all in. The corner Duane Reade that Alex would run to on winter nights; the nearby Stumble Inn, where we ate Juicy Lucy burgers, the patties oozing with bleu cheese; the 16 Handles ice cream shop we'd wander into on summer weekends. All of this had been our world.

Over the next few years, Alex would change careers and end up working in the same industry I now sought to escape. He'd climb the corporate ladder and reach the upper echelons of media planning, living in a swanky downtown Chicago apartment that he'd fill with yet-to-meet friends and future loves. In time, our old New York apartment would be completely rebuilt and expanded with a new family moving in. Our once-humble home would become unrecognizable, leaving no trace of the relationship that had unfolded there. Well, no trace, albeit one: that same radiator bench pushed up against the window—now repainted white—on which I had spent countless afternoons day dreaming of far-flung countries I hoped to one day see.

I watch as Alex walks into the street to hail a cab, the yellow car rolling to a stop at his feet. Opening the door, he turns to me with a look that seems to say, *Well, this is it.*

There'd be times that Alex and I would speak in the future,

checking on each other every so often via the occasional text or message, but this would be the last time we'd see each other. Holding back tears, I hug him and wish him well, gingerly closing the car door after him. For a few minutes, I watch as his cab speeds away, shielding my eyes against the glow of the sunset now enveloping his taxi.

"I promise I'll earn this," I say to myself quietly, and with that, I turn and walk away.

11

Monkeys and Travel Bloggers

Tanjung Puting National Park, Borneo, Indonesia

Why haven't I reached the river dock yet?

Before I can answer my own question, a rustle in the nearby bushes sends a jolt through my body. A wild bearded boar emerges from the overgrowth. He's massive, gray, and dirty, with two bone-white tusks framing his long snout. Atop his snout rests a nest of stringy yellowish hair. From what I can recall from my guidebook, this is the "beard" that makes this specific breed of boar so unique. Through squinted eyes, the boar looks right at me and loudly snorts as if to remind me whose home I'm in.

Noted, Mr. Boar.

I stand stock-still as the boar slowly ambles by. I read once that you should always avoid eye contact with grizzly bears so as not to appear threatening and inadvertently encourage a confrontation. This random fact comes to mind now, as I make the split-second decision to stare at my feet and hope the same rule applies to wild boars. Once the boar disappears into the bushes, I assess my surroundings. ·

Towering Belian trees rise above the pathway, their large bases flanked by lush green ferns tangled into the leaf-strewn ground. Around me, strangler fig trees and their twisted moss-draped roots rise from the jungle floor like gnarled hands shooting out of a grave. Strangler figs are a crazy tree; they are born from the seeds of a fig that attaches itself to a per-fectly healthy tree and then proceeds to germinate, sucking the very life out of its host like a vampire. Over time, this parasitic tree will eventually twist and grow until it cuts off the nutrient supply of its host tree and kills it. Somehow the beautiful, deadly strangler fig seems to perfectly encapsulate the dog-eat-dog world of the jungle.

Do I go left? Do I turn right?

I'm trying to remember my way back to the riverboats, but nothing looks familiar now. I stand still and listen, trying to pick up the sound of any other people in my vicinity. Surely, I should be able to hear talking or footsteps nearby, but in-stead, there's just that all-encompassing jungle soundscape: the rustling of leaves, the distant calls of howler monkeys, the buzzing of insects, the fading snorts of a lone, disgruntled boar. My stomach drops the way it so often does whenever I am hit with a tsunami of stress.

I'm lost, I think to myself, panicked. *I'm lost in Borneo.*

★

I never thought I'd visit Borneo in my lifetime. It is one of those places I grew up seeing on the covers of the *National Geographic*s my parents collected in the mid '90s. From those magazines, here's what I've learned about Borneo: the island's history has been a tug-of-war match between countries fighting for power. The Malaysian side of the island was once colonized by the British, while the Indonesian side belonged to the Dutch until World War II, when the entire island belonged to Japan. Today, Borneo is shared by three countries—Malaysia, Brunei, and Indonesia—and is the third largest island in the world. Beyond its political divisions and storied past, Borneo is super old, like 140 million years old, making it more historic than even the Amazon jungle.

Beneath its canopy of trees, the biodiversity of Borneo hides a well of secrets that naturalists and scientists are still constantly unearthing. Four hundred new species have been identified here since 1994, while over forty animals are native only to this island. This is a place so wild and so untamed that it has captured the imagination of explorers for decades—and now here I am, standing in the middle of the jungle, lost.

I arrived in Borneo a few days ago, landing in the small city of Pangkalan Bun, a jumping-off point for exploring Tanjung Puting National Park, considered a natural wonder of the world. I found Pangkalan Bun's low-rise buildings, red-tiled roofs, and gray-paved streets to be rather unremarkable except for one detail: the morning call to prayer. Two-thirds of Borneo's population is Muslim, and the city of Pangkalan Bun is home to over thirty ornate mosques, one of which stood proudly across the street from the small hotel in which I stayed.

Be it the ringing of the bells of Notre-Dame in Paris, the singing of tropical birds on a languid morning in Bocas del Toro, or the crescendo of waterfalls in Iguazú—I've come to realize that many of my travel memories are rooted in sound, and Borneo is no exception. While the jungle is marked by monkey calls and snorting boars, Pangkalan Bun plays a different tune. In the early morning hours, I woke to the hauntingly beautiful call to prayer summoning people to worship.

Stumbling out of bed, I rubbed the sleep from my eyes and parted the gauzy white curtains to reveal a dazzling sunrise illuminating the mosque. The next morning, I left Pangkalan Bun and boarded a riverboat en route to Camp Leakey.

In the two to three days it took for me to reach the camp, my appearance has changed as dramatically as my surroundings. The riverboats are rustic, to say the least. There are no rooms, only a large open-air deck on which paper-thin mattresses are scattered each night. Below deck, there is a small kitchen, a toilet, and little else. There's no shower onboard, so I arrived at Camp Leakey looking like a contestant from the show *Survivor*: dirty, smelly, tired, yet exhilarated.

I'm traveling in Indonesia as part of a creator trip, in which eighteen bloggers were invited by the Indonesia Tourism Board to explore the wonders of this country in exchange for creating content on their respective blogs. To snag a spot on this once-in-a-lifetime trip, I had to apply with an overzealous video touting the many ways that my blog, *The Pin the Map Project*, could help promote Indonesia to an American-based audience. After sending out my hastily edited video—a compilation of shaky clips from past trips, inspirational background music, and promises of all the blog posts I'd write about Indonesia—I tried to forget about the opportunity, sure they'd go with a more polished blogger with a bigger audience. A few weeks later, I received an email from Indonesia Tourism formally inviting me on this all-expenses-paid adventure, and so I dropped everything and said yes.

"I can't believe how remote this is!" I exclaimed to no one in particular as our group approached Camp Leakey's feeding and observation area.

Camp Leakey is one of the oldest animal research centers in the world, nestled deep in the heart of Borneo's jungle. It was established in the 1970s as an ongoing research project designed to explore the nuances of orangutan behavior. Today, this research center specializes in conserving and protecting wild orangutans, endemic only to this island and neighboring Sumatra.

The orangutan feeding area of Camp Leakey sits in the middle of the jungle, about twenty or so minutes hiking from the river docks, in a clearing that contains a handful of rickety wooden benches surrounded by a low-hanging rope separating spectators from animals. Beyond the rope are various wooden platforms on which piles of discarded banana peels rest. In some ways, the clearing acts as an inverse zoo, with the humans confined to a small area and the orangutans free to roam nearby, as though they're really the ones observing us. There isn't much to stop these great apes from stepping over the frayed nylon rope, except for what must be some level of trust or indifference they feel towards the people who've sat right here in this very spot, watching them for years.

"I don't think I've ever been somewhere so far-removed," remarked a fellow travel blogger as we walked through the dense jungle towards the clearing.

"It's unbelievable," I started to say. "We're totally and completely alo—"

My voice trailed off when the trees began falling away to reveal a bustling feeding area packed with more crowds than a Black Friday sale at Walmart. "What the hell?" I murmured, incredulous at the sight. Jam-packed in the small clearing stood dozens of tourists: families dressed like they were on a safari, wearing beige cargo pants and floppy green hats, couples posing with selfie sticks, teenagers holding up cell phones, impatiently looking for reception.

All I could think was how I had spent two days traveling by riverboat, living beneath a canopy of mosquito netting, and sleeping on a pillow consisting of my rolled-up jeans, only to arrive at Camp Leakey with sweat-slicked hair and a hundred layers of sunscreen and mosquito repellent on my skin, convinced I'd traveled to the farthest reaches of the earth. We shared looks of annoyance as all eighteen of us flooded the already crowded feeding area. As travelers, we are always searching for that elusive destination free of other camera-toting tourists—this was not one of them.

At the same time, I pity other travelers whenever our group arrives because suddenly, every sunset, mountaintop, and pristine beach is transformed into a photo shoot, replete with drones, clicking cameras, and endless idle chatter. Of the eighteen bloggers on this Indonesia trip, each one self-identifies as belonging to a specific niche. There are the luxury travel bloggers who pester our guides with requests for champagne, insisting their followers need to see them drinking poolside in a caftan. There are the video bloggers who schlep around a studio's worth of drones, tripods, and GoPros on their backs. It doesn't matter where we go, how far we hike, or—as in the case of our visit to Komodo Island a few days ago—how many hours we've spent searching for the eponymous dragons; these bloggers will whip out twenty different kinds of cameras in hopes of capturing their exploits.

Beyond adventure and luxury, our group further fragments into other genres of blogging. The foodies are so desperate for the perfect shot of your fried mie goreng noodles that they'll physically block your fork from disrupting their picture. The yoga bloggers will take thirty-one photos of themselves performing sun salutations on the beach, while the solo travel bloggers go to wildly great lengths to uphold the illusion of being alone in Indonesia, painstakingly taking selfies off to the side so they can hide the other seventeen people surrounding them.

Amid this cacophony there is me, somewhere on this broad

spectrum of blogging. I cringe at the selfie sticks our group holds above our heads when we hike and the way it makes us look like a flock of pink flamingos moving in synchronicity across a salt flat. I try to block out the conversations revolving around Instagram's latest algorithms and how they're "totally ruining my likes!"

Blogging is a funny world of storytellers genuinely keen on sharing their experiences alongside self-serving opportunists interested in flaunting free trips and collecting free swag. In the months since I'd quit my job in media buying, I felt I'd seen it all. On a trip in Asia, I watched as a travel blogger screamed at a bellhop for dropping a suitcase that he swore was "more expensive than his house." On an adventure tour in the Caribbean, I stared incredulously as another blogger whipped out a sparkly floor-length gown in the middle of an arduous jungle hike, posing for a selfie. On a visit to the Philippines, I listened to a travel blogger grappling with the dilemma of posting about the free fridge she simply *had* to accept but had no desire to write about.

Let me take a moment to knock myself off my high horse. I, too, have cringeworthy shots in which I'm inexplicably twirling in front of the Eiffel Tower or wearing a silky skirt while poised on slippery rocks in Belize. I, too, have Instagram photos accompanied by empty platitudes about how "not all who wander are lost." Hell, I've even written my fair share of sponsored blog posts touting some free hotel stay or a complimentary suitcase. How much judgment can I throw when I've played the game? The truth is, without blogging, I couldn't travel, especially now that I'm unemployed. Or rather, I'm self-employed by my nonpaying blog, if you're a cup-half-full sort of person.

After calling off my wedding, I quit my job at Inventif Media. I knew it was risky—I didn't have enough savings to cover rent, let alone my student loans—but I had emerged from both the canceled wedding and Iguazú jungle determined to take back my life—no matter the cost. The first step had been not to walk down the aisle and the next was to go after my dream of travel writing.

While blogging doesn't *actually* pay any of my bills, it does allow me the opportunity to see the world, even if it's with a gaggle of people in tow, talking relentlessly about their social media stats.

All that being said, I'm at odds with myself now—both enchanted by blogging and eager to move beyond it. When I look back at my career, it has always been about writing. From studying journalism in college to trying to get my big break in New York, my dream has always been to become a travel *writer*. When I couldn't immediately get a job as a travel writer, travel blogging seemed the next best thing. But the further I wade into this world, the more I find that writing can be about as far removed from travel blogging as Camp Leakey is from Pangkalan Bun.

With the rise of social media, I see bloggers now gravitating from writing towards well-edited videos and magazine-style photos. In fact, the act of blogging has seemingly become archaic nowadays, replaced by influencers and their curated imagery. I tried to get with the times, but I feel inherently awkward and self-conscious about taking selfies in public. On a trip in Jamaica, I set up my camera and tried seven times to get a "candid shot" of me walking down an oceanfront pier, hoping to mirror the idyllic travel images that have been flooding my Instagram feed, only to end up falling on my ass after being taken out by a wave. In my early attempts at YouTube vlogs, I tried to emulate other video bloggers and share the beauty of a destination, only to have the footage be out of focus or the scenery blocked by a zoomed-in image of my head. As the 2010s have seen blogging continue to move towards aesthetic appeal, I have stayed rooted in words, wishing that I worked at a travel publication where being on staff could afford me the opportunity to travel, a steady paycheck, and the ability to share my stories with millions of readers—all without needing to pose for a selfie.

★

"Helloooooo! Is anyone out there?"

There had been so many people in the feeding area, it seems impossible I've somehow managed to stray far enough to get lost. Back at the clearing, I had plopped down on a corner bench where I could watch the orangutans in peace away from the rest of my group and their chatter. *What's a good caption to go with this monkey photo? Can you get a shot of me with the orangutan in the background?*

As I sat with my Nikon camera poised, watching a female orangutan emerge from the surrounding jungle, I noted how her orange coat glowed a fiery tangerine, the afternoon sun bringing out the natural gold, crimson, and brown highlights in her fur. To her breast clung a baby orangutan, no larger than a football, its bald head revealing a smattering of fur the way a newborn human might have a soft tuft of hair. Nearby, a young lanky orangutan bundled bananas in his arms and slinked off into the trees as a larger male looked on lazily.

Watching the orangutans is like tuning into some sort of suburban family sitcom. In today's episode, the incorrigible teen raided his parent's stash of bananas, sneaking off into the wild with his loot as his bored father pretended not to notice and mom calmed the colicky baby. The very word "orangutan" means "people of the forest" in Malay—the official language of Brunei, Indonesia, Malaysia, and Singapore—and as I watched these great apes and their humanlike tendencies, I could see why.

I had been so hypnotized by the apes and their interactions that when I finally blinked and looked around, I didn't recognize anyone around the clearing. Somehow, my group had left without my noticing—and, apparently, without *them* noticing *my* absence. The clearing had a few remaining tourists, but I figured I could hike the twenty or so minutes back to the docks and catch up with my trip mates along the way. And so I left the Camp Leakey feeding area and wandered off into the jungle.

"Hellooooooooo!?"

I took a wrong turn somewhere, that much is clear. I hold up my water bottle to see I have only two sips left, and as if on cue, I begin sweating profusely. It's humid as hell in this jungle. The sort of humidity that feels as though you're wearing a damp wool sweater and soggy jeans. With the sun beginning to set, I try my best not to panic or imagine that my group has already sailed off without me downriver, or that I'll be stuck snuggling with Mr. Boar tonight.

On some level, I do have to laugh at the sheer irony of being back in another jungle, my voice once again ringing out over the treetops. But Tanjung Puting National Park and Iguazú National Park are nothing alike—for starters, it doesn't take days to reach the Iguazú waterfalls, and nearly all of Iguazú's trails (at least on the Argentinian side) are circular, defined, and about thirty minutes from the nearest parking lot. Also, there are no waterfalls where I am—just those towering Belians and strangler figs as far as the eye can see.

How much time has passed?

As I yell out into the jungle to no response, my voice becomes more panicked. I can't blame the group for losing sight of me. Our local guides had been playing the role of sheepdog this entire trip, wrangling us together and making sure we moved from hotel to airport, tarmac to destination, without straying. Between the luxury bloggers demanding bubbly and the adventure bloggers hanging off cliffs, it was only a matter of time before one of us got lost—I just didn't think it would be me.

I look at the dirt-packed trails ahead of me, which could extend for miles in either direction. Without any markers or signs to guide me, I can go right, left, or retrace my steps. To risk walking down any of these trails is a gamble that might lead me farther astray into the wilderness, and so I stand there weighing my options, fighting the twisting knots in my stomach. I decide that my safest bet is to go back to the feeding area; as I walk, I keep calling out.

"Helloooo?!" I shout again.

"Yes!" says a faint response. "Over here!"

My heart leaps. I look around; the sound seems to be coming from farther ahead. I follow the sound of the voice for several minutes until I reach a guide whom I recognize, escorting two tourists from the feeding area back to the docks. The three seem surprised and somewhat amused at the sight of me emerging from the dense bushes, sticks poking from my hair, dirt streaking down my calves. As my breath steadies and we approach the river dock, I spot my group ahead, settling into the two riverboats that ferried us here.

I'm so relieved at the sight of them, even the ones preoccupied with editing their latest pictures, undoubtedly wondering which cliché travel quote best compliments an orangutan photo.

When I see their posted images later, I'll wonder if we are even on the same trip. Their highly saturated photos will look like something straight out of a *Vogue* fashion spread. Somehow, their hair will appear perfectly blown out and their makeup intact despite three days without showers. The vloggers will share superbly edited videos worthy of the Travel

Channel. The solo bloggers will indeed look like they had ventured into Borneo solo, while the luxury bloggers will somehow make our rinky-dink riverboat seem like a glamourous yacht.

For as varied as my trip mates' social media and blog posts are on this trip, they all have one unnerving thing in common: the portrayal that travel is perfect. Our dirt-streaked clothing, the crowded feeding area, and our mosquito-net covered mattresses are all left unseen. The perfection will hide the mishaps—like, say, a stray blogger getting lost in the jungle—not realizing that it's these very moments that make a journey memorable.

As our boat pulls away from Camp Leakey, floating farther into the heart of Tanjung Puting National Park, I stare off into the jungle pensively. For the past few years, I had clung to my travel blog like a life raft, desperate for the joy and adventure it promised. *The Pin the Map Project* had not only sparked my passion for travel, but it had lit up a path to a career I hoped to one day have. Had I already started to outgrow it? I hadn't expected to become disenchanted with travel blogging so soon.

Far off, I swear I can hear the snorts of Mr. Boar as our riverboat cuts through the murky brown waters and the stars begin to dance overhead. As I watch the other bloggers settle, turning in for another hot and uncomfortable night on those godforsaken mattresses, I think about my career, the paths that led me here, and where I'll go next, feeling as though a part of me is still out there, lost in the wilderness.

12

I Promise to Always Have Pub Mix

Paris, France

When I'm in Paris, I'd like to picture myself as a left bank sort of gal: an aspiring writer better suited to the narrow, book-piled aisles of Shakespeare & Company or the wobbly sidewalk tables of Les Deux Magots over the glistening designer shops that line the Champs-Élysées. Given the choice (and means), I'd prefer to stay in a hotel overlooking Ile de la Cité with the tolling bells of Notre-Dame as my alarm clock. For me, Paris is a city where I can really nerd out and walk in the footsteps of my literary idols like Simone de Beauvoir, Sidonie-Gabrielle Colette, and Gertrude Stein, throwing back cocktails in bars where Ernest Hemingway and F. Scott Fitzgerald once drank.

If I could go back to any time in history, unsurprisingly, it would be Paris in the twenties. Back then (or so I imagine), being a writer was more romantic than it is nowadays. Prose that would withstand generations was fueled by cheap bottles of Beaujolais nouveau in cozy bars tucked away in Pigalle. Novel ideas were born from impassioned conversations in darkened corner bistros in the Latin Quarter. Poets and painters met in the cobbled plaza of Place du Tertre, the beating heart of Montmarte's bohême. There was no procrastinating on TikTok, watching one-minute videos of someone cleaning their apartment or sharing their latest Amazon haul. There was no tapping away on silver MacBooks as Starbucks baristas yell out coffee orders. I once read that Hemingway would stare out at the Paris rooftops when he had writer's block, just waiting for the city to inspire his next sentence. When I have writer's block, I turn on Netflix and watch reruns of *The Home Edit*.

I remember the very first time I came to Paris years ago when I'd been living with Alex in Normandy. While our weekdays were largely spent with Alex in class and me working up the nerve to walk a block away from our apartment, the weekends were when we ventured beyond Rouen. The first time I saw the Eiffel Tower, I let out an audible squeal. I am not one to squeal or even scream, mind you. I have only really squealed once in my entire life, and that honor belongs to Paris. I had exited the Metro, turned around, and saw the Eiffel Tower standing tall at the end of a quiet and cobbled residential street. It didn't matter that I had seen the landmark countless times in photos and movies; nor did it matter that I'd had an Eiffel Tower painting hanging in my college dorm for four years. Nothing compared to seeing the real thing in person. The more I traveled, the more this rang true for other recognizable monuments I eventually crossed off my bucket list. The Trevi Fountain, the Lincoln Memorial, Christ the

Redeemer—nothing compared to standing in the presence of these iconic places. But even so, only Paris made me squeal.

I hadn't imagined returning to France after Alex and I ended our engagement. For the past few years, he and his family had been my sole connection to this country and culture. It was Alex who took me on a road trip through the Loire Valley, visiting a dizzying number of crumbly castles and old châteaus. It was Alex who had introduced me to macarons, looking on proudly as I ordered my first one in Frenglish. It was Alex's dad who gave me my first tour of Paris and Alex's mom who got me hooked on the joys of a crisp glass of Sancerre and the oh-so-delicious Camembert cheese.

The first time Alex's mom cut me a slice of Camembert, she handed it to me with a cocked eyebrow and a warm smile as she warned just how pungent this particular cheese could be. For those unfamiliar with it, Camembert is seriously funky, boasting notes of cabbage, mushroom, and dirt. Appetizing, I know. The sign that Camembert is good is that the smell is so potent that when you open the fridge, it should feel like you've thrown open a barn door. I could understand why Alex's mom had warned me, assuming my "delicate" American palate was more accustomed, to say, Kraft Singles. Little did she know that I'd been raised for this moment, had grown up standing in the kitchen alongside my dad, wordlessly passing hunks of stinky cheese between us.

The next morning, Alex's mom came downstairs to find me munching on a slice of Camembert and a baguette for breakfast. I not only liked the cheese, I *loved* it. I loved Camembert so much that there exists a wooden cheese box with my and Alex's faces printed on it from when we traveled to the actual village of Camembert, where the 200-year-old cheese originated.

Under Alex and his family's tutelage, I had transformed into a full-blown Francophile. But my decision to call off our wedding had not only broken our relationship, it had ripped away his family and my ties to a culture that I'd come to love dearly (not to mention the promise of regular visits to France). Alex had been my only reason for coming here. I couldn't imagine returning to France without him or arriving in Paris without the promise of his family waiting to pick us up at Charles de Gaulle Airport, and yet here I am, walking briskly along the Seine River, fidgeting with a small gold lock I'd purchased for less than twenty euros at a nearby souvenir shop.

I'm nervous. Too nervous. I look down at the lock; it's maybe two inches in length and flat with a silver hook. Up ahead, Pont des Arts—Paris's Love Lock Bridge—dazzles with locks of every size, shape, color, and style. Some are gigantic, dripping with stickers and glitter glue flashing at passersby, impossible to miss. Other locks are small and simple. But despite the rich spectrum of locks on display, all of them have one thing in common: each represents a couple somewhere in the world who once came to Paris and locked a love they deemed unbreakable.

Today, I'm one of them. Such an innocuous act shouldn't feel so important, and yet this does. Months after calling off my wedding, I've come back to this country to lock a new love.

★

I'm here in Paris with Jeff, a stand-up comedian and film-maker who I'd met on Tinder back in New York. I wasn't looking for my next great love, or even my next great date (too focused, instead, on my next great trip), but at the behest of close friends, I decided to release myself from the guilt and depression I'd settled into after calling off my wedding, and download the dating app, figuring I could just *see* what's out there. On my screen unfolded a parade of eligible bachelors and their cringey selfies: shirtless men and nerdy men, men posing with exotic animals (so many tigers), men posing with beautiful women, men lifting weights at the gym, men staring broodingly off at a sunset, men flashing stacks of money, and men who apparently live in a tent somewhere in the woods. And then there was Jeff.

Jeff's Tinder profile revealed a good-looking thirtysomething man wearing a black V-neck T-shirt covered by an open checkered blue short-sleeve button-down. He was pictured sitting casually on a brownstone step, looking off to the side with an expression of amusement, as if a stranger had interrupted him midsentence with an unexpected compliment. Jeff was the first and only person I reached out to on Tinder, intrigued enough by his profile to make the first move. Our conversations and banter flourished across our screens. His humor was one rooted in nostalgia, with the sort of niche references that will have you looking up quotes from obscure early 1990s films, while his mind worked like a gigantic filing cabinet or the archival department of *The New York Times*. He was quick to pull information from an article he'd read five years ago or an offbeat show he once watched at age seven, constantly slipping in historical tidbits and pop culture comparisons.

I hadn't intended to meet anyone on Tinder. I'd downloaded it with as much expectation as I have for one day winning the lottery, and then I swiped right on Jeff. By that point I could see I'd long since fallen out of love with Alex, and yet I was still wading through the debris of our canceled wedding. To date anyone felt like a slap in the face to Alex, our families, and our friends. So, when Jeff suggested we meet in person, I immediately recoiled. Was it too soon to begin dating? What would people in my life say? Then there was the question of whether Jeff was actually who he said he was. When

I began dating Alex four years prior, online dating had been associated with catfishing and horror stories analyzed by Dan Rather on episodes of *60 Minutes*. Four years later, finding love online has become as commonplace as the falafel trucks parked on every street corner in New York.

Jeff asked me to meet him during prime dating hours on a Friday at 8:00 p.m. in the East Village. So, naturally, I countered with the senior dinner discount hours of Monday at 5:00 p.m. outside the Best Buy in Union Square, giving me the advantage of broad daylight, heavy crowds, and a quick escape should I need it. In the end, I decided to meet with Jeff out of both curiosity and intrigue; I loved speaking to him online and was eager to see the man behind the screen. On the day of our first date, I looked messy—not Parisian chic messy, but *actually* messy—like I had somersaulted off the bed, onto the subway, and directly out onto the streets of Union Square, gathering crumbs as I rolled. I had opted against wearing any makeup, instead throwing on baggy jeans and a loose-fitting crimson shirt with a hole in one sleeve from where my thumbs had pushed through. I reluctantly trudged to the subway for this date, fully prepared to discover the man I'd been speaking with was, in fact, a seventy-year-old retiree who lived with roommates in the Bronx and collected discarded subway cards as a hobby.

Instead, Jeff stood looking exactly like—if not better than—his Tinder profile photo. When I first saw him, he was leaning casually against the outside wall of Best Buy, in an easygoing stance similar to the one in that brownstone picture I'd since memorized by heart. He looked like a cross between the actor Penn Badgley and a young Mark Ruffalo, with dark Italian features and short brown hair that was haphazardly gelled as though he had given up styling it midway through. His eyes were almond-shaped and brown, and he had a smile that could expand from a sexy grin to laugh-out-loud big. Jeff was so cute that I instantly began attempting damage control, smoothing out my wrinkled shirt and straightening my messy hair.

Despite my initial reluctance (and ghastly appearance), our first date was perfect. From wine at a speakeasy hidden behind a Chinese restaurant to a first kiss at a dive bar in the East Village (followed by much more kissing on brownstone steps), we immediately clicked. Jeff was easy to talk to and be around. He listened earnestly. There was nothing pretentious about him. Instead, he was the sort of person you immediately felt comfortable with, as though you could feel the tension in your shoulders dissipate in his presence. All I wanted was to keep peeling back the layers of his personality.

As a comedian and filmmaker, Jeff spent most of his twenties and early thirties pouring his creativity into short films, stand-up sets, and documentaries. He was an artist without any of the irony or self-indulgence, only a passion for creating and making others laugh. At heart, he was a storyteller and observer, constantly absorbing words, feelings, and scenes around him that would later be spun into comedic gold. I was relieved to discover in Jeff a kindred creative, someone who could not only understand my desire to become a travel journalist but fully support my dreams of writing. This had been such a sticking point in my relationship with Alex that I found it almost strange to see Jeff revel in my plans for the future.

As days melted into weeks, things with Jeff felt easy in a way they had never felt with Alex—or any man before him, for that matter. Jeff and I slipped into those early honeymoon days as though sliding into a warm bath. "No games" became our mantra—a promise to say what we meant and skip the tricks that often befall couples. In practice, it was simple. If something was bothering me, Jeff would ask, "What's wrong?" Rather than me responding "Nothing," followed by hours of silent brooding, Jeff would say, "No games," and encourage me to cut through the bullshit, reminding me there was nothing we couldn't work out so long as we were open with one another.

It was an approach to dating that felt refreshingly different from any relationship I'd had in the past, in which there had been all sorts of games: jealousy games and gas-lighting games, passive-aggressive games and ego games, games in which the threat of a breakup would be used as a bargaining chip, and games where ultimatums were tossed out like confetti. Here instead was a truly adult relationship, with a foundation rooted in transparency. It was as though all the drama I'd come to associate with romance was somehow being expunged. And because we started from a place of honesty, everything that followed felt honest too. With Jeff, I could be honest about my wants in my career and my wants in the bedroom and not feel awkward about it. For years, it was like I'd been trying to force the wrong key into a lock, willing it to open the door to a romance that could stand the test of time. Then there was Jeff, offering something frictionless. It just suddenly clicked.

What I remember most about falling in love with Jeff is the glow of the multicolored Christmas lights strung up around his Astoria apartment. They cast a gauzy yellow-red glow over our early nights together, so I remember them now as though it were all a dream. It was far from Christmas, but those lights added an unexpected pop of whimsy to what was otherwise a mismatched bachelor pad with faded furniture, a framed poster from the 1984 film *The Toxic Avenger*, and a statue of a human-shaped butler with a dog head named Reginald.

I never expected to fall in love with Jeff. After breaking things off with Alex, I had found myself in that rarest of all circumstances: completely untethered. Family members re-mained pissed about the canceled wedding and financial fall-out, and friends stayed disgruntled about how I'd failed to confide in them. So, I reasoned, there would never be a bet-ter time to leave the country for good.

A few weeks after calling off my wedding, I applied for graduate school in London, rationalizing that a student visa would allow me to move abroad while a master's degree in journalism could only bring me closer to becoming a real travel writer. I chose to overlook the $30,000 I had already racked up in student loan debt from my undergraduate years at Indi-ana University or how a master's program would require an additional $70,000 loan to pay for courses, student housing, textbooks, and meal plans. I ignored the average salary of a travel writer and how it would take me decades to pay off the over $100,000 of student loan debt I'd be accumulating. I ig-nored all of it because Manhattan had become an unbearable city, a skeleton of a place marked by disappointment and dam-aged relationships. I ignored it all because after years of chasing my dream career, my eyes trained on that glittering horizon, I'd started to feel as if I hadn't come any closer to reaching it.

Before Jeff and I met, I had accepted admission to the City University of London, and had been planning to visit England in hopes of both touring the school and scouting a flat to live in. By the time of my first date with Jeff, I had already made plans to start classes the following spring semester. Meanwhile, Jeff had grown weary of New York and sought a sublet in Los Angeles, eager to try his luck with stand-up comedy on the West Coast. Separately, we had planned everything for our respective cross-country and cross-Atlantic moves, but had never accounted for swiping right on one another.

A week or two into dating, I met Jeff at another dive bar

near Union Square. We had yet to have any serious conversation about our future as a couple, instead just living in the day-to-day bliss of an early romance. Over beers, I made the impromptu decision to invite him to travel to London with me. The minute I suggested it, I internally berated myself. A trip to Europe suddenly felt too serious for a fledgling *something* that had yet to be defined. Not only had we not discussed our plans to move in opposite directions, but I had yet to share our relationship with family and friends, all of whom would be wondering about this man I'd be traveling with.

The following day, I remembered those Christmas lights and how they threw a warm glow over us, wrapped in one another's arms. I thought of those early moments in which Jeff had lifted me up and how strange and right it felt to be with someone who celebrated my ambitions rather than tore them down. Would I let something as arbitrary as timing affect our relationship? Would I push aside these feelings out of a fear of judgment from friends and family? How long would I punish myself for canceling my wedding?

"I think you should come with me," I said to Jeff a few days later, doubling down on my invitation.

"What about going to Paris too?" he suggested, eyes sparkling. "We might as well do both cities."

Soon enough, we were sitting side by side on a Norwegian Airlines flight bound for Charles de Gaulle International Airport, with a plan to spend a few days in Paris before going to London via the high-speed train.

In many ways, traveling is like a litmus test for couples, a way to gauge how well two people can relate and interact when thrown into unfamiliar circumstances and surroundings. When things go awry on a trip—as they so often can—a couple's ability to navigate, say, lost luggage or a stolen wallet can speak volumes about the relationship as a whole. Traveling brings out the best and worst in us. We can shift from inspired in one moment to overwhelmed the next, riding that spectrum of human emotion in a way that gives those around us whiplash. But with Jeff, traveling only accentuated the feelings that had blossomed between us back in New York. We moved through London and Paris with the ease and inherent trust of a couple who had been married for years. Everything felt comfortable and supportive, passionate and wondrous.

After a day or so in Paris, the two of us were standing in front of the Eiffel Tower, surrounded by couples swooning in the shadow of Paris's iconic landmark. As I stood holding my Nikon camera, its lens focused on the view ahead, Jeff turned to me.

"Move in with me?" he asked, pulling my attention away from the aperture and focus dials I was fumbling with through my knit fingerless gloves. He stood smiling, wearing a black knit hat and leather jacket that made him look only more handsome.

"Are you sure?" I asked tentatively. The question both thrilled and terrified me.

"Yes, I'm sure," he said warmly, pulling me in closer. "I love you and I'm set on you. This just feels so right."

Timing is everything, and in our case, it felt as though I had met the perfect man at just about the worst time. I looked towards the Eiffel Tower and thought for a moment. Since Iguazú, I had been learning how to find my inner voice, listening to my intuition rather than burying it the way I'd been doing for years. I knew I had both fallen in love with Jeff and wanted to see where this relationship would take us. I knew I could keep chasing my dreams of travel writing without taking on $70,000 of debt and moving across the Atlantic. I knew I wanted to stay in New York and fight for the life I'd been working towards instead of running away from the mistakes I made. I had emerged from the jungles of Argentina triumphant, intent on stepping into the light and regaining control of my life, but guilt kept pushing me further into the shadows. Now here was Jeff, throwing open a side door that invited me to step into an entirely new chapter with him.

"Okay, let's do it," I said, a smile spreading across my face.

★

As we approach the bridge, I begin to scan the railings and grates for a sliver of space where we can place our lock. Pont des Arts is a stunner, a pedestrian-only walkway that connects the river's left and right bank, making it easy to saunter from the Institut de France to the Louvre Museum in a matter of minutes. The bridge is wide with wooden floors and metal frames that stretch over the Seine River. Ever since tourists began placing locks on the bridge around 2008, Pont des Arts has been nicknamed Paris's Love Lock Bridge for obvious reasons. While it's unclear when or why the tradition of love locks started, there is one theory that comes from Hungary, where legend has it a woman who had lost her love during the first World War would place locks on a nearby bridge where they'd frequently meet, symbolizing an unbreakable romance that not even death could shake. Her act of devotion inspired a tradition that spread across Europe and eventually made its way to Paris and this very bridge.

I love doing the thing you're "supposed" to do when visiting a new city. What others might find cliché—riding a gondola down a Venice canal, donning tilted berets in Paris, tossing pennies into the Trevi Fountain in Rome—I enjoy tremendously. I can just imagine myself broaching the idea of locking our love looking like a caricature of a Francophile, holding a glass of red wine, wearing a striped shirt, and reading Flaubert at a bistro on the left bank. But as much as I love a cliché, I never thought to lock my love with Alex. During all those weekends when we'd ridden a train from Rouen to Paris or all those holidays when we'd flown in from New York to visit his family, I never once suggested we commemorate our love by placing a lock on the Pont des Arts. The idea simply hadn't occurred to me.

Jeff and I kneel by the side of the bridge now. We've chosen a spot towards the edge of the river where the bridge meets the left bank. Pulling out the black Sharpie in my pocket, I carefully write our first names and last initials on the front of the lock alongside today's date. Beaming, I hand the lock over to Jeff, who delicately turns it over in his hand and writes both our first names down but this time with a shared last name, his name: Cerulli.

"I vow to always love you and never take you for granted," he says now, looking at me and holding the lock as though getting ready to propose with it.

"And I vow that if anything goes wrong or we lose track of ourselves or this relationship, that we'll return to Paris," I promise.

"And I vow," he adds, smiling, "to always have pub mix at home."

I chuckle at this one. When I had first visited Jeff's apartment in Queens, he had pulled out an industrial-sized tub of pub mix, consisting of pretzels sticks, bagel chips, and cheddar cheese twists. Throughout the early days of us dating, that pub mix had been a constant, an unending form of sustenance that fueled every lovemaking session or late-night movie marathon. It wasn't that pub mix was particularly delicious (although I enjoy a good bagel chip), but rather, I'd come to love how pub mix reminded me of the playfulness of my and Jeff's romance. I understand this vow as him saying he'll never forget the little details, those imperceptible joys so often taken for granted. With that Jeff closes the lock on the bridge, saving a key for each of us as souvenirs, and then gives the third one to Paris, tossing it into the inky waters of the Seine River below.

★

After we landed in New York a few days later, I moved in with Jeff and officially stepped through the door of this next relationship. Together, we abandoned our individual plans for Los Angeles and London—he gave up the sublet and I withdrew from graduate school. California and England would always be there, after all. Following an evening flight from London Gatwick to JFK Airport, we took a cab back to his apartment, where I left my suitcases piled by the door and wondered, briefly, if we were maybe moving too fast. I thought about the broken road behind me, littered with heartbreak, and questioned everything, while Jeff held my hand patiently, letting me walk at my own pace. But soon enough, that bachelor pad became our shared home, a reflection of our love and creativity. The framed *Toxic Avenger* poster was eventually replaced with framed photos from all the places we'd one day travel together: Thailand, Vietnam, Japan, Italy, Kenya, Iceland, Belize. But Reginald, that monocle-wearing dog statue, would always remain.

A year later, we learned that Paris officials had cut off those love locks, insisting the pounds of metal weighing down Pont des Arts were beginning to threaten the bridge's integrity, which, of course, they were. A few of the locks were to be saved and temporarily displayed at the Palais-Royal, but most would be thrown away, including ours. In the end, it had never been about the lock or even the tiny silver key that still lay rusting at the bottom of the Seine. Rather, it had always been about those vows, about two people promising to do everything they can to stay together—from never taking the other for granted to always having a jar of pub mix on hand.

It was about the moment, about us hoping that a simple act would guarantee a lifetime together, and how on one chilly day in November, away from everyone and everything we had left back in New York, Jeff and I gave love another chance.

13

The Perfect Meal

Hanoi, Vietnam

Welcome to my place of dreams.

I had promised myself I would visit Vietnam before my upcoming thirtieth birthday, and now—a few months before I'm meant to cross the threshold into my thirties, I have arrived in Hanoi with Jeff. We've been dating for nearly three years now. In some ways, our small pre-war apartment in Astoria is a lot like Hanoi's Old Quarter—tight, ancient, but absolutely beautiful in its subtlety. To walk into our home is to know exactly who we are and what we love. Jeff and I are reflected in every corner of that Astoria apartment, from my tattered travel guides with their dog-eared pages to his off-beat DVDs and framed movie posters of documentaries he filmed. Ours is the sort of relationship I always dreamed of finding. Three years in, I can't imagine my life without Jeff.

Despite the many obstacles strewn across our path in those early days—the reluctance of my family and friends to accept our new relationship—he has stood beside me like a lighthouse standing tall against a storm.

Jeff and I are staying in a hotel in the French Quarter on Hang Bong Street—or is it Hang Gai? While I may not have the geography precisely nailed down, I can confidently say that our hotel is somewhere west of Hoàn Kiếm Lake in the Old Quarter. Hanoi's Old Quarter is, as the name suggests, old. This part of the capital reflects Hanoi's storied past, with ancient architecture and thousand-year-old streets dating back to the fifteenth century.

Hanoi's Old Quarter differs pretty dramatically from the French Quarter, which (naturally) looks and feels more like Paris. From the late 1800s to the 1950s, Hanoi was under French rule, which is reflected in the upscale French colonial buildings, broader avenues, and a city plan similar to what Baron Haussman created when transforming medieval Paris into the city we know today. The Old Quarter was left largely untouched by the French and is a busy, crowded, and crumbling part of town that is beautiful in its kinetic energy.

As you walk through the Old Quarter, rows of cramped buildings seem to encroach on the sidewalks, their bricks drawn together like the shoulders of two friends leaning forward and sharing secrets. Between the buildings are thick black cable wires strung with delicate paper lanterns swaying in the breeze, their colors a spectrum of ruby reds, golds, and dusty pinks. Along the Old Quarter are shops whose faded awnings promise everything from a steaming bowl of bun cha with its tempting smell of Vietnamese pork meatballs, to offbeat merchandise like vintage movie posters of long-forgotten films. Outside these storefronts, lining the sidewalks, is arguably where the real magic of Hanoi is found.

Scattered in front of the open, haphazard kitchens and restaurants are low red-and-blue plastic stools alongside vats of
bubbly phở, the steam from the iconic soup swirling upwards
in curly white wisps. The narrow streets are home to vendors,
shops, and motorbike parking; one wrong step and you'll fall
like a landslide, gathering plastic furniture and noodles as
you go. Even crossing the street in Hanoi requires some serious strategy, and they're not exactly conducive to the eyes-
glued-to-their-phone kind of tourists.

In Vietnam's capital city, there is little by way of traffic
lights; instead, the streets play out in a brilliant bustle of color
and sound and undulating chaos. There are very few desig-
nated crosswalks to promise safe passage for pedestrians across
the boulevards. Instead, to cross a street in Hanoi, you must
first step off the curb and ease into traffic slowly, like sliding
into icy water for the first time.

Just days before, on my and Jeff's first time crossing a busy
intersection in Hanoi, we sat staring at the oncoming traffic in
bewilderment. "Okay, on the count of three," I said as Jeff and
I teetered on the curb, toeing the street. "One...two...three..."

"Wait! Not yet!" urged Jeff, pulling me back on the curb
as a flurry of motorbikes came rocketing in our direction.
"This is crazy. Why is there no stop light?!"

"Okay, I think we can go now," I said as I tried to formu-
late a route. I was starting to feel like we'd live on this street
corner if we didn't get moving. "I'm just going to do it."

After a few long minutes, I stepped off the curb again, following a few other pedestrians, holding my breath until I
made it safely to the other side. When you cross the street in
Hanoi, you must focus your eyes on the opposite curb and
move steadily, ignoring the eternal flow of cars and motorbikes, and will one foot to step in front of the other. As you
walk, every nerve tells you to hesitate, but you don't stop;

you can't stop. To stop would surely cause an accident. Then, something magical happens. That drum of Hanoian life—a rapid beat of dusty motorbikes, compact cars, and cyclos with double panniers stocked high with produce—simply swerves to make room for you. They don't falter, and neither do you. Instead, you cross the street in Hanoi as though you were surrounded by a force field, and every single bike, car, cart, and motorcycle moves around you without breaking pace.

It is almost poetic how crossing a street in Hanoi requires a manual override of your most innate logic and fear. Being the romantic that I am, I can't help but compare it to the act of falling in love: standing on the edge of something, looking over your shoulder nervously, before you eventually step off the curb and move ahead anyway, trusting—despite it all— that your heart won't get crushed by an oncoming truck.

After I made it to the other side, I turned to look for Jeff, only to see he was still standing on the opposite curb, eyeing the traffic nervously.

"Just cross!" I yelled across the street, the cacophony of cars and motorbikes immediately drowning out my laughter.

Far behind Jeff sat a group of elderly Vietnamese men at an outdoor café, slowly sipping their steaming mugs of coffee, eyes twinkling in amusement as Jeff toed the street. They'd been watching us for the past ten minutes; two American tourists looking like kids on a playground waiting for the perfect time to jump in on a game of double Dutch. After a few moments, I watched as one of the Vietnamese grandpas pushed himself off the chair, stood up from the table, and walked over to Jeff. Without a word, he gingerly took Jeff's hand in his own, gestured towards the street ahead, and guided him across as his friends and I howled in laughter, Jeff looking both grateful and sheepish.

★

I fall in love with Hanoi easily. Too easily, almost. This is partly because I loved Vietnam before I arrived and partly be-

CALL YOU WHEN I LAND · 177

cause it's impossible *not* to fall in love with this country. There's an old American military slang known as "gone bamboo," said to have originated during the Vietnam War (or the American War, as it's called here) and used to describe US soldiers who finished serving and decided to stay in Southeast Asia. Over time, "gone bamboo" was adopted by the travel community and used to describe globe-trotters who've become so enamored by a destination that they'd drop everything—their jobs, responsibilities, belongings, relationships—to stay put. Throughout my twenties, I had dreamed of "going bamboo" on many trips, whether it was falling in love with Cartagena, sitting on a beach in Panama, or running away to Buenos Aires, and Vietnam is no exception.

I first encountered the phrase "gone bamboo" through the late, great Anthony Bourdain, that renegade writer, storyteller, and traveler. Not only did Bourdain author a crime novel titled *Gone Bamboo*, but the man was widely known by his reverence for a bowl of Phở piled high with herbs, and, of course, his love of Vietnam—a country credited with sparking his passion for travel. I consider myself a Bourdain fan—and not just because there exists a news clip of me teary-eyed, standing in front of the Les Halles memorial in New York following his death, in which I'm literally labeled "Bourdain Fan." Bourdain's ability to capture the essence of a place and transport a reader to some far-flung market in Marrakech was outmatched only by his knack for pairing emotional gravitas with travel writing. The man had talent, damn it, and I'll forever be sad that we missed out on all the tremendous reflective novels he would have undoubtedly penned in his golden years.

Bourdain's writing had me falling in love with Vietnam long before I landed at Noi Bai International Airport. Through his musings, I could practically feel my butt growing numb from sitting on a too-small plastic stool, knees up around my ears as I ate a dish of noodles and pork-infused broth. In many ways, Bourdain's words have inspired my own, setting the bar in my mind for what travel writing can accomplish. I was never drawn to the sort of travel writing you find in a *Lonely Planet* guidebook. Rather, my idols are the ones who can pair the magic of a destination with the emotions of being there, writers who can not only transport you to another city but can have you drooling over a soup being served on the other side of the planet. Writers like Bourdain.

Here in Hanoi, street food is a treasure trove. Even the coffee—Jesus, the coffee—is enough to haunt you, to ruin every subsequent cup of coffee you will have from now until the day you die. The egg coffee (cà phê trứng) is a sweet, sugary, and syrupy concoction topped with a homemade egg cream combining two raw egg yolks, vanilla, and condensed milk whipped into a thick, fluffy cloud. Before you wrinkle your nose at the thought of eggs in your coffee, know that cà phê trứng tastes like the finest Italian tiramisu and has the consistency of melted marshmallows in hot chocolate. The coffee is enough to make you want to drop-kick any Starbucks cappuccino.

It's nighttime in Hanoi, and Jeff and I are a few blocks from the Phoenix Hotel, hoping we'll stumble across a restaurant or café where we can pick up a quick dinner. We walk a few blocks until we spot a slew of low-lying plastic tables where a handful of Vietnamese men sit silently, their chopsticks poking at their red-and-white bowls of noodles.

Bingo, I think to myself.

I'm briefly transported to another trip altogether, where I was solo traveling in Mexico City and on the prowl for authentic tacos. In a sea of tourist-facing restaurants, I was hungry for a real deal taco, the kind that doesn't come with a picture menu (Bourdain travel tip #1: always avoid picture menus, a sure sign of a tourist spot). After walking around aimlessly, pacing the

surrounding streets of Mexico City's Zócalo Square, I spotted it: my white whale. There, tucked between the boutique
hotels and Mexican pharmacies, stood a blink-and-you'll-
miss-it taqueria with nothing more than a take-out window.
I watched as a group of construction workers nearby—their
dust-covered hard hats perched atop their heads—bit happily
into soft shell tacos overflowing with shredded chicken and
verdant cilantro, served alongside two plump lime slices. Following suit, I strolled right up to the taco window, making
my way through the surly men in stained overalls, and asked
for what they were having (Bourdain travel tips #2 and #3:
always go where the locals go and eat what the locals eat).

Now, after spotting the plastic furniture and Vietnamese
men, I lead Jeff to one of the empty plastic tables.

"Maybe we should go," suggests Jeff quietly.

I look up to see our fellow sidewalk diners staring bla-
tantly at us, their inquiring eyes thinly veiling their curiosity and—in the case of a few—annoyance. It feels as though
we've walked in on a private event or, worse, a conversation
in which we were the topic of discussion.

"It'll be fine," I assure Jeff, reaching for his hand across
the shaky blue table. Despite the stares, I'm unfazed. I know
that it's these very places, the ones that are seemingly invisible to tourists and left out of guidebooks, that offer the most
memorable meals.

In New York, Jeff cuts through the city with the confidence of a great white shark swimming through the ocean.
As a born and bred New Yorker, the city and its every nook
and cranny is his domain, whereas I can get overwhelmed by
the crowds and unrelenting soundtrack of sirens and honking
cabs. As an aspiring writer, my days are typically quiet, marked
by the whirring of my espresso machine as I pen another blog
post or dole out another freelance article. Anywhere else on

earth, my desire to explore a new place will override my innate coziness, pushing me to venture across foreign cities in pursuit of busy marketplaces or tucked-away shops, but in New York, I'm surprisingly a homebody. Jeff pulls me out of that comfort zone, taking me to underground comedy shows in Midtown West, dimly lit music venues on the Lower East Side, and film screenings in Brooklyn.

With Jeff, New York continues to surprise me even after nearly ten years. In return, I lead Jeff beyond his comfort zone, past his fear of flying, and out into the world. I've watched with unbridled joy as his eyes light up when he feeds elephants watermelon at a rescue in northern Thailand. He'll always find something to love about a country he'd never imagined visiting: the spectacle of life unfolding on Avenida Atlântica at Copacabana Beach in Rio de Janeiro or the feel of cycling through the chilly streets of Amsterdam in early spring. Traveling may be more my thing, but there is no one else on this planet I'd rather see the world with than Jeff.

Like most relationships, we have our quirks and certainly our flaws. Jeff can be stubborn while I can be pushy, two traits that sometimes clash in the most unlikely of places, like a bánh mì shop in Hanoi. One afternoon, I was pulling us in the direction of a lunch spot I had read about, eager to have my first taste of a true bánh mì sandwich. A bánh mì has it all—the crunch of a French baguette, the fresh herbs found on every table and bowl of soup, the pickled vegetables and spicy chilis. The unique clash of sour-spicy-sweet flavors that *just work*. I was desperate for my first bánh mì and adamant Jeff try it too. Jeff, on the other hand, was craving something different.

The more I pushed him to eat this sandwich, the more he dug his heels in, determined to eat something else entirely, leading him to discover one of the best meals of our trip: a turmeric-dusted fish with fresh dill and rice noodles known as Chả Cá Lã Vọng, found—of all places—at a hole-in-the-wall joint blasting Britney Spears's '90s hits from a dusty boom box sitting in the corner. When my pushing can rub up against his stubbornness, we challenge each other. He reminds me to go with the flow and not be beholden to some self-enforced ideal of how things should be. In turn, I give him a gentle nudge when it comes to trying new things he may not have otherwise done. Together, we can be like a clash of flavors on a bánh mì sandwich—it just works.

*

The sidewalk restaurant we're at doesn't have a menu or other food options; instead, we are given whatever the cook is making that day. Within a few minutes of us sitting down, a kind-faced, sweat-slicked elderly woman delivers two bowls brimming with thin vermicelli noodles, fresh mint, and shredded chicken breast floating like a raft atop a light and oily broth.

In one of his early books, Bourdain scours the globe for the perfect meal. From Michelin Star restaurants in Napa Valley to oyster beds in a sleepy French village, his search ultimately ends in the Caribbean. Sitting at a table across from his then-wife, Nancy, their toes pushed deep into the sugary sand, he describes eating tender but slightly crispy barbecue ribs and washing them down with ice-cold Caribs and Red Stripes. As it turns out, the perfect meal was never about the food, nor was it found on the tasting menus of Eric Ripert's Le Bernardin in New York City or at Thomas Keller's French Laundry in California (although I'm sure those meals are fabulous). Instead, he found truth in the old adage: the perfect meal is about the moment, where you are and who you're with.

Over the years, I had watched and read about this very kind of Vietnam sidewalk experience countless times, a simple yet spectacular meal so transcendent it is practically religious. But in reality, this moment is so much better—sure, the soup is fresh and complex, piled high with herbs that taste as though they were picked this morning, but the ambiance of the meal is where the real magic is. I am deliriously happy, and not just because the soup is a revelation, an explosion of flavors from the broth to the crunch of the crisp herbs to the sweetness of the hoisin sauce dancing across the soup's glistening surface.

With days of exploring Hanoi ahead of us and a flight to Tokyo after that, I'm taking time between slurps to appreciate this very moment. A country I've dreamed of traveling to, a relationship I dreamed of one day finding, a life of travel I dreamed of experiencing. Suddenly, I'm overwhelmed by gratitude for everything—this moment, this man, this country, this life. Sitting on this dark Hanoi street across from Jeff, hunched over plastic bowls, the rev of motorbikes and the *put-put-put* of passing cars behind us—this feels like the perfect meal to me.

14

Is This Japamala Working?

"You travel alone, miss?" the elderly man asks, smiling kindly though his rearview mirror. I don't know much about my driver, Ketut, but from his name I can glean he is the fourth child in his family.

In Bali, there are a lot of Ketuts. There are also a lot of Wayans, Mades, and Nyomans. Chances are that any local you meet—man or woman—will have a variation of one of these four names, because every Balinese child is traditionally named in accordance with their birth order. The first born is named Wayan, the second is named Made (pronounced "Ma-day"), the third is named Nyoman, and the fourth born is named Ketut. If a family has more than four kids, the cycle of these four names repeats itself with slight variations, such as Wayan Balik (which basically translates to "another Wayan").

If I'd been named according to Balinese tradition, my name, for example, would be Wayan.

Ketut is maybe sixty-five years old with wiry gray hair that struggles to cover his balding head. His skin—tanned to the point of looking like leather—is deeply darkened by the sun in the way only someone who lives on an island can be. Ketut oozes kindness, and even the etched lines around his eyes hint at a lifetime spent smiling. There is nothing that feels particularly threatening or off-putting about Ketut, whom I hired for the day to drive me the one and a half hours from Ubud to the Pura Ulun Danu Bratan Temple, and yet I'm suddenly unnerved by his question.

The short answer is yes, I *am* alone, Ketut. I am not only alone in Bali, but I'm also alone in the back seat of your car, rocketing in a direction I can only hope is the temple I read about in my *Lonely Planet* guidebook this morning. I am also alone without cell service or internet at the moment, since my once trusty Wi-Fi hotspot has decided to stop working entirely. Should anything go awry between now and when we reach the temple, I am not only completely disconnected, but I haven't let any loved ones back home know I was leaving Ubud for the day.

It's at this moment I consider how often we dole out trust when traveling—especially when solo traveling. We trust pilots to ferry us across oceans and continents in one piece; we trust hotels to have locks that work and sheets that are free of bed bugs; we trust restaurants to serve us Ayum Bumbu Bali chicken and hold the side of food poisoning; and now I am trusting Ketut (whom I've known all of fifteen minutes) to bring me to the Pura Ulun Danu Bratan Temple without detour.

"Uh, yeah, I'm traveling alone," I reply, wondering if I should have made up a lie.

"You no have husband?" Ketut asks, his eyebrows rising in surprise.

This is a question most women get when venturing into the world solo. Coming from a city like New York, it feels especially archaic. Ask a New York woman why she's out without a husband, and you'll be greeted with a scathing look and loud guffaw that says, *Who the fuck are you to ask me that?* New York women are fearless, if not a little scary. My and Ketut's cultures are very different. Beyond the tourists sipping beachfront mojitos, you'll find that Bali—especially in smaller villages—can be both conservative and patriarchal. I know that Ketut means no harm by his question; rather, he is genuinely curious as to why I'm currently seated alone in the back seat of his silver sedan without a ring on my finger or a man holding my hand.

"Not yet," I answer, thinking of Jeff back home in Queens. I imagine he is right now snuggling on our sunken brown couch with our tabby cat, Peeps. "Maybe soon." I smile to myself. "My boyfriend is back in New York."

"Ahhhhhh," says Ketut, drawing out the sound a little too long. It's a loaded "ahh," as if my answer were a coded message he is trying to decipher. "I have daughter your age, maybe."

Something about this makes me feel instantly better about being alone in his back seat, driving down empty roads through lush rice paddies.

"What's her name?" I smile, curious now.

"Ketut!" He laughs.

★

Chances are you may know Bali as both a quintessential honeymoon destination and one of the places featured in the best-selling memoir and subsequent film, *Eat Pray Love*, in which Elizabeth Gilbert (played by Julia Roberts) grapples with her divorce amid the rice paddies. I first read *Eat Pray*

Love the summer I met Alex. I'd sit on those steps of Columbia University and lose myself to Gilbert's travels, reveling in how she'd move through the world while simultaneously moving through the jungle of her emotions. I read *Eat Pray Love* again while solo traveling in Argentina, finding solace in Gilbert's words as I readied myself to confront myself and make a decision about my impending wedding day. I remember sleeping with the book in that hostel in Buenos Aires, having the spine pressed against my own as though the words could spoon and comfort me. Today, my copy of *Eat Pray Love* is so worn that the cover has quite literally fallen off.

Nowadays, the *Eat Pray Love* effect is in full swing. You see the "Eat" everywhere in Bali, in American tourists donning billowy sundresses while walking thoughtfully through the morning markets, searching for...*something* transcendent between the crates of mangosteens and durians. You see the "Love" in the couples emerging from tucked-away villas with satisfied smiles plastered across their faces. You find the "Pray" in the countless expat-run yoga studios selling Japamala necklaces that promise to encourage everything from kinder thoughts to higher productivity.

A Japamala is a necklace of 108 prayer beads that are used in both meditation and prayer. Similar to the rosaries we see in Catholicism, the Japamalas around Bali can be used for reciting mantras or counting during a spiritual practice. Walking around Ubud, I've seen a lot of travelers wearing Japamalas— and I'm somewhat embarrassed to say I've become one of them. A few days ago, I visited an Australian-owned yoga studio outside Ubud, in which evening yoga classes take place in full view of the surrounding rice paddies. I'd hardly consider myself a yogi. Back in New York, I'm about as active as a pet rock, but like I said: I love to do the thing you're "supposed" to do in a destination. As a traveler in Ubud, the word on the street is "wellness:" wellness of the soul (spiritual practice), wellness of the mind (meditation), and wellness of the body (acai bowls and yoga).

After a slow-moving yoga class in which we spent the first ten minutes sitting in a circle and just…breathing, I spotted a display of Japamalas, their delicate beads ranging in color from sunny yellow to fiery orange to tranquil blue.

"They each represent something different," said my yoga instructor, catching my gaze, a Japamala swinging from her own neck.

"What does that one represent?" I asked, pointing towards a necklace of light blue beads strung along a silky turquoise string that ended in a tassel of more blue strands.

"That's for better communication," she replied. "It helps you get the words out."

Now, I'm a sucker for advertising. A shampoo that promises to give me Farrah Fawcett waves? Sold. A not-so-easy-to-install bidet with chrome buttons? Done. A vibrating patch that swears to undo decades of bad posture? Count me in. As soon as my yoga instructor said "helps you get the words out," I practically threw myself at the display case. For a while now, I felt my writing growing stale as I grappled with outgrowing my travel blog. I was desperate for any inspiration to get my words flowing again, and was thus especially open to my yoga teacher's eager invitation to try out the beads.

"I'll take it," I said. God knows, I could use all the help on that front.

★

Pura Ulun Danu Bratan is a gorgeous temple, standing on the edge of Lake Bratan, flanked by the nearby mountains of Bedugul. The twelve-story pagoda rises above the crystalline lake like a series of opened umbrellas stacked one on top of the other. This multi-tiered roof is known as a Meru tower and is unique to Balinese temples. Pura Ulun Danu Bratan is iconic, by which I mean it is the image most closely associated with Bali; it's even on the cover of my guidebook. The whole scene is stunning, like a Bob Ross painting—the mist coming off the nearby hills, settling over the still waters of Bratan like little wisps of cotton, the reflection of the pagoda perfectly mirrored in the lake, the verdant greenery of the manicured gardens against the cool blues and deep purples of the mountain silhouettes.

After leaving Ketut in the parking lot, I walked towards the lake and plopped down on a stone bench facing the temple, where I'm now sitting, just feet from the water. I love the colors. I love the temple. I love the stillness of Lake Bratan and how it'd be the perfect place to skip stones. I notice tourists are beginning to fill the walkways and pour onto the temple grounds. I beat them by thirty minutes at most. I say a silent thank-you to Ketut and his driving skills.

Because my Wi-Fi hotspot has failed me, I have no idea about the deeper history or story behind Pura Ulun Danu Bratan. I think about going back to the car to ask Ketut, but am reluctant to give up my bench to the flock of Australian teenagers who seem all too eager to take my seat.

Instead, I pull out my dog-eared guidebook and flip to the page about the Pura Ulun Danu Bratan, where I learn it's a Hindu-Buddhist temple dedicated to the Balinese-Hindu Goddess of the water, Dewi Danu. The temple was originally built in 1633 and has since become emblematic of Bali, even appearing on the currency.

I wonder about this Goddess Dewi Danu and what the legend is there. Who was she? Why is she the goddess of the lake? What did she do to earn such a stellar temple? I've always loved legends—even as a kid, my favorite pastime was to pore over Greek mythology books. When I travel, I love to learn the stories that surround important landmarks and places, finding that the details are always fantastical, passed down from generation to generation like a millennia-long game of telephone.

Reaching for my notebook and pen, I begin to imagine the possible origin stories of Dewi Danu. I could picture the Goddess as once being a woman ahead of her time, pushing against tradition and balking at the idea of being married off to a local farmer. I envision her trying to sail away from her fate, only to end up capsizing and drowning in this very lake. Perhaps the gods admired her tenacity and decided to turn her into something immortal, like this iconic temple. Maybe Dewi Danu herself is a sort of patron saint of wayward travelers.

"Hey Ketut, what is the story behind Dewi Danu?" I ask once back in the car.

"She's a goddess of the water," he answers cheerily. "For the rivers and lakes too."

I wait for Ketut to continue, but he doesn't elaborate. Maybe that's all there is to it. Like Athena in Greek mythology, maybe Dewi Danu was born into her goddess status the way some kids are born to celebrity parents.

"Terima kasih, Ketut," I say, using the only Indonesian phrase I've memorized. *Thank you.*

I pull out my little notebook, studying its red-and-turquoise fabric cover, a recent purchase from a shop in downtown Ubud. It feels good to have written *something* down, even if it's a factually inaccurate history of Bali's famous temple. Fingering the necklace hanging around my neck, I wonder if this Japamala—and its purported powers—is working.

*

In recent months, my travel writing had started to resemble one of those cracked desert floors following a year-long drought. I was parched for words and desperate for inspiration that apparently only a $60 Japamala necklace (as in $60 American dollars, not Indonesian rupiah) could bring. Before

Borneo, I had quit my job in advertising, deciding I'd throw myself fully into my dreams of becoming a bona fide travel writer. At the time, this felt like a sound decision. I mean, how could I ever be a travel writer if I wasn't traveling? I argued that my job at Inventif Media not only held me down, but kept me from ever pursuing the career I wanted. It was time to cut my losses and bet on myself—just as I had done when calling off the wedding—and so, I handed in my two-week notice. With no available travel writing jobs to be had, I threw myself into building *The Pin the Map Project*, hoping that I could one day parlay it into a full-time gig and use the blog to showcase my work.

By this point in time, *The Pin the Map Project* had grown enough that I could travel to places like Borneo on the wings of my writing. But there was still the (rather large) obstacle of actually monetizing my words. While working in advertising, this hadn't been an issue—I had a regular biweekly paycheck deposited into my Chase bank account, leaving me free to enjoy the perks of travel blogging and to chase that next story. Except, as it turns out, I couldn't *actually* enjoy the perks because so long as I accepted that regular paycheck, I was beholden to ten vacation days a year. Suddenly, my frustration with my job blossomed into full-blown resentment. Blogger trips rolled in with invitations to Asia and Africa, South America and Europe—but I wasn't free to accept any of them. How does the saying go? Water, water everywhere but not a drop to drink? Well, it was like that, and I was thirsty. So, I quit.

For a month or so, my decision to quit advertising felt incredibly freeing, until I realized that the only thing more limiting than ten vacation days a year was having no money, ever. I spent every waking minute trying to monetize *The Pin the Map Project* while simultaneously pitching freelance story assignments and applying for on-staff jobs at travel publications. Emails for potential brand partnerships went unanswered or were met with the same boilerplate responses of "Sorry, we have no budget" or "How about a sponsored post in exchange for free swag?" Freelance pitches went largely unanswered too, or at best garnered a succinct reply weeks later with the one-liner "Not a fit, thanks." Applying for jobs felt like tossing my resumé out the window, with no publication interested in hiring a writer with a dusty journalism degree and only a few blog posts and bylines to her name.

To make matters more frustrating, nearly every travel blogger I followed seemed to be both successful *and* living full-time off their content creation. Whether they had second jobs, a robust savings account, or a trust fund, I couldn't say, only that they seemed to travel in Dubai one week and the Maldives the next. What was I doing wrong? I tried to follow by example, spending what little money I had on redesigning *The Pin the Map Project*, reasoning the fees were an investment in my future. I tried to apply some of my advertising experience to my blog, building glossy media kits that spoke to the reach and audience of my website. But while I could leverage *The Pin the Map Project* to fly around the world, try as I might, I couldn't get it to pay a penny of my rent. This proved a problem: my dream of becoming a travel writer was rooted in the belief that I could be paid to combine those two passions. If I couldn't sustain *The Pin the Map Project*, hack it as a freelance writer, or find a job at a travel publication, then I'd have to go back to working in advertising, but if I went back, then I'd have to give up the freedom to travel (and in turn, my ability to find stories to write about).

The more I pushed my writing to pay the bills, the more I felt the words fizzle and fade. This is the thing about trying to turn your passion into a career: if you're not careful, the more you demand of it, the less you enjoy it. All of this was going through my mind as I wandered into a café on the outskirts of Ubud on my last afternoon in Indonesia.

The breeze gently blew across the rice paddies and billowed through the open-air café, puffing out the tented ceiling like a balloon. I watched as the flowers from the canang sari lifted into the air, a few petals carried off in the wind. Ubud is considered the spiritual heart and cultural center of Bali. It's a town surrounded by rice paddies and steep ravines, and dotted with ornate Hindu temples and shrines decorated with delicate Balinese offerings known as canang sari. These colorful handmade offerings consist of a woven leaf basket in which flower petals, fruit, incense, and sometimes coins are placed as gifts to the Hindu gods.

These blessings have become one of the things I love most about Bali—you see them everywhere: in front of shops and outside restaurants, on temple steps and on sidewalks outside homes. At the guest house where I've been staying, every morning I come downstairs to find the elderly woman who lives there sitting at her kitchen table and assembling leaf baskets—one after the other—in preparation for putting out the day's canang sari.

My favorite part of the Ubud café—aside from the calming view and fresh pots of ginger tea I've taken to drinking—are the two gray-striped tabby cats who've become my companions. As I sat cross-legged on the intricately woven floor pillows, those two kittens snuggled up against my elephant-print pants, their delicate and lean bodies curling into snail shells against me. I felt defeated and deflated. I had reached the end of the page—literally and figuratively. I could no longer afford to keep travel blogging or freelance writing while ignoring the mounting late notices I was getting from student loan lenders, T-Mobile, and Oscar Health Insurance. On top of that, I knew I wasn't being fair to Jeff. He'd been extremely supportive of my decision to quit advertising.

"I'm proud of you," he said. "You should do what makes you happy."

But the more my bank account dwindled, the more the scales tipped towards him. If I kept at it, Jeff would be paying my half of rent by the end of the month.

To add to the mix, I had officially grown tired of my blog. Maybe I was sick of constantly trying to make it a success, pushing it up a hill like Sisyphus pushing that boulder. Perhaps I'd grown weary of the very act of blogging. Writing for *The Pin the Map Project* had begun to feel like I was now mumbling to myself about the feelings and revelations I had long ago grown tired of rehashing. I wanted to turn the spotlight outward and write about other people's stories instead of my own. As those two little cats pushed their tiny paws against my shin, their soft purrs vibrating through my pants, I pulled out my laptop and searched my email.

Before coming to Indonesia, I had applied for a job that felt perfect: a travel editor role for a London-based publication called *The Global Journey*, set to open their first New York office in the coming weeks. The position felt like the center of a Venn diagram, a perfect compromise between working full-time and still advancing my career aspirations. It had been weeks since I applied for the position, and there was still no response. I couldn't say I was surprised. My job history felt sporadic and inconsistent, a clear representation of a twentysomething woman stumbling her way through the workforce. From a brief stint in marketing to an even briefer time in public relations, I had tried on jobs as if shopping for dresses, tossing each ill-fitting gown over my shoulder. Nothing worked except for travel writing—everything else just felt scratchy against my skin.

Standing up to leave the café, I walked away with one glaring truth: it was time to grow up. My dreams of becoming a travel writer were one thing, but collapsing beneath the palpable weight of defaulted student loan payments and debt collectors was quite another. Maybe I'd go back to serving tables, writing on the side and traveling when time allowed. Or perhaps I'd (reluctantly) trot back to advertising, letting a paycheck help finance my travel blog and grow my writing experience.

Whatever I decide, I promised, *I won't lose track of myself again.* I'd pour my passion into travel writing, regardless of what job was paying the bills, and I'd revel in simply being happy with Jeff.

And then, a day later, 39,000 feet over the Pacific Ocean while en route back to New York, I finally got an email from *The Global Journey* asking me to come in for an interview.

A week later, I had the job.

15

The Big Bad Wolf

Bogotá, Colombia

I've never been to this part of Bogotá before. I'm somewhere on the outskirts of the city, where the neighborhood streets are dirty and dusty, covered with a layer of beige soot that kicks up each time the wind blows. A far cry from the art-splashed walls of La Candelaria, the buildings here are drab and painted in muted hues of grays and browns. The sidewalks are empty, the doorways are darkened, and the windows are covered by metal bars—all of it giving the sense we've landed in some postapocalyptic neighborhood that has since been abandoned.

I'm sitting in a black SUV with two men: my driver and fixer. Fixers are vital to reporters; they're on-the-ground contacts who help foreign journalists arrange interviews, gain access, and get the information needed to write a story. My fixer, José, is a young and eager journalism student I was referred to back in New York when researching fixers. My driver is Alejandro, my grandma's go-to Uber driver.

For the past week, I'd been staying with my grandma, Clarita, who owns apartments in both Miami and downtown Bogotá. Clarita is a wild and, at times, outlandish woman living out her golden years with the same energy as a twenty-one-year-old on spring break. To some in my family, Clarita is a controversial figure: a person seen as frivolous and gaudy. But I admire my grandma's knack for putting up a fight against time. Picture a grandmother, and chances are you'll probably imagine an elderly cheerful woman wearing orthopedic slippers and an oversized fleece sweater with a well-placed brooch, much like my paternal grandma, Amparito. Clarita goes against that stereotype.

Clarita is lean and tanned, usually wearing black leggings and an off-the-shoulder blouse styled with one of those chunky belts cowboys sometimes wear. Her hair, dyed a honey-eyed brown, is kept straight and in a short bob. On her wrist are enough gold bangles to rival an Egyptian goddess, while her nails are usually painted some sort of dark red, bordering on black. Her makeup is always the same: black-lined eyes and drawn-on brows with coral lipstick that pops against her tanned face.

She'd kill me for writing this, but Clarita is old, although only in a numerical sense. Her energy is young and sprightly, throwing parties and drinking champagne, dancing in heels, and dating silver foxes that she adds to her stable of rotating "boyfriends." She puts up a fight against time using all means necessary: workouts, healthy eating, and, of course, a little plastic surgery. But of all the ways Clarita—who asked me at a young age *not* to call her Grandma so that she wouldn't seem old—fights against time, it is her spirit that is the biggest tool in her arsenal. Clarita is sparkly and spunky, constantly laughing her way through life.

★

"Honey, Alejandro is going to pick you up," said Clarita, her voice loud and crackling through my iPhone. I had just arrived in Bogotá, exhausted from a day spent flying from New York, through Miami, and onward to Colombia.

"Who?" I asked.

"Alejandro, honey, Alejandro!" She said this as if I'd just asked who my brother was. "My Uber driver, sweetheart. You'll see him." I had never heard any mention of "my Uber driver" from her before, but figured I'd find out soon enough.

"Sure," I said, and made my way towards baggage claim.

As it turns out, Alejandro is an Uber driver my grandma had happened upon one afternoon ride. When Clarita loves something—be it a Michael Kors tote bag or a carpet in Istanbul—she takes it, and so Clarita pulled Alejandro right off Uber, offering him money to be her personal driver. I turn towards Alejandro now, who is looking warily around the sketchy street. Clearly, he got more than he bargained for with today's ride.

"Okay, let's do it," I said, turning towards José, the fixer. "Alejandro, we'll be back in a half hour or so."

José and I jump out of the car and amble towards a commonplace building with black bars placed over the windows and doors. One knock and the metal door swings open to reveal a stoic-looking security guard wearing all black.

"Si?" he asks with a deep grunt.

Before I can respond, my fixer springs into action, explaining in rapid-fire Spanish that we're here for a media interview. Whenever I visit Colombia, I am eager to flex my Spanish-speaking skills, as it's usually my only opportunity to dust off the ol' conjugations. But here, looking at that grim-faced guard, I'm grateful to José for taking the lead.

The guard nods and gestures for us to step inside. A dark hallway leads to a glass-encased conference room in which a young woman sits motionless, waiting beneath fluorescent lights, her eyes staring blankly at the rectangular table in front of her. Flora—who opted to go by a pseudonym—can't be more than thirty years old. Her face is round, and her hair, which is cut into choppy layers, is streaked with red-and-purple highlights framing her face. She is wearing a dark hoodie with her hands sunken into the pockets, as if she's trying to disappear into the folds. Flora is hardly intimidating enough to warrant such security, but then again, I remind myself just who it is I'm speaking to. Flora is an ex-FARC fighter, as in, the guerilla group that killed nearly 260,000 people across Colombia, as in, the guerilla group that may have murdered my great-aunt, Adita.

★

I'm on assignment in Bogotá for *The Global Journey*, where I've been working as an on-staff travel editor and writer for about a year now, tasked with overseeing their travel section. While I had chased the dream of being a travel writer, I found the role of travel editor to combine the thrill of writing and traveling with the promise of steady pay. When I began working for *The Global Journey*, I was joined by a handful of other editors, each of whom had been given their own genres to spearhead: art, sports, fashion, design, wellness, health, food, and music. Out of a shared sense of camaraderie that befalls anyone joining a start-up, I instantly bonded with my coworkers, especially Esme, Amber, and Rachel.

In a funny way, each of us perfectly embodies our respective genres. Esme, the wellness editor, is statuesque with features reminiscent of an actress. She is one of the few people I know who not only enjoys working out, but has experienced *all* forms of workouts, wellness trends, and energy cleanses. For *The Global Journey*, Esme had done it all: she's sat in a salt cave for an hour; she's had a photo taken of "her aura" (which seemed to me a rainbow polaroid with her face in the middle); she's tried all forms of therapies—including cryotherapy, hydrotherapy, and massage therapy. Esme has even taken an "orgasmic meditation" class, which, years later, we'd come to find was part of a cult.

Rachel, too, perfectly encapsulates the art genre. Her go-to color is black, which she can accent with a bold lip and a chunky pair of combat boots. Rachel just *looks* like an art editor, effortlessly chic and cool without any of the pretension that comes with the art world. She never judges me for being baffled by the significance of Duchamp's signed urinal, nor does she mock my limited knowledge of art history, which stops at Picasso.

Amber is the editor for home and design. She is confident in an enviable way and probably the most educated of all the editors, holding a master's degree in liberal arts and women's studies. While her stories cover design-adjacent topics ("How Cast Iron Transformed SoHo, from Factories to Fancy Lofts"), she frequently pushes for articles that fascinate her, injecting her own interests into her genre. Come to think of it, all of us push the envelope of our genres in one way or another, publishing stories that go beyond the slideshows and listicles we've been tasked with creating. This is what thrills us: the ability to shape our sections and send stories into the world that we hope will likewise thrill others.

Inspired by my team, I want to continue going beyond the mind-numbing repertoire of "10 Places to Visit in [insert destination]." Within my first month of working at *The Global Journey*, I saw the difference in my being a full-time travel editor versus a travel blogger. The first difference, of course, is money. Here was a job that was paying me (regularly!) to write about travel and edit travel stories. *The Global Journey* wasn't a one-off assignment that would pay $150 three months from now, nor was this another unpaid blog post I had spent two hours writing for *The Pin the Map Project*. This was a bona fide job that could pay my rent.

The other difference was a glorious thing called having a budget. As a member of an editorial team, our publication would expense travel costs. Expense. Travel. Costs. While I was allowed to accept periodic press trips at my editor-in-chief's discretion, I could now take individual trips too (not using my vacation time) in pursuit of a story—all while getting paid to do it. My mind reeled. Beyond the joys of being paid to write and travel, there was one more difference between *The Pin the Map Project* and *The Global Journey*: my stories now reached a big audience.

On its best day, my blog could reach maybe a thousand people, which is no small feat, but also not a figure that moves mountains. *The Global Journey*, on the other hand, reached thousands upon thousands upon thousands upon thousands of readers worldwide. I began to pursue articles that were rooted in interesting places and addressed stories I felt were important. I traveled as far as Iceland to write about whaling, eager to investigate how consumer demand for whale meat (of which there was virtually none) was greatly outweighing the supply of meat sitting in storage units outside Reykjavik. I ventured as close as Bleeker Street to meet with a women's rights activist for a feminist walking tour that highlighted all the overlooked monuments that honored New York women. Not only did my words now have monetary value, but I had been given an audience with whom to share them, and I knew exactly the next story I wanted to tell.

★

"Hola," I say, sliding into the seat across from Flora. "Mucho gusto."

José plops down into a chair on the other side of Flora. My

questions today are entirely too important to be left to my wobbly Spanish.

"Thanks for talking to me today. I'm going to be recording this conversation," I say, gesturing towards my iPhone lying on the table. "Should you want me to stop the recording or not include something you said, just say 'off the record' and I'll pause."

As José begins translating my words, Flora nods nervously, her eyes never leaving the surface of the table, her hands still plunged deep into the pockets of her hoodie. Flora is undergoing a reintegration process, a controversial program that has been put into effect following a historic peace deal signed by President Juan Manuel Santos and the FARC, transforming this once-deadly narco-terrorist organization into a political party with guaranteed seats in the Colombian congress and senate. The peace deal—which was voted against by the majority of Colombian citizens—has drawn intense criticism for its leniency towards the FARC, creating a fiery debate about what is more paramount: obtaining justice or having peace. At the center of this hot-button issue sit people like Flora, who have spent their entire lives living in the FARC camps hidden inside Colombia's jungles.

Right away, I'm nervous. Not just because this is one of the more serious articles I've pursued, but because I have a personal stake in this story. I think back to my childhood and how the acronym FARC came to represent so much misfortune in my family. I think back to a few days ago when I met with Margarita, one of Adita's surviving daughters. My dad had put me in touch with Margarita, encouraging me to sit down and ask her about her late mother. Margarita showed up at my grandma's apartment wearing a white button-down blouse tucked into a pair of slim-fitting blue jeans. Her near-perfect English was heavily accented as she began to tell me about my great aunt, slowly unraveling the knotted threads that had surrounded her murder.

★

Once upon a time, Adita had been a dentist and a painter who lived in the beachside town of Santa Marta with her husband, whose family owned a massive plot of farmland that had been passed down from generation to generation. Back in the day, this farmland had been used for all the usual things—growing crops and raising cattle—but was one day overtaken by FARC guerillas who invaded the property and claimed it as their own. Slowly, the FARC began to sell off pieces of the land to other buyers, using the profits to finance their illicit activities.

Adita's husband—a lawyer, at the time—tried his best to get his family's farmland back. As he proceeded to navigate a corrupt legal system, an on-paper battle between his family and the invading guerillas was created. As Margarita explains, the FARC took that fight right off the page and sent threats to Adita's husband, shooting him (nonfatally) and scaring him just enough so that he never returned to the farm again. Once he eventually passed away, Adita decided to resume her late husband's work and get the family land back by evicting the FARC from their property. This is where an already compli-cated story becomes more convoluted.

"I was talking with my mother," recalled Margarita, sit-ting on my grandma's cream-colored couch. "She told me she was going to try and talk to this man and agree on some-thing soon."

"This man" was apparently a nearby landowner who had allegedly purchased a plot of Adita's land from the FARC il-legally and was abhorrent at the prospect of giving it up.

This is where the theories begin to swirl.

My dad believes the FARC killed Adita for trying to re-claim her land. Margarita thinks this landowner hired people to rough her mother up in hopes of getting her to abandon her legal efforts. All we know for sure is that one morning, Adita was kidnapped and taken to the Sierra Nevada mountains, where she was killed and found hours later.

"It was a very big rock that they used," said Margarita flatly, her eyes faraway, remembering how she'd had to identify her mother's body, noting the trauma to her head.

I sat silent. I had finally learned how and why Adita had been killed, but the question of who did it remained unanswered. In the immediate aftermath of her murder, the landowner was never questioned, and to layer in more mystery, Adita's kidnappers turned up dead. These facts just bred more questions. How long after she disappeared was the body found? How did they know her kidnappers were the ones who turned up dead? How could police not question the landowner? None of it made sense and perhaps it never would. And, just like that—as has so often been the case in Colombia—my great-aunt's death was swept under the rug.

"Do you blame the FARC?" I asked Margarita, wondering if she, too, saw them as the big bad wolf.

"Some people in Colombia just do what they want," she sighed. "The laws are so soft, and there is no punishment."

★

I think of these words now as I sit opposite Flora.

"Okay, let's begin." I nod towards José to signal the start of the interview. "Let's start with how you came to join the FARC?"

José snaps into action, translating the question and leaning close to Flora so he can relay her answer.

"Many young people decided to enter into the FARC because they didn't have other opportunities," explains Flora, shifting uncomfortably in her chair. Her voice is a near whisper, small and quiet, as though she were a child being reprimanded for bad behavior. "It was normal for my community to make this transition from their families to the guerrilla groups."

As she speaks, I'm a little surprised to feel a pang of sympathy. Flora joined FARC at fourteen for no greater reason than they promised her food, security, and shelter at a time when her family couldn't. She wasn't a gung-ho Marxist spewing ideologies or a vigilante intent on overthrowing the government. She was just a kid. Flora's early life—like that of so many other child recruits—had unfolded within the guerilla group. In Colombia's jungles, she had her first period, fell in love, lost her virginity, and even gave birth to her first child (a baby she promptly had to give up due to the FARC's strict rules against soldiers having children). I had come to today's interview expecting a villain, but am instead met with a wide-eyed woman, desperate to reconnect with her now fourteen-year-old daughter.

"If my own child thinks I'm a monster, it's easy to understand why the rest of the society thinks the FARC is full of terrorists and murderers," says Flora sadly. "Reintegration is a process."

Here, on the outskirts of Bogotá, Flora is being prepared for civilian life. She's been set up with everything from a bank account to a cédula, which is comparable to a Social Security number in the United States, in order to help reintroduce her to Colombian society.

The half hour interview passes quickly, and soon enough, José and I are walking back onto the dusty street towards Alejandro and that black SUV. I decided not to bring up my family history to Flora. Partly because it felt unprofessional and partly because I'm not sure what good it would have done. A few days ago, while having dinner in downtown Bogotá with some relatives, I learned of the term "Locombia," which combines the word loco (crazy) with Colombia, used to describe the chaos of the country. Walking away from my interview, I think of this term now and the stories I've uncovered during my trip here: a child being inducted into a terrorist organization; a woman being murdered for trying to take back what is rightfully hers. There is just no rhyme or reason to my homeland. In my own writing, I love to have those perfect endings that tie everything together in a way that leaves no stone unturned. But by the time I leave Bogotá, theories about Adita's murder unravel. I must learn to live with the unfinished story.

Alejandro starts the engine and pulls off, all too eager to head back towards the city center. For the longest time, I'd understood travel writing as only being about travel: where to go, what to pack, what to do, and where to sleep. Sure, travel writing is all of those things, but working at *The Global Journey* has shown me that it can also be about so much more. A travel article can encourage human connection and help people better understand the country and culture they are visiting, along with its history. I think about Flora and I think about my great aunt Adita, trying to make sense of the nonsensical. Both Adita and Flora had been crushed by the ambitions, greed, and political agendas of men who had manipulated, taken advantage, and killed countless innocent people in their own corrupt interests.

I wonder how many other women have stories like this to share.

PART THREE

Landing

Landing: The last part of a flight, when an airplane returns to a steady surface after a voyage.

Varanasi, Jaipur, New York City, San Juan La Laguna, Masai Mara, Iguazú

16

Royally Screwed

Varanasi, India

I'm tempted to drop my grandma's silver bracelet into the Ganges River, but the truth is, Amparito would have hated that. For her, cleanliness was close to godliness, and even after all this time since her passing, I could picture her wrinkling her nose and widening her eyes in horror at the image of her fine jewelry being thrown into a river in India, no matter how holy the waters are said to be. Her reaction would be akin to the countless times she'd guffaw at how I'd wipe my dirty hands on my jeans as a kid, rubbing the grease from a Domino's pepperoni pizza slice or crumbs from a bag of Lay's BBQ chips onto my sides. Still, I let her delicate silver bracelet hover precariously above the Ganges River, watching its inky waters flowing downstream, interrupted only by the offerings of floating candles that look like stars on a cloudless night.

As I've come to learn from a local guide, the Ganges—or Mother Ganges, as it can affectionately be called—is like a main artery of Hinduism in India. People come from all over to bathe in its waters, embracing the forgiveness the river offers as it washes away their transgressions. To live a life without soaking in the Ganges River at least once is considered in Hinduism to be a life incomplete. Here in Varanasi—a city *Lonely Planet* once described as "the India of your imagination" because of its rich beauty and spirituality—it is believed that when one drops the ashes of a loved one into the river, the water will ferry their soul to heaven and break the cycle of rebirth. This concept—known as "Moksha"—holds enormous weight in the process of reincarnation. Of course, Amparito would have hardly appreciated this as a devout Catholic, so devout that she once burst into tears when I gave her a twenty-euro rosary I had purchased from a gift shop at the Vatican. Hers was a reaction so genuinely earnest that the Pope himself may as well have blessed the gift.

Growing up, I was never religious. The closest my family came to faith during my childhood was when my dad promised God he'd go to Sunday mass if he passed his medical board exams. Sure enough, after passing the test, he dragged my teenage self to church the following Sunday, where I stared in bewilderment at grown adults eating crackers they believed were real manifestations of "the body of Christ." While my family never practiced or taught any religion to my siblings and me, my grandma, on the other hand, kept a bust of a pained-looking Jesus in a crown of thorns a few feet from her bed—a statue so terrifying that my dad and I would toss a dish towel over it whenever we visited her apartment, which was a short twenty-minute drive from our home in Chicago. While we never talked about religion on these visits, I'd see it reflected in the little details surrounding her—holy iconography scattered across her one-bedroom home, a laminated card of Mary perched on the dashboard of her car, a silver necklace depicting a saint that always hung from her neck.

I've never embraced or fully understood religion, but I have always appreciated it in some nebulous way. I can get down with the need to find beauty and meaning in the chaos of life. I have my own Nikki-branded version of spirituality: I believe in some sort of higher power, because to think otherwise feels depressing. I believe in destiny and fate because I love the romantic notion that certain moments were written in the stars. I believe in superstitions passed down through my family, such as always throwing salt over my left shoulder and knocking on wood. I don't go to church (unless I'm visiting a historical one in Europe) but will pray on occasion, although usually with one-off asks like "Dear God, please let me have a safe flight" or "Dear God, please let this check clear." While my praying sometimes feels like I'm hitting up a genie for wishes, my hodgepodge of spirituality works for me, and here, in Varanasi, I can admire how the raw beauty of religion unfolds on the banks of the Ganges River.

★

I'm feeling incredibly reflective right now, partially because it's hard *not* to feel pensive while traveling in India and partly because my career is (yet again) in flux after having just recently been let go from my job. I won't pretend that working for *The Global Journey* was my dream, but being a travel editor and writer certainly had been. I'd spent the better half of my twenties with arms outstretched towards a career that had eluded me. I finally landed my first on-staff editorial role for the digital publication where I'd been working for the past three years, and with colleagues I genuinely enjoyed working with. Getting laid off was the biggest shock of my life, although somehow, not entirely unexpected. For months the company had been going through rounds of layoffs, and for months I'd been biting my lip with anxiety, wondering just when my name would be called.

I could point my finger at the media industry, a shaky field in which digital and print publications are being pushed onto landmines left and right and getting blown to smithereens. I could blame the company itself and how its CEO was more concerned with positive online reviews than maintaining a healthy work environment. Or I could blame myself for starting to push for harder-hitting stories that led one of my managers to respond to a pitch of mine with, "Just what the hell does she think this is? *Vice*?!" The truth is, I had been trying to turn *The Global Journey* into the sort of publication I imagined it could be versus the publication it had become— a place where listicles went to die (or thrive, depending on whom you asked).

The day I was laid off, I had been working from home, busily preparing for this very trip to India. The opportunity to travel to India hadn't even arisen through *The Global Journey*, but through my blog, *The Pin the Map Project*. Like that trip I'd taken to Indonesia years prior, this was another blogger trip in which travel bloggers were invited to a destination in exchange for creating content inspired by their experiences there. In this case, it was to be an all-expenses-paid adventure to travel aboard the luxury Maharajas Express train, a five-star hotel on wheels that would take us from Delhi to Jaipur, Ranthambore to Agra, Khajuraho to Varanasi, and eventually back to Delhi over the course of a week. Although I didn't need to cover the experience for *The Global Journey* and planned to go either way, I wanted to both represent them and (admittedly) write the time off as a work trip versus a vacation. And so, I excitedly shared the opportunity with my managers, thrilled when they not only approved the time off but seemed excited at the stories I could write for their website.

A week or two before my flight to India, I was working from home while the office—unbeknownst to me—was in mayhem. Everyone was scheduled for a brief check-in with the office manager, but quickly realized that anyone meeting before lunch was getting promoted while everyone meeting after lunch was getting terminated. Our office was a small open-plan space in SoHo with three tiny conference rooms encased entirely in glass. Word spread through the office quickly as everyone tried to avert their eyes from that afternoon's lay-offs, doing their best to avoid staring at the meetings happening behind glass walls mere feet from their desks. Blissfully unaware of the day's events, I was scheduled to meet with the office manager, Ed, at 5:00 p.m., and so logged on to our video meeting, eager to share my story ideas around my upcoming trip.

"Hi, Ed!" I started cheerily, sitting cross-legged on my bed.

"How are you, Nikki?" he asked coolly.

"Great!" I responded. "I'm just getting organized for India and have some story ideas to run by you."

"Listen," said Ed, averting his eyes, "we don't need you to come in on Monday."

"Sorry, what?" I asked, puzzled.

"We no longer need you working here."

My face blanched as I absorbed his words. *Holy shit, I'm being fired.*

"Wha…what about my things?"

My mind immediately flashed to my desk, the framed photos of Jeff and me, all my little trinkets, my "be grateful" coffee mug. Then the video call dropped. As I tried to rejoin the conversation, I realized, in horror, that the company had already shut off my work email, leaving me no time to salvage any in-progress stories or important conversations. I checked my personal inbox, where Ed had sent a new video link.

"I can pick up my things," I offered, holding back tears. I refused to let him see me cry.

"That won't be necessary," he said awkwardly. "We'll just ship them to you."

"No, really, I'm happy to come by after hours to collect my things," I pushed, trying to keep my voice light. "I'll even come by on the weekend."

The idea of my boss shoving framed photos of Jeff and me into repurposed Amazon boxes seriously irked me. I couldn't say why I was so concerned about my belongings, only that picking them up myself felt like retaining my last shred of dignity.

"That won't be necessary," Ed said, more firmly this time. "You don't need to come back to the office at all. HR will be in touch." And with that, he ended the call.

I sat atop my comforter, staring at the blank screen, tears swelling up as my jaw hung slack. Jeff, who had been sitting in the living room with our cat came in and wrapped his arms around me as I choked out that I was now out of a job.

"Don't worry," he said, nodding and pulling me in close. "We'll figure this out."

★

When I had started working at *The Global Journey*, they'd just opened their New York office—the first North American branch. Those early days found me and my colleagues assembling our own desks and chairs, excited to be part of building something from the ground up. Before my fellow editors and I had been hired to oversee our respective genres, *The Global Journey* had largely consisted of contributed articles without any real editorial direction or voice. Each of us were thrilled to help shape our verticals and, to our manager's credit, were largely given free rein to do so. I had gone from desperately trying to become a travel writer to suddenly being handed a travel section that I could not only shape but edit and write stories for that reached an international audience.

By the time I was laid off, *The Global Journey* had become something I'd poured my heart and soul into. While I understood the need for layoffs (the media industry is such that mass layoffs are announced practically weekly), I couldn't fathom the lack of gratitude the company had shown towards the people who built the very foundation on which the CEO now stood. It wasn't so much that I'd been let go as the way it had happened: without a single iota of empathy, a "good luck on your next endeavor," or even so much as a "thank you" for the three years I'd given the company. Instead, I'd been made to feel like an unwelcome intruder, a threat to an office I had once lovingly decorated for holiday parties and even purchased a champagne fountain for as a surprise.

With shaking hands, I messaged my coworkers and learned they were already gathered at a bar in SoHo commiserating over the layoffs like weary soldiers toasting fallen comrades. Over the years, our motley crew of editors had become very close—we ate lunch together every day, stood in line for coffee at Dean & Deluca every morning, grabbed snacks at the downstairs bodega every afternoon, nursed happy hour wine every evening, and spent time together on the weekends. The idea of no longer seeing my coworkers regularly saddened me more than the dawning realization that I was now out of a job. After I arrived and began drowning my sorrows alongside them, I began to think back to that video call. The more I replayed my ex-manager's words, the more agitated I felt.

Standing up to tearfully hug my friends goodbye, I walked outside, letting the cool air dry my damp cheeks. As I traversed the few blocks to the Prince Street subway station, I stopped walking. *The Global Journey*'s office was just three doors away…and so was my stuff.

"I'm going to get my goddamn things!" I slurred to no one in particular.

It was nearly 9:00 p.m. then, and while the building would be open, I figured the office would be empty. Instead, there sat one of the other office managers—Ed's right-hand man—whose eyebrows practically leaped off his forehead at the sight of me pushing open the front door.

"I'm just getting my stuff," I said a little too loudly, trying to mask my awkwardness with overzealous confidence. Clambering over to my desk, I began collecting my belongings, gingerly placing them into my tote bag: the framed photo of Jeff and me in Paris the day he'd asked me to move in, the little knickknacks I'd brought from home, that "be grateful" mug now permanently stained with coffee. I then waltzed to the door, throwing one last look over my shoulder at the office that had once brought me so much joy.

"Good luck to you," said the manager flatly, still sitting at his desk.

"OH! I'll be fine. And you can tell Ed," I called across the room, my voice rising an octave as I reached for the doorknob, "to royally *fuck* himself."

And with that, I left *The Global Journey*, supremely pleased that I'd used the word "royally" as I felt it gave a cheeky nod to the management team over in London, who would surely hear about it the next day. Waking up the following morning, head pounding from the previous night's drinking, I reached for my iPhone to find a coworker had sent a flurry of images. I zoomed in on the photos and immediately recognized it as the security desk that sat at the entrance to the SoHo office building, where a kind but bored-looking security guard would wish me good morning as I waited for the elevator. There, hanging above security like an FBI Most Wanted poster, was my LinkedIn profile picture printed on a large piece of paper as a warning for security to be on the lookout. My royal "fuck you" had already made its way across the Atlantic.

I laughed at the absurdity of the picture, even sending the photos to my mom with a "Can you believe this?!" But between the laughs rose a sinking feeling, a nausea heightened by my hangover. Who was I kidding? I may have been the one to tell *The Global Journey* to royally fuck itself, but I was the one now royally screwed. I was out of a job and tossed from an industry I had spent most of my twenties pursuing. I had wasted ample time trying to monetize my travel blog to no avail. I had tried to hack it as a freelance travel writer, only to find I could not afford to travel without a paycheck, pay my bills with the less than $300 I earned from stories, or secure enough article assignments to cover my rent. Would I ever be a travel editor again? Could I even write about traveling without a steady paycheck to support me? It was then that I remembered my upcoming trip to India.

*

Varanasi is one of the holiest cities on earth and the oldest in all of India. It's a place unlike any other I've traveled to in recent years, a city that seems to encapsulate both the beauty and tragedy of human life. On the banks of the river, over 300 bodies are cremated each day in open-air crematoriums. A line of stretchers, each holding a body draped in orange marigold flowers and white shrouds, is pushed into the thrashing flames and billowing gray smoke. Beside the roaring fires sit piles of human ash, still smoldering, ready to be pushed into the Ganges so they can journey onward to heaven. After sunset, this haunting scene is contrasted by the Aarti Festival taking place downriver, a nightly festival of bright lights and loud music that brings locals and travelers together in gratitude and celebration of the river. The delicate tinkling of chimes and the rising Sanskrit chants fill the air as people arrive in droves to witness this dazzling display.

The duality of Varanasi—how Life and Death coexist as neighbors on this river—captivates me. Sailing downstream, you can almost imagine Death wearing a black woolen cloak and standing on the river's edge, personally ushering souls out of the fire and into the water. Meanwhile, Life, joyful and exuberant, throws a nightly party and invites everyone from near and far to dance, chant, sing, and be merry. To sail down the Ganges is to witness the human experience on full display—from death and mourning to life and celebration. It's impossible to not feel reflective as your boat cuts through the slow-moving waters.

Thinking back on my life so far, certain moments remain so vivid. The dirt-packed trails of Iguazú National Park as I walked off into the jungle solo and decided to call off my wedding. The pained look on Alex's face, his eyes filled with tears as we sat silently picking at our Agata & Valentina feast. The holiday lights hanging in Jeff's apartment, casting a glow over the two of us as we fell in love. The last time I saw Amparito alive, lying on a hospital bed in Chicago, the sound of her heart monitor letting off a slow and steady beep. I remember her hands—the deep blue-purple of her veins and her skin, delicate like a too-thin crepe. I had come to say goodbye, and as I left her room and stepped out into that quiet and fluorescent-lit hallway, I remember ripping off my hospital mask, damp from my tears, and just staring at the dark mascara smeared across the light blue fabric.

As I survey the banks of the Ganges now, I try to make sense of all of it: those collections of moments that sum up a life. There is no running from time in Varanasi or hiding from life's harsher realities; there is only the calm of this river reminding us that we are born, we live, we age, we die, and it should all be approached with unwavering gratitude. I stare at my grandma's bracelet again and weigh the symbolism of dropping it into this river against the nature of the woman I knew her to be, and then tuck it back into my pocket. She would have hated this.

★

As my boat slowly approaches the Aarti Festival, gliding down the river, I think back to a few days prior when I had arrived in Jaipur. As the capital of India's Rajasthan state, Jaipur is known as the "Pink City." History tells us that the reason behind Jaipur's rosy hue was inspired in 1876 when Prince Albert (the husband of Queen Victoria) visited the city. Pink is a color that represents hospitality in India, so the gesture of repainting Jaipur was thought to strengthen ties with the British monarchy and welcome Prince Albert in style. Walking through Jaipur, I spotted buildings ranging in color from terra-cotta to dusty pink, but of all the buildings, none impressed me more than the Hawa Mahal, whose honeycombed windows are said to have allowed royal women to peer out on the streets without ever being fully seen by outsiders.

When the Maharajas Express pulled into the Jaipur Junction Railway Station, our group was loaded onto coach buses and driven to the heart of the city center, where we got off and were immediately thrust into a kaleidoscopic spectacle of dazzling colors and harmonious sounds. Our tour of the city had crossed paths with a street parade that felt more like a carnival. Everywhere I looked, people moved forward in an endless stream of brass instruments and jewel-toned saris, their shimmering aquamarine and canary yellow fabrics catching the afternoon sunlight with each twist and turn. As crowds swelled and banners flapped high above me—their golden hues and sunset oranges contrasting with the bright blue sky—I was suddenly overwhelmed with emotion.

Since getting laid off, I had spiraled into depression. It felt like *The Global Journey* had not only taken away my career but had stolen my dreams with it. I was untethered in a way I had felt too often throughout my twenties and had hoped to not feel again now that I was in my thirties. I had spent years searching for a job like the one I'd had and now wondered whether I'd have to spend another ten years trying to break back into the industry. For days, I felt both anxiety's clutches (how would I pay my bills?!) and insecurity's vise grip (what if I'm not good enough to get another travel editor job?) tightening around my windpipe, reminding me of all the time I had spent chasing this career. But standing in Jaipur, something near-magical happened. There, amid the *brrr brrr brrr* of blaring gold trumpets and the *swish swish swish* of ethereal saris, I felt the metaphorical clouds break. Happy tears filled my eyes as I took in the vibrancy of the street parade swirling around me, my heart suddenly bursting.

I'm in India! For the first time on that trip, I let the thought fill me with joy. I'd come on my own merit. I hadn't gotten this trip through *The Global Journey*. Rather, I'd been invited to India—just as I had been invited to Indonesia years prior—because of the work I'd done on my *own*. Standing in Jaipur, I realized I didn't need permission to experience the world or a job title to chase my passion for writing. Despite being let go, I was still out here traveling, soaking in the brilliance that other countries offer. I may have been unemployed and lost (again), but I hadn't lost my shimmering horizon. I knew I'd have to figure out the next steps of my career and sort out the financial fallout from losing my job, but being in Jaipur had reminded me that the thrill of travel would always be there, as would my dreams of travel writing. No one—not even the management team of *The Global Journey*—could take *this* dream away from me.

17

Unearth Women

I'm having an out-of-body experience, as though I've floated up out of this rigid chair and am watching my job interview from above. There I am, a disingenuous smile affixed to my face, fervently nodding in agreement with everything the interviewer says, hands fanned out as I respond, eager to impress this man who is eerily reminiscent of *The Global Journey*'s CEO. Everything about his appearance seems modeled after the start-up founders of Silicon Valley—his relaxed posture of one ankle crossed over his knee, his casual button-down shirt and blue jeans, his satisfied smile. He's a peacock of a person, exuding an overtly masculine aura that suggests he wants everyone to feel like they're in the presence of pure genius.

I'm interviewing for an editor role at a start-up called *Trip Your Way*, whose offices sit in one of those WeWork-type spaces where you can rent a cubicle by the month. This room—the entirety of the company office, as far as I can tell—has exactly three tables and is roughly the size of a studio apartment. There are two desks, each occupied by one eager-looking twentysomething girl sitting within earshot of my interview, and there, positioned like a gilded throne in the center of the room, is his desk.

"So, you see, we're going to be creating these fantastic digital travel guides, and we could definitely use your help editing them," he says, eyes bright.

I can't help but envy his innate confidence, as though he is the first person in history to come up with an online travel guide. He pauses for dramatic effect as he speaks, as though he expects me to jump up from my seat and clap like a trained seal.

It reminds me of a lunch I once had with the CEO of *The Global Journey* to discuss the travel section. The meeting was meant as an opportunity for me to share ideas about growing the website's travel content, but instead morphed into a monologue about how he'd switched careers and became the founder of his "very successful" media company. We had left the office and walked to a nearby park, where we sat on a bench for a lunchtime chat. He shoveled carry-out sushi into his mouth, speaking in between bites about the company's origin story (a self-indulgent tale I had heard ad nauseam). As he spoke, his chest puffed out with pride. A grain of sticky rice had found its way from his takeaway platter to his cheek, where it sat stationed throughout the remainder of the conversation. I wanted to laugh, but instead, I leaned in with furrowed brows, pretending to hang on his every word, wary of interrupting his story by pointing out the rice grain. I was tap-dancing for an entitled start-up founder then, and I'm doing it for one now.

"I could definitely help with your travel guides!" I hear

myself say enthusiastically. "I can even pull from my other work experience to help grow the company in other ways!"

I'm pouring on everything I've learned over the past decade—from working in advertising to my stint in public relations to my role as a travel editor.

"That would be great," he says. "We haven't hired a social media person yet, so if you have experience there, that would be awesome. Like any start-up, this is a real all-hands-on-deck operation."

In the course of my job interviews, I've come to learn that "all-hands-on-deck" is just corporate speak for "We expect you to do whatever is needed for this company—even if it's not part of your job description—for no additional pay." And yet, I'm desperate. Since getting laid off, I've found that being a travel editor is like snagging the last seat in a game of musical chairs; those with jobs are unlikely to get up anytime soon.

"No problem!" I say. "I can definitely help with social media!"

★

When the interview is over, I walk out onto the red cobbled streets of Dumbo, the curve of the bricks rubbing up against my too-thin ballet flats as I unscrew the fake smile I had plastered on for the past hour. Up ahead, I spot a group of people with selfie sticks thrust into the air at the intersection of Washington and Water Street, where the Empire State Building sits in distant view and perfectly framed beneath the oxidized Manhattan Bridge. This spot always draws a bevy of tourists all eager for this quintessential Brooklyn photo.

Despite the crowds, I love this Brooklyn neighborhood. Like Manhattan's West Village, Dumbo feels like an idealized version of New York. I love the old warehouse buildings now converted into restaurants and pizza parlors; I love the overpriced indie coffee shops selling specialty brews; and

I love the ornate design of Jane's Carousel, with its forty-eight intricately carved wooden horses so beautifully painted they could stand alone as individual works of art. Named for its owner, Jane Walentas, who spent over twenty years restoring the carousel, the ride looks plucked from the Belle Epoque with its gilded mirrors and painted frescoes. One of the things I appreciate the most about New York is how even in the midst of glistening glass and impenetrable steel, pockets of the city transport me to another decade entirely. From the aged Fraunces Tavern, where George Washington once bid farewell to his officers, to the towering St. Patrick's Cathedral on 5th Avenue where F. Scott Fitzgerald married Zelda Sayre in 1920—I don't need to search far to find the past hidden amid the present.

Today, the clouds are heavy and gray as I make my way to the Dumbo ferry stop, eager to get back to the comfort of my Astoria apartment. It's the gloomy sort of day that promises fall and all its autumnal glory are just around the corner. Just the kind of day I love. It's a pain to get from Queens to Brooklyn, especially from Astoria to Dumbo. By subway, the trip can take almost an hour. An Uber or taxi to Dumbo may take half the time, but costs upwards of $40 to $50 (not ideal if you're unemployed). I've always felt the ferry is an underrated mode of public transportation in the city: it's cheap, has an onboard concession stand, and boasts unbeatable views of Manhattan and Brooklyn.

I watch as the ferry approaches the dock, groaning in the landing, and lowers its ramp for passengers to disembark. I find myself a seat against one of the water-streaked windows facing the Manhattan skyline and reflect on the job interview. I had spent an hour rattling off all the ways I could make the founder and his company a success in exchange for long hours, a shitty salary, and doing the work of an editor, social media manager, and marketing assistant. I knew he wanted to hire me because of how little he'd have to pay in exchange for how much I had promised to bring to the table. It was an uneven exchange, but one he knew he could swing because I had been desperate to become a travel editor again.

I wonder what it would look like to return to my own projects. A few years back, I had designed and printed a single issue of *Pin the Map* magazine, pulling stories from my then blog. The idea was simple: the magazine focused on combining travel stories with those that spoke to the human experience across the world. For weeks, I had worked on designing *Pin the Map*, only for it to come out looking like a half-assed brochure I'd designed in Microsoft Paint, which, of course, I had. While the stories weren't half-bad and even featured articles from women who had guest-written for my blog, the production quality was laughable at best.

Pin the Map arrived roughly the size of a placemat or Monopoly board and was missing a back cover. After weeks of designing it, I had forgotten to place any sort of end page on the magazine, so it arrived looking like the last page had fallen off in shipping. While the issue never saw the light of day (thank God), the idea of it sat on a sill in the back of my mind for years, percolating. *The Pin the Map Project* had fallen by the wayside, sacrificed on the altar of my becoming a travel editor and eventually turning into a time capsule of another era in my life entirely. But suddenly, *Pin the Map* magazine—in all its flawed glory—takes center stage in my mind.

What would it look like if I poured all of that effort and experience into my own travel magazine? My instinct is to brush away the question. *Me? Start a travel magazine? Yeah, right!*

The thought is audacious for someone living off unemployment benefits with virtually no savings. I have no family trust fund to pull from or a close relative I'd dare burden with asking for a loan. And yet, the idea of starting a magazine is tugging at my sleeve like an incessant toddler demanding their mom pay attention. *Look at me*, it seems to beg, *just LOOK at me*. I think back to that interviewer, the epitome of all the men who had laid stake to an idea that at one point must have seemed outrageous, to which the world (and its investors) responded by rolling out the red carpet.

I think back to the Women's Travel Fest I'd spoken at a few weeks prior, an annual conference bringing together women passionate about travel for a series of workshops and keynote speakers. This year, the conference took on a deeper meaning in light of the recent #MeToo reports that had begun to dominate the media. As women stood up in unity, calling out toxic men, a veil of defiance had settled across the globe. Each industry seemed to have its own reckoning, from Wall Street to Hollywood, and yet the travel industry had remained largely mute. That is, until the Women's Travel Fest.

A week before my trip to India, I arrived in the Lower East Side, set to join a panel on "Sexism in Travel," an honest discussion about the myriad ways that women experienced discrimination within the travel space, both professionally and personally. I had been meant to represent *The Global Journey* on the panel, but instead arrived unemployed and insecure about it, sitting alongside working editors from *USA Today* and *CNN Travel*. Onstage, I listened with rapt attention as my fellow speakers described heartbreaking instances in which they'd been undermined in the office or sexually harassed while traveling. It seemed that nowhere on earth was safe for women, particularly women of color. As they spoke, I looked out at the audience, noting the intensity in their eyes as they hung on the panelists' every word. Their heads shook in fevered agreement with lips pursed in frustration. Their physical reactions said it all.

After the panel ended, women ran up to the speakers, eager to share their own experiences with us. As I traveled across India, I chewed on their stories of being cat-called on the streets of Paris, enduring inappropriate touches on a subway in London, or being harassed by a male colleague in their Los Angeles office. I replayed the look on their faces as I flew back to New York. I remembered moments in my own life where I'd been made to feel uncomfortable on the street or a line had been crossed at the office. In the weeks since I'd been laid off, these somber stories had coalesced, and their frustrations had fanned the flames of my defiance. I wanted to do something outlandish. Something as downright insane as launching a new type of magazine: one that would champion women.

★

Stepping off the ferry near Astoria's Socrates Park, I finally return home to that cozy corner of Queens that Jeff and I now share. It had been years since I moved in, years since this one-bedroom apartment looked like the mismatched bachelor pad it once was. I kick off my shoes and amble over to the bedroom, tearing off my interview outfit a little too vehemently before pulling out my pajamas. Jeff is away for the evening, onstage at one of his weekly comedy shows.

"It's just you and me tonight, Peeps," I say to our tabby cat. He's sitting perched on his ivory-colored cat tree, his owl-like green eyes watching my every move. He lets out a gentle trill as if to say hello, and then follows me to the kitchen as I pour myself a generous glass of red wine and hand him a few treats.

What would it look like if I poured all of that effort and experience into my own travel magazine?

The words pop into my head again, but this time, it hits differently. The wine has begun to wash away the doubts that usually attack such a question. Without a job, I have nothing *but* time (time and at least three months of unemployment benefits) on my hands. If ever there was a moment to try something new, now is probably it.

I reach for my laptop. My head feels wonderfully fuzzy now, swirling with excitement. I open a Word document, staring at the blinking cursor, waiting for something to come to mind. The fragments start gelling: *Pin the Map* magazine, my dream of sharing global stories, a desire to lift women's voices, the revelations I'd found back in India, my frustrations felt during today's interview. Something is taking shape; what it is, I'm not quite sure yet, but a single name floats to the top now, and so I type it out: Unearth Women.

18

Glitter

New York, New York

Elsie Rooftop sits like an illuminated crown inside a display case, high above the streets of Midtown Manhattan. It has an Art Deco design, reminiscent of those dazzling Jazz Age flappers with their drop-waist dresses shimmering on the dance floor. Inspired by Elsie de Wolfe, one of the first female interior designers, this rooftop is undeniably feminine, from the curve of that delicate swirling gold chandelier to the plush pink lounge chairs scattered across the wooden parquet floors. I can't think of a better venue to celebrate the official launch of *Unearth Women* magazine than one paying homage to a legendary woman. For weeks, I had organized this launch event, taking into account every detail—the step-and-repeat and red carpet at the entrance, the gift bags bursting with brand-donated items—all of it planned for this coming-out party; a veritable debutante ball meant to announce to the world (or at least to Manhattan) that *Unearth Women* has arrived.

I'm making my way around the room, flitting like a butterfly from flower to flower, hovering between excitement and nervousness. My dress—a four-day rental from Rent the Runway—is a cap-sleeve navy blue number with a gold hem and a "cold shoulder" accent. It's nearly time for my toast, so I slide up to the gold-and-white bar and order myself a "She-hattan" (a play off a regular Manhattan cocktail). All along the bar, I had placed laminated signs featuring the *Unearth Women* logo and our She-hattan cocktail with its ingredients listed below—French single-malt whiskey, vermouth, a dash of bitters, and a Luxardo cherry. I'm glad I pushed for this signature drink, the cases of whiskey donated by the woman-owned Brenne, where the founder had gone from ballet dancing to one of the few women running a distillery (a story we planned to feature in our second issue). With my She-hattan in hand, I scan the room and spot my fellow cofounders and grab the microphone, waiting for the DJ to lower the music.

"I just want to thank everyone for coming out tonight," I start, my voice ringing out. I've always had a knack for public speaking, although I've never been particularly comfortable with it. My voice might come out confident, but underneath I'm shaking.

"Less than six months ago," I continue, "*Unearth Women* started as a mere idea on a page…"

★

Unearth Women began as nothing more than a wild notion, a pipe dream born from the depths of my unemployment and wineglass. My first step in starting the travel magazine had been to come to terms with my innate strengths and weaknesses. Sitting cross-legged in my pajamas, drinking vino, and ideating my dream magazine, I realized I couldn't do this alone. If that sad little copy of *Pin the Map* had shown me anything, it was that while I could edit and write, I couldn't design, photograph, budget, market, or even sell a product. I needed a team, but not just any team. I needed a group of intelligent, skilled, connected women who were as crazy as I was to want to start a print magazine in the digital age. Enter Elise, Kelly, and Jess: three women who followed me down the rabbit hole.

Elise, whom I met during a family vacation in Mexico at age ten, had been my oldest friend. We immediately hit it off when we met at the hotel, spending our days eating French fries on the beach and splashing around in the pool. When it came time to check out, we were thrilled to find our families lived just fifteen minutes away from each other back in Chicago. Thus started one of my most enduring friendships.

Elise is statuesque with defining features, startling ice-blue eyes, and near-platinum blond hair, which looks good in just about any cut and length (all of which she has tried, from a short crop to wild curls). Elise has always exuded confidence and levity in a way I envied throughout high school; she always managed to just be *cool*. If a boy broke her heart (which they rarely seemed to do), she didn't pen her last will and testament the way I often did. Instead, she'd flip her blond hair, shrug, and get over it, just like that. No drama, no furious diary entries, no cryptic AIM away statuses pulling from the latest Third Eye Blind lyrics. While I was rimming my eyes with jet-black eyeliner, listening to Nirvana, and smoking secret joints while my parents slept, Elise was generally less dramatic.

Elise could walk into any room in any city in any country and leave an hour later with a gaggle of new friends—that's who she is. On the other hand, I have always been guarded—an aspect of my personality that has only sharpened with years of living in New York City. Since graduating high school,

Elise and I had made a point to see each other during holiday breaks, but once college ended and I moved to New York and she to Aspen, we began to drift apart. This had changed recently when we sparked a sort of pen pal email relationship. In the past few months, I'd learned that she was working in a job she was tired of in a city she was growing antsy to leave, while I was out of work in a city I couldn't afford to keep living in without a steady paycheck. I knew that both Elise and I were lost in our careers and looking for the next big thing, whatever that might be, and so she was the first person I reached out to about *Unearth Women*.

Once Elise joined, I emailed two other women I knew and revered: Kelly and Jess were professional acquaintances I had met in New York's travel scene. While we weren't close, I admired their work from afar: Kelly had created the Women's Travel Fest conference (along with a series of woman-focused travel guide books and a women's tour company), and Jess had gone from writing about travel and food to becoming a host of an Emmy-winning show out in Philly. Both were creative by nature, pushing out content and creating experiences that championed other women. Together, the four of us made a dream team: Elise would lend her entrepreneurial spirit to help *Unearth Women* from a business development side. Kelly—a whiz with crafting brand partnerships—would leverage her rolodex of connections to grow awareness of *Unearth Women* and connect it to brands in hopes of creating profit. Jess and I—both writers and editors in our own right—would shape the content, defining the publication's voice while selecting impactful stories to publish. From the core team, we'd hire a freelance graphic designer to take on the aesthetics of *Unearth Women* magazine, turning our work into a visually appealing publication that we hoped people would want to go out and buy.

The idea of *Unearth Women* was straightforward: it would be a print and digital publication dedicated to *unearthing* women's stories around the globe with pages that combined thoughtful reportage with the sort of wanderlust content you'd expect from a travel magazine. There would be compelling stories about remarkable women doing remarkable things, stories that for one reason or another never seemed to make their way to mainstream media but deserved the spotlight nonetheless. There would be features on destinations and the women who shaped them with dedicated guides that pointed travelers in the direction of women and BIPOC-owned businesses, which had historically been left out of guidebooks.

Our stories wouldn't demean readers with obvious suggestions on visiting the Statue of Liberty in New York or the Eiffel Tower in Paris. Instead, we'd tell travelers about that feminist bookstore in London hosting stellar community events or the woman immigrant-owned kitchen in Queens working with refugees to cater cuisine from Syria, Myanmar, and Senegal. For every in-depth story about a woman's triumph or plight, there would be a visually enticing piece with the sort of advice you'd hope to find inside a travel magazine, like how to stay safe while traveling solo or how to plan a road trip through Iceland's West Fjords. *Unearth Women* would hit that sweet spot of exciting, profound, helpful, and lighthearted, all while championing women and their oft-overlooked stories. We filled our heads with inspiring platitudes about *Unearth Women*, a new kind of magazine where feminism met travel.

For each issue, we planned on orbiting the stories around a unifying theme. In the case of our first issue, resilience, the articles highlighted women's strength in countries worldwide. The stories were a combination of pieces we wrote and commissioned from freelancers whom we paid out of pocket. They included an interview with South Africa's all-woman anti-poaching unit known as the Black Mambas, a republished article by a young Gloria Steinem (which her team had generously allowed us to run), and a colorful guide to Buenos Aires focused on highlighting women-owned businesses. We combined harder-hitting stories with wanderlust—a destination guide through Germany's wine country or a beauty tour through Marrakech's medina. The first issue of *Unearth Women* had a minimalist design that mirrored *Kinfolk* or *The Cut*. To stand apart from other travel magazines, we put a woman on the cover instead of a destination, making it clear that this publication was, first and foremost, a celebration of the ladies. And in case readers had any doubt that *Unearth Women* was also a travel magazine, we printed a line above the cover title that read: "A Travel Magazine For Women, By Women."

Once the issue was designed and written, we turned to Kickstarter to raise $5,000 (in retrospect, a measly amount) in hopes of printing just 100 copies to sell via our website, unearthwomen.com. Thanks largely to Kelly and her connections, we exceeded our Kickstarter amount by maybe $2,000 and soon had enough funding to print just one run of our first issue. All at once, the floodgates burst open as our little magazine received a welcome reception. Brands reached out, eager to support a woman-founded publication laying claim to a male-dominated space, while the press generously interviewed our team about the magazine we had created.

Soon enough, *Unearth Women* appeared in *The New York Times* and in *Good Morning America*, earning digital coverage in the likes of *Travel + Leisure* and *Vogue Spain*. I'd wake up each morning with such an eagerness to check my inbox, excited to see what sort of opportunities would be waiting there—publicists asking for new-on-the-scene celebrity clients to appear on upcoming covers, writers keen to contribute to an upcoming issue, the possibility of a book deal for an *Unearth Women*–inspired guide, invitations to speak at conferences, an investor who had dreamed of creating such a magazine and who was now eager to put $50,000 into the company. All the doors in the world felt like they'd been flung open. My life began to feel exquisitely exciting. The meteoric rise of *Unearth Women* was more intoxicating than any drug. What once felt far-fetched and impossible had started to feel as though it could hardly fail.

From $5,000 raised to $50,000 newly invested, our team sat back in wonder as more opportunities rolled in, including an invitation to distribute our magazine internationally. Our first issue had caught the eye of Curtis Circulation, one of the largest magazine distributors, responsible for placing titles like *Travel + Leisure* in airport shops and bookstores. Eager to distribute *Unearth Women* to a broader audience, Curtis promised that our second issue—what would become our International Premiere issue—would be sold in stores across the United States, Canada, and in select cities overseas, so long as we redesigned the magazine and made it more commercial-friendly. Our minimalist design wouldn't cut it, so we hired a new graphic designer and revised the cover to stand up better against other legacy titles.

Sticking to our guns to keep a woman on the front, we were lucky enough to snag CNN's Lisa Ling of the hit show *This Is Life with Lisa Ling*. We paired her interview with articles on visiting Lithuania and adventures in the Dominican Republic, alongside stories of iconic women like the late intrepid explorer, Barbara Hillary (the first Black woman to travel to both the North and South Poles). We went from selling 100 copies of our first issue online to printing 15,000 copies of our second issue, which made its way into hundreds of Barnes & Noble stores across the country, a few Walmarts, and independent shops throughout Canada, Europe, and Australia—and it had all happened in less than a year.

★

"I want to thank my cofounders and everyone in this room for believing in *Unearth Women*," I say, gripping the microphone a little tighter. "And I'm thrilled to share that our second issue will be internationally sold in bookstores starting next year!"

The room bursts into applause, a sea of smiling faces and glasses raised in toasts. Behind me, my cofounders are brimming with pride because *we* did this together. We went from a group of women sitting on the floor of a Barnes & Noble in Union Square, flipping through magazines as we jotted down notes of what we wanted *Unearth Women* to be, to now standing in a room toasting the launch of our publication, which was about to be sold around the globe. Suddenly, I understand how that parade of male start-up founders I had worked for remained so damn confident. When the world validates your ideas, you begin to feel like the fabled Rumpelstiltskin, spinning every forgotten straw into glistening strands of investment-worthy gold.

As I listen to the applause, my cofounders and I stand together smiling in sleek jumpsuits and cocktail dresses, toasting our signature "She-hattan" drinks in this gorgeous venue. Looking around the rooftop bar reminds me of one quote from Elsie de Wolfe: "I'm going to make everything around me beautiful—that will be my life." I want nothing more but to do the same, to inject the world with beautiful stories and inspiring words and let that be my legacy. For the first time, that dream feels possible with *Unearth Women*. It's as though everything in my career—leaving advertising, starting a travel blog, getting laid off from *The Global Journey*, being thrust into unemployment—had somehow brought me to this very night when I feel I've finally made it in New York.

Standing in this gilded jewelry box of a room, I feel too

lucky to breathe. Too lucky to notice just how high I've risen above the clouds, glitter strewn across my eyes. It feels like we've accomplished the unthinkable—and perhaps in some ways we have—but developing an idea is one thing; sustaining a company is quite another. There comes the point in every great idea where the reality of it begins to eclipse you. You think you know exactly how it will play out, but something always catches fire.

19

Killing Your Darlings

New York, New York

What a scene.

One year later, I'm sitting on the floor, surrounded by broken glass and ripped-up paper, tears streaming down my face. Moments ago, I snatched that framed *New York Times* article off the wall and smashed it to the ground, the glass tearing through the picture of me and the inky headline celebrating *Unearth Women*. I remember the morning that article was printed and how that color photo of my face took up half the travel section of the Sunday paper. All around the city and beyond, I imagined people grabbing their morning lattes or ordering their egg sandwiches at bodegas and seeing that photo plastered across the *Times* while flipping through the newspaper stacks. Everything felt possible back then. That was clearly my problem. I got too comfortable basking in *Unearth*

Women's inevitable success, so it was too late when I realized it was falling apart. I couldn't stand to look at that framed news article a second longer. The mocking headline celebrated all that I had let slip through my fingers.

This is the end of dreaming.

These words, albeit dramatic, have been ringing through my brain on repeat. If I weren't so devastated at this moment, I'd probably laugh at myself crying on the floor like some goddamn Greek tragedy. The problem is, it *does* feel like the end of dreaming. I couldn't sustain *Unearth Women* magazine, and after just three issues, we could no longer afford to keep printing, let alone sell it in stores. Despite the interest and excitement that had swarmed the magazine at the beginning, it simply hadn't translated to sales: people weren't buying the magazine enough to offset the costs of printing.

A swell of anger floods my body as I grab another issue and rip through its spine. I had adored the feel of *Unearth Women* once. We had sprung for a premium paper stock that was velvety to the touch, glossy, and, in retrospect, entirely too expensive. I had prided myself on that paper choice, wanting the magazine to feel more high-end than a supermarket tabloid but soft like a copy of *AFAR*. My team and I had gone to a printer in Manhattan in those early days. It was an ancient place with groaning, rusted machinery that looked like it was a relic of another era. We had been considering local printers long before we realized printing stateside came at an exorbitant cost. Ripping apart the magazine now feels deeply cathartic. I'm finally giving in to my emotion, however ugly, watching as shredded pages fall to pieces around me.

When *Unearth Women* flatlined, I hadn't seen it coming. Sure, I knew money was tight, but I figured we'd simply have to scale back to two issues a year; I never imagined we wouldn't have money to keep printing. I was distracted by pulling together our next issue, a celebration of diverse stories and voices centered around a unifying theme of inclusivity. Of the three issues we had put out, I was the most excited for this fourth one, which seemed to encapsulate everything I hoped *Unearth Women* could stand for. The pages of the next issue wove a dazzling fabric of travelers—from LGBTQIA+ to BIPOC—whose stories lacked the chance to be represented in the travel space, particularly in bookstores across the globe. With the magazine written, edited, and designed, we needed only to send the final PDF file to our printer, who would then ship 15,000 copies to our distributor. We were one click away from sending over the next issue—*one click away*—when I realized we'd hit a wall. Our bank account had zeroed out, and we had no money to keep printing the magazine. We had no money to keep doing anything.

It all came down to the numbers, in the end. The goddamn numbers. I wouldn't consider myself a business-savvy person or even good at math. When I declared my journalism major back in college, I was distraught to find that a statistics course was one of the requirements for my degree. Part of the reason I had declared myself a journalism major was the hope of never again having to feel the cold beads of sweat run down my neck as a sadistic calculus professor announced a pop quiz on a Monday morning. On some level, I can understand why people enjoy math in much the same way I can see the appeal of working in IT—there's an innate satisfaction in untangling a problem that others struggle to solve. I am not one of those people.

Throughout my childhood, my standardized testing scores mirrored what I already knew to be true: I was good at writing and reading comprehension and abysmal at math and science. I had long suspected that the math problems I was forced to solve would never serve me in my adult life. Problems like:

if Bob sells 100 salads worth $6.50 and Fred sells 500 sodas worth $2.50, what is the total revenue of...who the fuck cares? For the most part, I was right; I didn't need math. There was a tipping app ready to calculate 20 percent of every restaurant check and TurboTax for filing complicated tax returns. I never needed a grasp of numbers until I started *Unearth Women*.

From the get-go, I had shrugged off any desire to handle *Unearth Women*'s finances, instead relegating the numbers to the other team members so I could focus on the things I'm good at. Without realizing it, I had already committed a fatal sin of launching any sort of start-up: turning my back on the bigger picture. I chose to zoom in on the aspects of *Unearth Women* that brought me joy, like editing and writing. I started treating *Unearth Women* like a full-time editorial job I had just been hired for, trusting I could focus on the words while other people handled the company operations. As time passed and our issues printed, I was pulled into different facets of the company I did not enjoy as much: sales calls and awkward partnership negotiations, marketing conversations and weekly team check-ins. I wasn't entirely blind to what was happening, yet flatlining surprised me nonetheless. I still had glitter in my eyes from our meteoric rise; I still believed success was inevitable.

While *Unearth Women* was written about in the press, published by a major distributor, and sold worldwide, money was slow to come in. The costs of mass producing a magazine outweighed the revenue of selling it, and the money spent on paying freelance writers outweighed the print subscriptions. We covered all of the up-front costs of producing and printing *Unearth Women*, and in turn, our distributor paid us a percentage of the magazines sold, of which there were few. The harder we pushed to sustain *Unearth Women*, the more my cofounders and I burnt ourselves out. Because we weren't actually earning enough to pay ourselves, we balanced full-time jobs with building *Unearth Women*, spending evenings working on our company, taking calls during lunch breaks, and attending conferences on weekends, only to be back at our desks by Monday morning. We balanced jobs that paid the bills with the hope that *Unearth Women* one day could.

When it came to the magazine's design, editing, and writing, those costs fell on us. When it came to the printing, shipping, and distribution, those costs fell on us too. When all was said and done, we were hemorrhaging money. In retrospect, we should have switched from a quarterly magazine to a bi-annual one, allowing ourselves more time in between issues to raise money and gain advertising. We should have scaled down the number of copies we printed and bookstores we were sold in, realizing we'd be better off selling fewer copies in a local market than peppering the world with a magazine they'd yet to hear of.

I remember having a conversation with a start-up founder recently whose company had expanded into a nationally respected food publication. When I asked him how he got started, he recounted how he and his cofounder had scrapped together $50,000 to launch their idea. They'd grown their publication slowly and intentionally, allowing it to gain a cult-like following in New York before expanding to other cities. I reeled at the number. It was the exact amount that had been invested into *Unearth Women*. The exact amount that I'd somehow managed to squander.

I wish I had let *Unearth Women* grow slowly and organically, gaining traction over a few years until it was ready to expand to other cities and countries. Instead, I allowed the idea of *Unearth Women* to eclipse its own reality. Scaling back had felt like giving up, and so we pushed forward.

By the skin of our teeth, we put out three print issues,

hoping—against all odds—that each one would bring in higher sales or attract more advertisers (they didn't). By then, we had ballooned the number of copies we were printing, afraid to tell our distributor we needed to scale back for fear they'd drop us. As I focused on editing our next issue, I turned a blind eye to the lights beginning to flicker around me. In its heyday, *Unearth Women*'s team had been fifteen people strong, all capable women working remotely on contract. But soon enough, it was just Elise and me, holding tight to an idea that was beginning to blow away.

Yet Elise still stayed, the two of us holding the flapping tarp as the hurricane beat down upon us, protecting my silver lining the way she had done throughout our childhood. This pain was as much hers as mine, for she, too, had poured her heart into *Unearth Women*, genuinely believing it could ferry us into the future. Frantically, we approached additional investors, ran crowd-funding campaigns, and reached out to brands who had celebrated *Unearth Women* publicly but had yet to spend a penny on partnering with us. We applied for business and personal loans while racking our brains for creative ways to turn a profit, but the two of us had flatlined as much as the company's finances, depleting our resources and pouring from an empty cup.

Now, after months of pretending everything was fine, I've finally collapsed to my knees on the floor of my apartment. As I start ripping another magazine in half, the front door opens and Jeff walks in. His eyes grow wide as he takes in the scene in front of him. My running tears. The broken glass. The shredded pages. My emotional levees have finally broken.

Jeff had celebrated every moment of *Unearth Women*. He never wavered in his support, listening with rapt attention as I discussed the next issue, stuffing gift bags for our launch party, and carrying boxes of back issues to a nearby storage unit. The first time I saw *Unearth Women* in Barnes & Noble, Jeff proudly held the camera as I kneeled with a bundle of copies in my arms like a mom holding her newborn child, ecstatic to see my magazine alongside titles I'd grown up reading and admiring. I'm embarrassed that he has to see me like this, brushing glass off my bare knees.

What will everyone think?

It's the last thing I should be worried about, but suddenly, I feel like I've let everyone down. I'm reminded of my decision to call off my wedding to Alex years ago and how the aftermath had so painfully rippled across my life. I had disappointed a long list of over 100 people then—friends, family, acquaintances, relatives. Now I am letting down a list of hundreds of people—magazine subscribers, freelance writers, designers, printers, photographers, the women whose stories we featured, my cofounders, our families, our friends. I think about our single investor and how she had generously poured $50,000 into our company, an amount I assumed could carry us for years. Now every penny of that investment is gone, eaten up by the cost of printing a magazine that didn't sell. I think about the people I admire who came to raise a glass to *Unearth Women*'s launch and my loved ones who had been so proud of what I had accomplished. What would they think of me now?

There was no choice but to fold *Unearth Women* magazine. I'd have to make an announcement and apologize to everyone who supported us, believed in us, and paid to buy magazines from us. We'd issue refunds to those who had preordered issue four and the many who had already preordered issue five, which (rather ironically) we'd planned to center around the theme of Hope, spotlighting women who were shaping the future with new ideas. We'd offer our next issue digitally and pull *Unearth Women* from over 800 bookstores. We would take an example from the many publications that had folded their print issues and instead focus on the website, promising the same women-empowering stories online.

I knew that sustaining *Unearth Women* magazine wasn't viable—but somewhere along the way, reason gave way to emotion, and the magazine became my obsession. I had poured everything into its birth, and then there she was in all her glory—all 130 pages of her glistening with the promise of a bright future ahead.

There's a common piece of advice given to writers known as "killing your darlings." It refers to authors forced to ax a beloved character or superfluous plotline in favor of the larger story. This is one of the more painful parts of creative writing: collapsing something you've spent time cultivating. Folding *Unearth Women* magazine was my darling to kill, smothering a magazine I had learned to love fiercely but that had never truly been needed. Staring at the glass and paper around me, I realize I've done more than fall. I'm mourning. I had let my darling take too much from Elise and me, inhaling our energy and finances, consuming our lives and well-being, and now she could not live a moment longer.

20

Someday Soon

San Juan La Laguna, Guatemala

The clouds above Guatemala's Lake Atitlán are wispy, hanging like lace veils over the mirrorlike surface. The lake's bank is drizzled with dense verdant forests and rising volcanoes, their A-frame silhouettes running along the perimeter. Sunset is the most dazzling time at Lake Atitlán, when those still waters absorb the rosy pinks, deep purple-blues, and burnt orange of the sky as though it were a canvas dripping with fresh paint. Between the volcanoes and forest are a bevy of Mayan municipalities bordering the edge of Lake Atitlán, each one boasting a distinct personality, drastically different from the next town over.

After driving three hours from the nearby city of Antigua, I arrived at the lakeside town of Panajachel, a backpacker's haven that serves as a jumping-off point for exploring the rest of Lake Atitlán. Panajachel is a small but bustling city with a main street offering all the typical tourist trappings—shopping, rowdy hostels, indie bars, and local restaurants. I didn't stay long in Panajachel, instead hopping on a small white boat and making my way to nearby San Marcos La Laguna. Compared to Panajachel, San Marcos La Laguna is a laid-back "hippie" village and, in my opinion, one of the more beautiful towns around the lake. Back in the 1960s, communities of hippies settled around Lake Atitlán's edges, drawn by the palpable energy and reported healing properties of these volcanic waters. These villages merged local Mayan philosophies with their New Age movement, and when a spiritual center arrived in the 1990s, Lake Atitlán pulled in aspiring shamans and healers the world over, cementing this corner of Central America as a wellness destination.

As much as I'd love to be balancing out my chakras in San Marcos La Laguna, today I'm exploring the nearby village of San Juan La Laguna instead. Stepping off my boat onto a rickety wooden dock, I see San Juan La Laguna rising before me, its main road inclining sharply in a way that reminds me of San Francisco's hilly streets. San Juan La Laguna is delightfully artsy, with its colorful homes and a slew of galleries slanted along the central thoroughfare. As I make my ascent, feeling the growing burn in my calf muscles, I spot Indigenous Mayan women wearing traditional huipiles, standing in the entrances of their shops, flashing an amused-yet-friendly smile as I huff and puff up the hill.

All around me, I spy shy stray dogs, napping in the shadows of the buildings and peering curiously from behind trees. Their sweet faces remind me of my own dog, Chico, whom Jeff and I had adopted while traveling through Central America a year prior. We had been staying on the island of Caye Caulker off the coast of Belize City, spending our mornings relaxing by the ocean and our afternoons walking the dogs of a locally run shelter where a man named Kenny lives side by side with a group of rescued dogs and cats. In the years that we'd been dating, Jeff and I had bonded over our shared love of animals. Whether we were bathing rescued elephants at a sanctuary in Chiang Mai, visiting a cat rescue beneath the ruins of Rome, or bringing supplies to a dog shelter in Mexico, we now always sought opportunities to volunteer with animals when we traveled, and Belize was no different.

During our stay in Belize, visiting the Caye Caulker Animal Shelter had become my and Jeff's favorite pastime. Every day at sunset, we'd bike over to the shelter and offer to walk the dogs. As Jeff and I strolled hand in hand down the beach, we'd thrill at the elation these pups had at simply rolling around in the sand, burying their snouts in a mound of washed up seaweed, and frolicking in the surf. From the moment we opened that shelter's gate with its hand-painted paw prints, the dogs would rush over in excitement, tails wagging.

We hadn't planned on adopting a dog in Belize, but after a few days of visiting the beachfront animal shelter, an all-consuming idea grabbed hold of me: *this* was where we needed to adopt our dog from. Jeff and I had been talking about getting a dog for years, bringing it up every time we saw a couple walking a fluffy pooch down the sidewalk back in New York. But we'd always come up with a myriad of reasons why it wasn't the "right time" to get a dog.

"I don't think we're allowed to have dogs in this building," Jeff would say, searching the lease agreement he'd signed long before I moved in.

"Okay…but what about the super and his family?" I'd remind him. "They have that yappy toy dog downstairs."

"Right," he'd start with a sigh. "But if we adopt a dog, they need to check with our landlord that pets are allowed in this building, and I'm not sure the super will sign off on that."

Eventually, we'd both abandon the conversation. But in Belize, I couldn't think of a better time or place to adopt a dog than from that very island and shelter. We had taken to Caye Caulker quickly, falling in love with the little island in a way we hadn't always fallen in love with previous destinations. Something simply clicked. And then there was Chico.

When we first saw him, Chico was small—a little ball of dirty brown fur with oversized ears shaped like New York pizza slices. His eyes were wide, rimmed with anxiety, and his paws—like those ears—were laughably big compared to his tiny body. Chico had arrived at the Caye Caulker animal shelter a few weeks prior when he was found on the streets of Belize City alongside his two sisters and brother. Kenny had a knack for naming his dogs and cats, but for those who had yet to be named, he'd simply refer to them as "chico" or "chica" (the Spanish words for "boy" and "girl"). When we decided to adopt a dog from Kenny's shelter, we kept Chico's name as a nod to where he had come from. Whenever I travel now, I see Chico's face reflected in the stray dogs sleeping along the dusty streets.

★

I've been invited to Guatemala as part of a women-only trip run by a woman-founded tour company called Purposeful Nomad. I'd first come across them while looking for stories to feature on the *Unearth Women* website. In a sea of woman-founded travel companies, Purposeful Nomad stood out to me for its mission of curating bespoke group tours keen to leave a positive impact on the destinations they visited. I had spoken to its founder, Caitlin, for an interview on *Unearth Women's* website, as part of a new series called "Women to Watch," but I had yet to actually travel with Purposeful Nomad. In exchange for coverage on *Unearth Women*, Caitlin generously invited me to join this Guatemala trip as her guest.

It is my first time traveling since Elise and I decided to fold *Unearth Women* magazine a few months prior, a decision that still feels too tender to the touch. Come to think of it, it's my first time traveling in a while. Between my ambitions for becoming a travel editor and my dreams of starting the magazine, I had turned my passion for travel into a never-ending job. In recent years, I had blurred the lines between traveling for myself and traveling for a story, making it harder to enjoy trips the way I had once done in my twenties. Every trip had become a self-imposed assignment in which I tried to siphon off social media content, story ideas, and inspiration that I could use. And then, with *Unearth Women*, the traveling stopped almost entirely.

In the time I'd spent trying to grow *Unearth Women* into a media company, I'd stayed in New York City, pouring every minute and dime into that fledgling idea, desperate to make it a success. It'd been months since that day I sat in a sea of broken glass and ripped-up magazines. But eventually, I had to stand up and clean up that mess. I had to, as they say, face the music and announce to every reader, subscriber, follower, and fan that we could no longer print the magazine but would forge ahead as a digital-only publication. I kept the messaging upbeat, as though we had been the ones to make this choice rather than having it forced upon us by mismanaging our finances. Many subscribers were bummed, saying they'd miss the feel of the magazine, but that they'd look forward to the digital stories we'd continue publishing.

I wondered just what I had expected that day sitting on the floor, tears rolling down my cheeks as I tore through past issues. I had dreaded the thought of people who had supported *Unearth Women* now coming for my head, dragging my lifeless body behind them as their stilettos marched down Madison Avenue waving a sign that read: FAILURE. Instead, their messages were wistful and encouraging. The overall reaction was simply, "We're glad *Unearth Women* magazine existed and are sorry to see it go." Looking back, it wasn't any different from my response to the many magazines I had once loved but had long since faded away.

But even though the paper and glass had been cleared, the emotional fallout from folding *Unearth Women* took much longer for me to brush off. While I was glad the overall response to the decision had been supportive, I couldn't shake the reality that I'd been the one to drive my dream into the ground. I couldn't stop blaming myself. For months, I'd felt caged by my disappointment and shackled by my guilt—I was glad that people could forgive the magazine for folding, but I was still grappling with how to forgive myself.

Everything changed the day we put an end to the magazine. On some unspoken level, Elise and I stopped trying to turn *Unearth Women* into something it simply wasn't meant to be; we stopped trying to run it like a company. After the magazine's collapse and subsequent recall from bookstores, all our efforts to build *Unearth Women* abruptly fizzled out. We no longer had a team of people. We stopped knocking on brands' doors in hopes they'd work with us, tired of throwing darts that never hit their mark. We stopped commissioning stories from freelancers, no longer able to pay for stories or photography. I'd even stopped writing for the website, feeling completely parched for ideas or inspiration.

Separately, Elise and I needed to retreat to our own corners and back to our respective careers. I had let my finances and editorial aspirations freefall, distracted by the dazzling hopes of one day walking into an office where the plaque above the frosted glass reception desk read *Unearth Women Media*. Now I needed to get my life back on track: find a new editorial job, focus on my well-being and relationship with Jeff, and straighten out the ship of my life, seeing as once again I had let it veer off course. Soon, Elise stepped back from *Unearth Women* entirely. Her role had been to develop the business, while her title had been Publisher, but with neither a viable business to develop nor a magazine to publish, there simply wasn't anything left for her to do. She had given the company everything she had, and then some, and was now ready to walk away and find her next project, relegating *Unearth Women* to a special ride we'd once shared.

For months, I grappled with feelings of abandonment and frustration. I couldn't help but feel like I was left sitting alone with my Frankenstein, a beast of a thing I had created one stormy wine-fueled night and now resented, unsure of what to do with it. I was eager to discontinue *Unearth Women* entirely, to wash my hands of the whole experience. But on the flip side, I'd discovered something about *Unearth Women* these past few months that I'd lost track of back in the excitement of its early days: there was beauty in what I had created.

★

I continue scaling San Juan La Laguna's main street when a sign catches my eye. A hand-painted wooden board proudly reads "Asociación de Mujeres," with a few succinct Spanish sentences below that introduce a female-only artisan group whose workshop rests a few feet ahead. I look around and spot a few more similar signs, all advertising woman-owned businesses or a female artisan cooperative in town. San Juan La Laguna is an enclave for Mayan women running their own businesses, from weavers to healers.

I'm breathless, having finally reached the top of the main road. Turning around, I can take in the entirety of this lakeside village: the incline of its street, the slanted buildings, the bevy of stray dogs sunbathing in shadowy corners, the wooden dock jutting out into the shimmering waters of Lake Atitlán, volcanoes rising in the distance. I'm headed for a hand-painted sign that reads "Casa Flor Ixcaco," one of those women artisan cooperatives in the village. This particular co-op was started back in the 1950s when founder Teresa Ujpan Perez began learning the traditional Mayan art of backstrap weaving, a labor-intensive process requiring a backstrap loom and hours spent painstakingly hand-weaving over the course of a month.

Nowadays, the Indigenous textiles known to Guatemala are being mass-produced and sold on the streets and in souvenir shops for a fraction of the cost. Machine-made huipiles are sold for $20 to unwitting tourists convinced they're supporting local artisans by taking home an "authentic Mayan garment." Unable to compete with these low prices, Mayan communities have begun to lose their centuries-old weaving tradition.

This is where artisan groups like Casa Flor Ixcaco matter; they educate foreigners on the value of Mayan weaving, and more importantly, create a space for Indigenous Mayans to carry forward the tradition. Perez formed this group of women weavers with the goal of commercializing their hand-made products and offering sustainable income to their families. Casa Flor Ixcaco—"Ix" meaning "woman" and "Caco" giving the nod to cocoa and the color of a Mayan woman's skin—honors the ancient traditions of Guatemala's past while pointing to a more progressive future in which women can earn a living autonomously.

Sitting on a wobbly wooden bench in the workroom of Casa Flor Ixcaco, I meet a beautiful young Mayan woman named Johanna, who's holding a spool of hand-spun cotton to show me her weaving process.

"We use only cotton from the plants that we grow in the community, and we use only natural dyes," she says proudly in near-perfect English, gesturing towards a series of red clay bowls in front of her, each containing spun cotton of a different color. "We get the color from local plants, flowers, and fruits."

Some of the colors we're shown are expected—guava turns the cotton a baby pink and indigo turns the cotton a deep oceanic blue—while other colors are more surprising, such as the deep purple derived from walnuts or the sunny yellow resulting from carrots.

This is exactly the sort of story that would have made an issue of Unearth Women, I think to myself, feeling a pang of nostalgia for the magazine.

After the demonstration, I wander through the gift shop, where I pick out a one-of-a-kind indigo-blue-and-white woven bag that was hand-dyed and handmade by one of the women in the cooperative. With the bag swinging from my arm, I start walking back down that main street when I spot Caitlin sitting in the window of an otherwise empty coffee shop.

"How are things going with *Unearth Women*?" she asks as I plop down on a stool next to her and place my new tote bag on the table.

It's the question I dread above all else lately. I'm aware that from the outside looking in, *Unearth Women* still seems impressive. From its initial press coverage to the rapid scale in print issues to the hundreds of stores we infiltrated, the reputation of *Unearth Women* precedes it, regardless of the magazine ending. For such a question, I usually have my locked-and-loaded response, but for some reason, I can't ham it up this time.

"It's okay," I smile, hesitating. Caitlin and I aren't exactly close friends but professional acquaintances: two women who have admired one another's work from afar. I'm wary of complaining but desperate for solace from another woman trying to make her business work. "It's been a struggle since the magazine folded. I've just been wrestling with where to go from here."

She sighs in a way that seems to say, "Girl, I get it." And the thing is, she *does* get it. As I come to learn, she's been struggling with her company. As with any self-run business, the chase for profit and customers has proven relentless, while the fluctuations of an ever-evolving travel industry have been hard to keep up with. I find solace in listening to her speak now. Hers is a company I've long admired, and to hear about its challenges doesn't make me think less of her or what she's accomplished. In fact, quite the opposite. Her candor makes me respect her and her endeavor all the more because here she is, on the edge of Lake Atitlán, running another women-only tour and still pushing her dream out into the world. Despite it all, she is *still* trying, and perhaps—in the end—that's all that matters.

Growing up, my dad would sometimes tell me I was "drowning in ankle-deep water" anytime I was too lost in the details of a situation to look up and see the bigger picture. It's only now that I realize I've been drowning in ankle-deep water for months, struggling to lift my head against the pressure of what I labeled a colossal failure. Maybe *Unearth Women* didn't become the next Fortune 500 media company I hoped it would be or the next *Travel + Leisure* I imagined it could become, but it did turn into something worth celebrating.

Maybe it's the women I just met at Casa Flor Ixcaco, the fact that I'm traveling again, or listening to Caitlin, but I feel as though I see it all through a different lens now. *Unearth Women* may no longer exist as a magazine, but what matters is that it still can exist. It can still occupy a corner of the virtual world, celebrating women and holding up their voices. It didn't matter that the magazine no longer stood alongside *Vogue* or *AFAR* on shelves across the country, because it had never been about the magazine, anyway. It had always been about the stories. Like diving into those healing waters of Atitlán, I feel as though something deep inside my heart is mending. *Unearth Women* was and is still my playground, a place where I can run wild with the kind of storytelling I love, my veritable field of dreams. For all the pain that had come after it, so much beauty had grown from it too.

Thanks to *Unearth Women*, Elise and I had a book deal with Penguin Random House, crafting a women-centric guide that would carry the torch of what our magazine once shared. It was because of *Unearth Women* that I was able to snag another travel editor job, using all I'd accomplished as a way to continue growing my career, and it was because of *Unearth Women* that I was now standing in Guatemala. Since that day it all fell apart, I'd put myself away, closed all the doors, drawn all the curtains, and let the world be still around me. When the intimidating vistas of my life weren't looming over me any longer, I could pause and answer that most elusive of all questions: What had it all meant?

In the end, I couldn't say what I'd taken away from the meteoric rise of *Unearth Women* or the pain of losing the physical magazine—only that this experience had carried me forward in a way I hadn't expected. If anything, these past two years have shown me what I'm capable of and how far I can take a dream. There were still endless roads to discover anew. Here in San Juan La Laguna, where women seem to be defying every obstacle in pursuit of their passions—from the Mayan weavers, to the healers, to Caitlin and her group of travelers— I feel a flicker of inspiration. I'm still learning to put one foot in front of the other, still grappling with all the career lessons these past few years have brought, but I'm also optimistic that someday soon, I'll find solid ground.

21

Don't Let The Lions Hear You

Mara Naboisho Conservancy, Kenya

"I hope the jeep doesn't break down right now," says Jeff nervously.

As if on cue, the car engine sputters. Through the darkness, I can just make out the silhouette of our safari guide, Steve, trying to force the ignition. With each twist of the key, the jeep seems to shrug and give up, emitting a scraping metal-on-metal sound.

"Holy shit," I whisper, laughing to cover up my growing nerves. I've always been the sort of person to awkwardly laugh in uncomfortable situations, and this is no exception.

"I called it," says Jeff. "I knew this would happen." A few days ago in New York, Jeff had confided his concerns of being eaten by a lion. Naturally, I laughed upon first hearing this.

"Let me get this straight." I'd raised my eyebrows. "You *actually* think you could be eaten by a lion on this trip?" For days, I'd playfully teased Jeff about his fear, but now, sitting in a windowless jeep at night, stranded feet away from a pride of twenty lions devouring a wildebeest, his once ludicrous worry suddenly seems very valid.

★

For the past few days, we'd been traveling with the safari company Basecamp Explorer in Kenya's Mara Naboisho Conservancy, which borders the national Masai Mara Reserve. Since arriving in Nairobi and making my way to the Masai Mara, I've learned from my guide just how many benefits there can be to booking a safari in a private conservancy like Mara Naboisho over the national parks. The Mara Naboisho Conservancy is made up of 530 individual plots of land belonging to local Maasai families. Every month, Basecamp Explorer—in partnership with fellow safari tour companies operating in the conservancy—pays a leasing fee to the Maasai families, introducing a revenue stream that proves a more sustainable alternative to agriculture and livestock. This win-win model has set a precedent in Kenya—and Africa, as a whole—of what can be accomplished if safari tour operators work with the local people instead of simply exploiting their land for tourism. The partnership not only encourages the Maasai to protect the animals and conservancy but also generates income for the communities (seen in the construction of new schools, water tanks, and even satellite dishes), and directly employs the Maasai at its safari camps, paying for safari guide training should it be of interest.

Unlike the national parks, private reserves usually have fewer crowds and restrictions, meaning more activities like off-road game drives, walking safaris, bush meals (dining and happy hours in the wild), and night safaris. I especially love the night safaris because they give us the chance to spot predators after dark, using infrared lights (so as not to disturb the animals). Although similar to our afternoon game drives, the night safari feels more exhilarating and eerie as we glide across the plains with nothing but that red spotlight scanning for lions, cheetahs, and hyenas.

Our safari camp is set up like luxury glamping, with elevated canvas tents perched atop raised wooden platforms, equipped with large beds, working toilets and showers, and even a "roof" that retracts so you can see the stars at night. While staying at the camps, I never get used to seeing wild predators nearby. So far, we'd spotted a cheetah sunbathing mere feet from where we eat breakfast, we'd seen hyenas trotting past our tent, and we listened to lions roaring unnervingly close in the middle of the night. As magical as being on a safari is, the experience is far from relaxing. Since leaving Nairobi a few days ago, Jeff and I have yet to enjoy an undisturbed night of sleep. Granted, this is largely my fault as I've been shaking him awake with an urgent, "Did you hear that?!" every single night.

On our first night in the bush, I listened with bated breath as a large animal was munching right outside our tent. The creature seemed to pull down the limbs of a tree—the branches creaking and breaking with the force—before ripping off leaves and chewing them loudly. From the sounds, I assumed it was an elephant, water buffalo, or perhaps a hippo (all of which, I knew, could easily kill if startled). The next night, I woke Jeff in a panic when I scanned the outskirts of our tent with a flashlight and spotted two lionesses walking straight in our direction.

"JEFF!" I whispered loudly. "Grab the walkie-talkie. The lions are coming!"

This is what we'd been told to do should a lion decide to pop over to our tent for a nighttime snack: ring the front desk on our in-room walkie-talkie and wait for someone to run over wielding a giant spear. In fact, before and after sunrise, we need to be escorted to the main lobby tent with a guard holding a spear should a predator come ambling across our path.

"Hello. Hi. Sorry to bother you," I whispered evenly into the walkie-talkie, not wanting to reveal my panic. "I see two lionesses coming straight for our tent. Would you mind please sending someone over?"

Within minutes, one of the Basecamp staff came strolling up to our elevated tent, his flashlight scanning the fields beyond.

"No lions," he said definitively. "Just warthogs." And with that, he turned on his heel and went back to bed, his flashlight growing faint as he retreated back into the bushes.

"Babes, I *know* what I saw," I said urgently, scanning the outskirts of our tent, but Jeff had already fallen back asleep, too tired to listen to the girl who cried lion.

By this point in our safari, Jeff and I have become strung out on adrenaline, from racing across the plains in pursuit of giraffes during the day or startling at the sound of hyenas cackling outside our tent while lying in bed. Fun fact: hyenas not only cackle but let out a "woo-oo" sound when calling to other hyenas in their group, alerting them to a recent kill. Throughout the night, you can hear these "woo-oos" punctuating the night, like the hooting of owls. But of all the sounds we've heard on safari so far, none have compared to the lions ripping flesh from bone mere feet from our stalled jeep.

★

I'm transfixed, watching as the lions tear and break down a wildebeest carcass, chewing through satisfied roars and guttural grunts. It's a gnarly scene, like something out of a zombie apocalypse film. The male lions are closest to the carcass, getting the first bites of the wildebeest while the lionesses (who did the work of killing the animal) look on patiently, waiting

CALL YOU WHEN I LAND · 265

their turns. The males are soaked in blood, their paws and jaws red as they pull at intestines and crunch on bones, the feet of the wildebeest waving through the air with every tug and pull. When one of the male lions gets up, presumably to walk off his full stomach, a lioness slides in for her share of the kill. At the bottom of the totem pole are the cubs, clambering around the outskirts of the feast, waiting to have at the scraps. Every once in a while, one cub may try to edge his way in, only for dad to growl threateningly in between bites.

Watching this feast, I realize just how much nature documentaries gloss over the visceral details of the wild. The most I'd ever seen a lion do on screen is trudge off into the bush with a dead antelope hanging lopsided from his jaw. Nothing could have prepared me for the sounds and sights of an entire pride demolishing a wildebeest. Perhaps this wildebeest was roaming the plains that very morning on our walking safari, stumbling across the bones of a largely intact giraffe or the weathered horns of a long-gone water buffalo. Or maybe these lions were the same ones we'd spotted napping during our afternoon game drive, their golden-brown fur catching the sunlight as they lay snoring beneath the shadow of an acacia tree, looking as cuddly as a house cat.

For the most part, the lions pay no attention to the safari vehicles, probably regarding them the same way as other bumbling, nonthreatening animals. But, as Steve makes very clear now, if one of us were to jump out of the car or make any loud noises, this act of stupidity would surely be our last. We're surrounded by two other safari vehicles. One is starting to drive away, and the other begins to pull up alongside our car. It's then I realize that the other jeep is holding the rest of our travel group from Basecamp Explorer. Steve instructs Jeff, me, and a fellow traveler and Canadian journalist named Domini to clamber into the other car without making a noise or touching the ground.

"Don't let the lions hear you," warns Steve urgently from the driver's seat, not making any move to exit the vehicle.

"Wait. What about you?" Jeff asks, turning to Steve with rising concern.

"I'll stay with the car," he replies, unfazed.

Steve—who chooses to go by the easier-to-pronounce name rather than his actual Maasai name—is not only a trained safari guide but a member of the semi-nomadic Maasai, an Indigenous group that once killed lions as a rite of passage to manhood (a tradition that has since been abandoned in lieu of protecting lions). In the past few days, Jeff and I have really taken a liking to Steve—and not just because of his uncanny ability to deliver the absolute best game drives. He's also as funny as he is knowledgeable, the perfect kind of tour guide.

"Steve, you don't have to stay, man!" urges Jeff. "We have room in the car!"

"This happens all the time," says Steve, smiling nonchalantly. "Don't worry."

While it's hard to imagine that a car breaking down within feet of a lion pride is something that "happens all the time," we trust Steve and reluctantly clamber into the neighboring jeep, which takes us back to the safety of our camp.

When traveling on safari, you're beholden to a schedule: you wake up around 6:00 a.m. for a walking safari or morning game drive to survey the animals (which can last about three to four hours) before returning for breakfast and some midday downtime. In the late afternoon, once the midday heat has subsided, it's time for another game drive. Some afternoon game drives end in sundowners or bush meals, while others return to camp for dinner and drinks.

The next morning, we make a beeline for Steve's jeep.

He's leaning against the dusty car, texting on his cell phone, the red of his traditional Maasai shuka cloth popping against our otherwise muted wardrobe of khaki, green, and brown.

"Steve! What happened last night?" I ask, relieved to see him.

"Oh, not too much," he replies casually, as if he were updating us on the load of laundry he'd just finished. "I waited for the lions to stop eating, and then me and another guide got the car working."

"You...*waited* for the lions to stop eating? For how long?" Jeff asks incredulously.

"About an hour," says Steve. "Ready to go?"

And with that, Steve jumps into the driver's seat, ready for another day of chasing wildlife across the African plains. As he maneuvers the jeep, he checks his phone frequently; other safari guides are sending him messages about nearby animal sightings, and lions have just been spotted.

"Let's go. There are more lions," he says excitedly, and speeds the car across the field, sending red-and-brown dirt up in the air.

★

Later that evening, our jeep pulls over into a field interrupted only by twisted acacia trees. The sun is beginning to set, casting a blue-and-yellow glow over the surrounding landscape, marking the end of another thrilling day in the bush in which we saw giraffes, lions, hyenas, cheetahs, zebras, antelope, and even baboons. In the distance, I spot a herd of wildebeest walking in a single-file line on the edge of a hill, their shadowy silhouettes outlined by the setting sun. Steve and the other safari guides set up folding chairs and pull out chilled Tuskers (a beer made with local ingredients, including barley sourced from the Masai Mara) and place them on the hood of the cars. It's happy hour, but without the rowdy, crowded bars and Bud Lights. Here, you're surrounded by nature.

Grabbing two of the Tuskers, Jeff and I walk a few feet away from the jeeps and take in our surroundings. We've come to Kenya on the wings of my writing, as part of a press trip I'd been invited on a few months prior. In the years that I'd been working in travel media, I'd stopped accepting every press trip invitation, as I had in my twenties, choosing to travel less often but more meaningfully. Learning to be more discerning about when and where I journeyed for work has rebalanced my love of travel. I can now savor the vacations that are just for me and Jeff and better appreciate the trips that come through my job.

Over the years, I'd noticed a few common themes around the press trip invitations I received. During a regular week, I was likely to get at least two to three press trip invites in my inbox, most of which touted a free stay at a recently opened hotel in Detroit or Toledo in exchange for writing a story. Occasionally, I'd get a press trip invitation for a US city that needed more attention, so I could share the joys of visiting, say, Laramie, Wyoming. Once in a while, I'd get a press trip invitation to a country in the Caribbean (an easy flight from New York) at the behest of some tourism board or major resort looking for editorial exposure. Even more rare were the press trips to cities in Europe, South America, Africa, and Asia—all of which called for longer flights and bigger budgets.

Of all the press trips I'd received over the years, plus-ones were usually never offered. The only other time I could remember bringing someone was when I invited my mom to the Dominican Republic. When I received this invite for a safari in Kenya *with* a plus one, I nearly fainted from shock. This invite is the Halley's Comet of press trips and one I'm unlikely to come across for another seventy-five years. Of course, Jeff's trip wasn't entirely free. While my airfare and travel expenses were covered as a member of the media, Jeff's safari costs and flights were deeply discounted. Still, the invitation allowed us to enjoy a bucket list item we'd otherwise have to wait years (decades?) to afford.

Standing in the middle of Kenya's Masai Mara, I reflect on how my career and *Unearth Women* have converged. I am now thirty-four and in the three or so years since I stood on the edge of Lake Atitlán, I'd focused my energy into moving forward: building my editorial career while simultaneously keeping *Unearth Women* alive. I'd continued writing stories that excited me and uplifted women. I published a book called *Wanderess*, inspired by the women-centric guides on *Unearth Women*'s website. I spoke at nationwide travel events and conferences, pouring my experience and the journey of launching *Unearth Women* into impassioned talks that encouraged others to pursue their own dreams. I had even learned to embrace and speak candidly about the mistakes made and lessons learned in launching *Unearth Women* magazine, offering those revelations to others starting their own businesses.

With time, *Unearth Women* morphed into a beautiful project that both supported my career as a travel editor and, as it turns out, held me up. When the COVID pandemic struck in March 2020, throwing me and millions of others into unemployment, I still had *Unearth Women* to give me a sense of purpose. When the travel industry screeched to an unprecedented halt thanks to quarantines and travel restrictions, *Unearth Women* gave me an outlet to share pandemic stories of women working on the frontlines as nurses and teachers, women-founded distilleries churning out hand sanitizer, and laid-off chefs who had created food trucks to feed their communities.

When the pandemic finally began to give way to normalcy, *Unearth Women* was what I showcased on my résumé, pointing to the work I'd done during a year and half of unemployment. Eventually, I landed a new job as a senior editor for *Fodor's Travel*, a legacy company whose guidebooks had been around since the 1930s and whose digital website reached millions of readers worldwide. I'm here in Kenya to write a story for *Fodor's Travel* on the reasons to book a safari in a private conservancy, and I'm here to write a story for *Unearth Women* on the ways Basecamp Explorer empowers Maasai women through its social impact programs. In the end, *Unearth Women* carried me forward in more ways than I could have imagined. Between my work as a travel editor and my love of *Unearth Women*, I'd somehow managed to craft the very life I'd long ago hoped to have: one defined by travel. And somewhere along the way, I'd managed to find the very person with whom I loved sharing these adventures: Jeff.

There's a quote from the Austrian poet Rainer Maria Rilke that reads, "Let everything happen to you: beauty and terror. Just keep going. No feeling is final." Traveling in the bush, I've had moments of profound beauty—like watching the morning sun bounce off the Maasai's spears as they led us through the grasslands or seeing giraffe heads floating above a sea of acacia treetops. I've also had moments of breathless terror, like the sounds of those lions devouring a wildebeest or the rustling of a big animal moving past our tent in the dead of night. But between the beauty and terror, there is something else, something transcendent. An undercurrent of gratitude for this opportunity, and a peace that I am *finally* exactly where I'm meant to be, doing what I'm meant to be doing, and standing next to who I'm meant to be standing with.

22

Iguazú, Eight Years Later

Iguazú National Park, Argentina

If he's going to propose, this is the moment, I think to myself.

Jeff and I are standing in the very spot where I was eight years prior in the only decent photo I have of me from my first trip to Iguazú National Park. In that picture, I'm off to the side, smiling broadly in front of a line of waterfalls stacked out into the distance. The waterfalls are partially shrouded by dense green foliage, a jungle wall against the cloudless blue sky overhead. Admittedly, it's not the best photo—one side of my face is overexposed with the sunlight, while the other half is plunged into shadow; my messy waves are pulled back from my face by a ratty old bandana that I've since lost; and I'm wearing a green jacket with faux leather sleeves. It wasn't the most practical outfit, but it was the only outfit I had brought with me on that impromptu trip from Buenos Aires.

Looking at the photo now, my expression says it all: pure unbridled joy and triumph. I remember the moment clearly. I had arrived at Iguazú that very morning, choosing to hike down the lower circuit trail to the panoramic viewing platform of the falls. By the time I saw the waterfalls, the inertia of my spontaneous trip to the Brazil-Argentina border had been traded for something else: a swelling of pride. I had known on some level that I needed to come to Iguazú because there was something in the jungle waiting for me, a moment of solitude that would reshape my life. In my wildest dreams, I never imagined coming back here. Partly because Iguazú is logistically so far from New York, but also because I had found what I was looking for. And yet here I am.

Almost everything is the same as I remember it. The thunderous roar of the waterfalls, the elevated walkways that still hover above the cascading river, the mist that still billows up in the sky like smoke, the wooden signs that still have those weathered trail maps. Even those sneaky coati with their long snouts and raccoon-striped tails are still roaming about. Nearly everything in Iguazú is the same as I remember it, and yet it is all completely different.

Devil's Throat, where the vista of the Iguaçu River looks as though it's been gouged by an ice cream scooper, has taken on a reddish-brown hue today due to a recent storm pulling sediment from the surrounding jungle, dyeing the water a brick-colored auburn. Now it looks less like a waterfall and more like an enormous desert storm, with cascades resembling puffs of red sand shooting up into the air.

There are also more people in the park than I remember. The walkways feel extra-crowded, clogged by large families, couples, rowdy children, and tourists. Seeing the bevy of travelers, I wonder how I managed to find a quiet corner to walk alone all those years ago. The idea of hiking along one of these trails while talking aloud to myself seems laughable now, much less yelling into the trees about how I didn't want to get married. The irony of being back here again, hoping for a proposal, does not escape me.

I sense Jeff is nervous; there's palpable energy coming off him like the fizz atop a freshly poured soda. He seems too jittery for a day of hiking and keeps looking over his shoulder, as if we're being followed. All around us are families, a few of which have boys swinging from the railings like capuchin monkeys swinging from the overhead branches. I don't know if Jeff plans to propose today, but I can confidently say he is not one for spectacle. He hates to bother the waiter if he receives the wrong order. He'd never insist on having a birthday party. He doesn't like to draw too much attention to himself, which is at odds with his love of performing stand-up comedy. I've always known that if he were to propose, it would be a private occasion. Dancing flash mobs in Grand Central Station and signs on the Jumbotron screen in Yankee Stadium? Forget it. Jeff getting down on one knee at a popular vista, in front of howling teenage boys and their irked parents? Not happening.

Plus, I think to myself, *where would he have put the ring?*

As the resident "travel expert" in our home, I have a meticulous packing method. I adhere to the fine art of rolling one's clothing to maximize space, while Jeff (who insists on traveling with one big backpack) haphazardly stuffs his clothes as though he were simply traveling to the nearby laundromat. Because our trip would take us from Buenos Aires to Iguazú to Rio de Janeiro, across climates, and from cities to the jungle, packing one bag would require a strategy. And so, I began rolling—tucking jeans next to shorts, tightly coiling sweaters next to loose-fitting T-shirts, fitting hiking outfits next to ones we could wear to upscale restaurants in Copacabana.

As I sat rolling our clothes like a challenging game of Tetris that I was determined to win, I realized there was no way I'd overlooked a ring box. I had packed every inch of his backpack, as well as my own, using all the space so that he could hardly stuff an extra roll of socks inside.

I did wonder about the shoes, though. Back in Buenos Aires, Jeff kept locking his "fancy shoes" in the hotel safe, a habit I found odd. These black leather dress shoes were hardly fancy enough to merit him lovingly wrapping them in plastic, let alone locking them in a safe. In fact, the very shoes he was now protecting like a family heirloom had sat gathering dust in our closet back in New York for months, if not years. Only on this trip had he become invested in their safety, running to the lockbox every time we returned to our hotel room to ensure they were still there. Rather than pry, I let it go, giving in to the thrill of returning to a country I hadn't planned to visit again.

Now, at the waterfalls, I'm standing with one foot back in August 2014 and one foot firmly planted in August 2022, straddling my past and present as I wax poetic to Jeff about my memories of first being here. I pull up that old photo of me from my first visit, trying to recreate it with a picture of me today, standing in the same spot.

"Who took this photo?" Jeff asks as he tries to take a picture of me, playing with angles that mirror the original shot.

"Some stranger," I respond nostalgically. "This family saw me struggling to take a selfie and must have taken pity, I guess."

"How's this?" Jeff passes my iPhone over as I compare today's image with the one taken eight years ago. The photos are near-identical: the same wall of cascades behind me, the same jungle foliage, the same tangle of trees stretching towards the sky. Of course, I'm older than the girl in the 2014 photo, but my expression of pride and happiness remains.

"It's perfect." I smile back.

So much had changed since that first trip to Iguazú. Over the years, my relationship to travel had evolved from a love affair to an addiction to a career. In becoming a travel blogger, I had turned my trips into performances for faceless followers staring into a screen. In becoming a travel editor, I had milked every journey for a story. In starting *Unearth Women*, I had completely exhausted my love for travel, emptying the glass I once held so sacred in the hopes of building a brand. In many ways, my love for travel mirrored Shel Silverstein's *The Giving Tree*. Throughout the years, I kept taking from it, kept demanding success of it, kept emptying its well, until—much like that poor tree—my passion for travel felt like an overused stump. Only now do I turn towards it as one would an old friend. Not because I need a story or a social media post, but because in the past decade, travel has given me everything I value most—experiences, a career, love, friendship, even my pets.

After leaving the viewing platform, Jeff and I walk down the lower trail. Like the other walkways, this one is crowded, but as we keep moving, the travelers seem to disperse until it is just us standing in front of two twin waterfalls known as the Salto Dos Hermanos, the two waterfall sisters. There are 275 waterfalls in Iguazú National Park—most are concentrated by Devil's Throat, while the others are scattered throughout the jungle, nestled amid the greenery like diamonds waiting to be discovered. The Dos Hermanos waterfalls are smaller than those by Devil's Throat, but stunning nonetheless. They stand side by side, their waters falling in elegant synchronicity, as though dancing in unison.

Like the other big waterfalls, the Dos Hermanos are reddish-brown today, their waters tumbling down into a rust-colored pool. Jeff and I are at the top of the two falls, standing on a higher viewing platform that is level with the sisters, giving us a side view of the cascades. It's then I realize that we are alone. For the first time all day, we are free of the crowds bustling around the park. The pathways around us are clear. We've managed—however briefly—to find a corner of Iguazú to call our own, just as I had eight years ago.

"I love you," says Jeff, taking my hand, his eyes swimming with tears, a smile spread across his face. "You are my best friend."

It's happening. I feel hit with a tsunami of excitement.

"Is this really happening?!" I blurt out.

For years, I had dreamed of Jeff proposing, but although we spoke of one day getting married, life kept getting in the way. Losing and gaining jobs, starting and collapsing *Unearth Women* magazine, and a global pandemic had made the timing of a proposal and wedding less than ideal. Towards the start of our relationship, I had been consumed by the idea of getting married to Jeff, eager to lock down this man who I felt—deep down—was my match in every way. But as the years progressed and our relationship deepened, that desire to marry became less urgent. While I still wanted it, I knew in more ways than one that we were already bonded for life, that marriage was merely a formality for something we'd long since decided: we were set on each other.

"I want to spend the rest of my life with you," Jeff continues. "Will you marry me?"

Kneeling on one knee, he pulls out a small wooden ring box from Brilliant Earth and flips it open, revealing a dazzling princess-cut diamond in a platinum setting. By now, I have one hand flung across my face, failing to hide the tears rolling down my cheeks. We're frozen in this moment, as though time has slowed down, allowing me to capture every vivid detail: him, on one knee, holding the ring box open with both hands; me, standing up, head tossed back; the roaring sisters behind us, throwing mist into the air.

"Say yes!" Jeff chuckles. "My knee is starting to hurt!"

I let out a laugh. I had forgotten to answer his all-important question amid my own cascade of emotion.

"Yes!" I exclaim with giddy laughter. "Yes!"

Jeff stands up and takes me in his arms, gently placing the ring on my finger before pulling me in for a big kiss. We're so lost in the high of getting engaged that we don't even notice we're no longer alone. A family has come trudging up the walkway, their two teenage daughters peering at us with curiosity, taking in the scene. My tears. Jeff's smile. The ring box.

"Felicidades!" the girls scream, rushing over to hug us both. Their parents rush over to hug us too, congratulating the two of us on our engagement before offering to take a photo of us by those sister waterfalls, my hand extended out in delight, showing off the ring. As they walk away, I sit with Jeff on a nearby bench, wanting to stay in this moment a bit longer.

I'm overwhelmed by gratitude now—for Jeff, for this moment, for this place, but above all else, for the girl who came here eight years ago, who ran to the farthest corners of South America, desperate for one last gulp of fresh air before she walked down the aisle. The girl who, despite burying her guilt and confusion in whiskey, plane tickets, and men, couldn't outrun a growing sense of unease that her life was rocketing in the wrong direction. Yes, that photo of me in Iguazú had shown pride and joy, but it had also shown fear. Fear because I was about to learn something deep in this jungle that I couldn't unlearn: that it was okay to choose myself and walk away from the wrong relationship and wrong career because this was *my* life to live. That saying yes to make others happy had only left me stuck in a reality that looked nothing like me, and how it was only when I was honest with myself that everything else began to fall into place.

I wish I could reach back through the years and hug my twentysomething self. I imagine running up to her on that dirt-packed jungle trail, her backpack hanging off her shoulders, her eyes wide from having just screamed into the trees that she didn't want to get married and the daunting realization of what she'd have to do next. I'd throw my arms around her and say, "Don't worry, I promise it will all be okay. Better than okay, actually."

I'd tell her how in a few weeks, she'd tearfully tell Alex goodbye, standing in an empty apartment that had once been her home, and promise to earn all the pain from calling off the wedding. I'd tell her how she would, in fact, go on to earn it, and how her dreams of becoming a travel writer hadn't been in vain but would one day become her career. That she'd go on to become both an editor and writer for a well-respected travel publication and fly around the world on the wings of her writing and, unlike those early days spent working up the courage to explore France, she'd confidently venture through countries like Indonesia, Guatemala, and Vietnam. I'd tell her how she'd even launch her own travel magazine, and while it wouldn't turn out the way she imagined, it would lead to wonderful opportunities—including a book telling her very own story.

I'd tell her how in a matter of months, she'd meet a beautiful man who was creative and kind, loving and supportive, and how they'd lock their love on a bridge in Paris, deciding they'd found The One. How all the heartbreak that littered the road up until now—the Jaspers and Augustinos—had been leading her to her future husband. I'd tell her how she and this man would travel the world together, filling their lives with stories of walking alongside the Maasai in Kenya, exploring the streets of Tokyo, and chasing the northern lights in Iceland. I'd hold her close and assure her that her family would eventually get over the canceled wedding and would one day love this new man like a son and even count the years until he proposed.

And finally, I'd brush the hair off her face and tell her she'd be back in Iguazú one day. How at age thirty-four, she'd find herself with that same marvelous man, walking through these very jungles she was now standing in, and how beneath the same canopy of trees she had just shaken with her shouts of not wanting to get married, she would ecstatically say yes to marrying that man. I imagine she'd look back at me incredulously, as I'd tell her how she'd go on to become one of those brides who smiles anytime she introduces her new fiancé or tears up when she imagines walking down the aisle.

I'd tell her how wedding planning would be different this time; how she wouldn't be wracked by fear and guilt as though looking for an escape path, but would plan every detail of the soiree alongside her mom, who let out the most wonderful squeal upon learning she was engaged again. How together, they'd pore over catering menus and wedding dresses, swooning at custom cocktail napkins with illustrated photos of her yet-to-be-born dog, Chico, and tabby cat, Peeps. I'd turn to that lost twentysomething girl standing alone in the heart of Iguazú National Park and simply say, "Thank you. Thank you for doing what you did today. For releasing us to enjoy this future—*our future*—and all the love, adventure, and happiness it promises to bring."

★ ★ ★ ★ ★

ACKNOWLEDGMENTS

First, I want to thank my literary agent, Katelyn Dougherty. When I first approached you hoping to write a travel memoir, it is no exaggeration to say that I had nothing but a rough idea. Rather than send me on my way, you spent months helping me pull together a book proposal that eventually became an essential roadmap during my writing journey. I can't thank you enough for your unwavering belief in this travel memoir—and in me as an author. With your support, I feel confident to keep putting stories out into the world.

Thank you to my brilliant editor, Grace Towery. From our first conversation, I knew you understood what I envisioned this travel memoir could be. I'm forever grateful for your superb editing and thoughtful direction throughout my writing process. Writing *Call You When I Land* was a truly cathartic experience that had me revisiting difficult memories and rehashing emotions I'd long since buried. With your guidance, I found the strength to walk through the jungle of my past and bring forth beauty. Similarly, I want to thank the Hanover Square Press family, especially Azim Remani, Jennifer Stimson, Sean Kapitain, Justine Sha, Bonnie Lo, and Dayna Boyer. Thank you for your thoughtful edits, feedback on my manuscript, designing my dream book cover, and your efforts to help spread the word.

Writing a memoir is a personal endeavor that inevitably touches the lives of others who played a role in my story. Thank you to Alex for supporting my decision to write this book. Years ago, standing in our empty New York apartment on East 79th Street, you told me to earn the pain I'd caused after calling off our wedding. I hope you feel that I have.

I want to thank my dear friends Esme Benjamin, Rachel Gould, and Amber Snider. Thank you for always being there to support my wildest dreams and for never failing to defend my silver lining. I also want to thank Elise Fitzsimmons for her enduring friendship and unshakable loyalty throughout the years. Starting *Unearth Women* with you was one hell of a ride, and there is no one else I'd rather have done it with.

I want to thank my parents Axel Vargas, Yana Nedvetsky, Karen Hull, and Chris Bertelsen. I am the woman I am today because all four of you instilled in me the confidence to chase my dreams around the globe. To my step-father, Chris Bertelsen: Throughout this process, you've eagerly asked questions about my writing, helped to brainstorm book titles, and applauded every single milestone, from the signed book deal to the first finished draft. I am grateful to have you in my corner and for the joy, laughter, and love you bring to our family.

To my stepmother, Yana Nedvetsky: When I was eight years old, you gave me my very first journal and encouraged me to start writing. I remember it still: a blue notebook with Bugs Bunny smiling on the cover. Thank you for all the times you pushed me to read more, write more, and immerse myself in the literary work of others. To my mother, Karen Hull: Thank you for supporting this book. I know my calling off the wedding left a well of hurt. There was frustration about what happened, about why I couldn't say something earlier, and questions about why I kept running away. It wasn't an easy road, but I'm happy I took it, for here we are today. I hope this book makes you proud.

To my father, Axel Vargas: You have encouraged me to go after what I want since I was a little girl. As I hope is made clear throughout my book, you're a source of inspiration, a touchstone for my ambition, and a reminder to never compromise on who I am and what I want. So much of who I am today comes from you. I am endlessly grateful and proud to be your daughter. To my brother and sister, Jan Vargas-Nedvetsky and Natalie Nedvetsky: I am completely in awe of your passion, talent, and creativity. I hope my book inspires you never to stifle who you are and what you want out of life, for it is *your* life to live.

Thank you to my grandmother, Clarita, whose thirst for life is unmatched. I hope to age with as much laughter, spunk, and grace as you have. To my late grandmother, Amparito, I can still feel your hug and hear your laugh as you dance throughout the kitchen. I miss you and hope that wherever you are, you feel proud that this book honors your memory.

Finally—and most importantly—I want to thank my fiancé, Jeff Cerulli, who, by the time of this book's publication, will be my husband. You are the light of my life and, by far, my biggest adventure. Thank you for the countless nights you spent listening—and I mean *truly* listening—to me read every word of this book. Thank you for not only offering thoughtful feedback but for encouraging me to keep on writing at times when I felt uninspired, stunted, or intimidated.

Thank you for looking past the many times you'd come home to find me hunched over our desk, guzzling coffee or wine, donning pajamas, hair sticking out in every way, inaudibly mumbling, "I'm in the writing zone." Thank you for simply kissing me, saying you're proud of me, and making sure I ate dinner. This book is our love story; the tale of who I was before you, how we crossed paths, and who we became once we found each other. One of my favorite songs puts it perfectly: "The simple secret of the plot is just to tell the world that I love you a lot."